Valley Lines

The People's Railway

The Inside Story of a Train Business 1983–1993

John Davies & Rhodri Clark

© 1996. John Davies, Rhodri Clark and Platform 5 Publishing Ltd.

Published by Platform 5 Publishing Ltd., Wyvern House, Sark Road, Sheffield S2 4HG, England.

ISBN 1 872524 85-0

All rights reserved. No part of this publication may be reproduced in any form or transmitted in any form by any means electronic, mechanical, photocopying, recording or otherwise without the prior permission of the publisher.

Printed in England by Walker & Carson Ltd., Wreakes Lane, Dronfield, Sheffield, S18 6PN.

FOREWORD

by the Rt. Hon. Neil Kinnock
European Union Commissioner for
Transport and formerly MP for Islwyn

The 1980s was a difficult time for the communities of the South Wales valleys, a decade in which the loss of thousands of steel jobs, economic recession and a long and bitter miners' strike were followed by mass unemployment and closure of most of the area's remaining deep coal mines. One of the assets which helped to mitigate these hard economic blows was the local rail system -but it might not have been so.

When John Davies assumed responsibility for managing the Valley Lines, three of the routes that had survived the early closure programmes – in the Rhondda, Taff and Rhymney valleys - were under threat. By reducing the fares to match the pockets of each individual town and by marketing the trains aggressively, he was able to reverse the fortunes of the lines and prove that, even at a time of growing car ownership and considerable investment in new roads, people are happy to use local public transport as long as the product suits the market.

Photo: Shelia Barrett

Two valleys which had lost their trains after the fall of the Beeching Axe welcomed back their services as a result of this innovative approach to running railways. Without contributions from the European Regional Development Fund, Mid Glamorgan County Council would probably have been unable to restart the Aberdare and Maesteg services. Today the European Union is more committed than ever to the view that public transport must play a central role in meeting growing demands for travel and must be the key to reducing the costly congestion, the rate of accidents and the increasingly harmful pollution in the road system. To turn that vision into reality, however, local action – driven by imaginative and practical people like John Davies and his team – is absolutely crucial.

This book illustrates the methods and pitfalls of running a successful local railway with minimal call on the public purse. I commend it to anyone who is following the transport debate in the late 20th century, whether in South Wales or elsewhere.

INTRODUCTION

Little has been written about what I call the "business" side of running a railway and especially in regard to local rail services. I was in the privileged position of being in at the start of the "regional" rail service revolution which has taken place on Britain's railways and when the time came in 1991 to move on to other fields within BR, I felt that some day I would write a book about those uniquely exciting times.

I recounted my experiences to Rhodri Clark – a journalist working for the Western Mail, Wales's national daily newspaper. He put together the book in a readable style and structure, using direct quotes to convey the immediacy of the situations I had described. He added a brief historical background and notes of his own impressions from time to time. Rhodri himself spent some time working in the Regional Railways Cardiff office after completing his university degree course. While being brought up in the Rhymney Valley he was a frequent user of the local rail services in that valley so has a considerable inside and outside knowledge of what went on for some of the period of this book.

Creative tension is the term I would use to describe the atmosphere of the times we are writing about. Such massive changes both those imposed and those made willingly were bound to create much debate and argument but also led to decisions based on the tremendous inspiration engendered by those times. My single minded determination to make Valley Lines the best commuter service in the country made me many friends and enemies on the way but the fact that it got so far pays great tribute to many within the railway industry and outside who helped to make this possible. The pioneering work done by Provincial Services at all levels within almost impossible constraints was probably the saviour of regional rail services in this country. I am proud to have been associated with it.

I pay greatest tribute of all to Alan Beardsworth who in varying roles, worked with me from 1982 to 1990 and contributed so much to the success of the Valley Lines. Sadly, Alan passed away on 25th November 1990 and it is to his memory that this book is dedicated.

John Davies, Sketty, Swansea, September 1996

CONTENTS

This Barry Island to Merthyr service, seen leaving Cadoxton, illustrates the standard formation of locomotive and five ex GWR non-corridor coaches which was introduced as part of the 1953 timetable change referred to in Chapter one of this book. Standard Class 3MT 2–6–2 tank locomotives were used on passenger trains in the Taff and Rhondda valleys until diesel trains were introduced in 1958. The coal wagons in the background are on the former Barry Railway route from Pontypridd which was built as part of the original development of Barry Docks.
John Hodge

CHAPTER 1

THROWING OUT THE BABY WITH THE BATHWATER
The Valley Lines before 1983

It takes a century or two for a great oak to grow from a small acorn but it can die or be felled in a much shorter time. This is true of the greatest oak to grow from an acorn planted in the South Wales valleys, the mechanically-powered train. Although the device saw extensive use in the area for more than a century, the fact that it germinated in the valleys is no guarantee of permanence there.

The concept of hauling tramway wagons using a self-contained mobile power unit was first demonstrated in 1804, when Richard Trevithick's awkward-looking steam locomotive lumbered along the Penydarren tramroad beside the River Taff. Although its significance was not fully appreciated at the time, this machine was to bring immense social changes in various parts of the globe within half a century.

In South Wales, steam-powered railways were the catalyst for a burst of industrial growth. Entrepreneurs realised that the railways unlocked new markets for the rich coal seams lying beneath the valleys. Instead of being used simply to fuel the local iron furnaces, the coal could now be transported not only to the rest of Britain but to any part of the world from the coastal ports at Cardiff, Newport and Swansea. The mushrooming of coal mines fuelled parallel booms all around. The ports flourished into highly mechanised facilities adjacent to thriving towns. The iron works expanded and people surged in from rural Wales, Ireland and other parts of western Europe to take up the thousands of jobs on offer. Nonconformist preachers had never had it so good.

Coal was the lifeblood of this huge symbiotic organism and railways were the veins and arteries that kept the whole system alive. The Taff Vale Railway, the principal train operator in the valleys, became the most profitable railway company in the world. There was room for more companies, too. New lines were built to try to tap the Taff Vale's coal traffic and switch it to other, purpose-built ports or even other parts of the docks at Cardiff. When each valley had been saturated with railway lines the prospectors began building routes that ran across the grain of the valleys, routes that tunnelled through ridges and soared over the valleys on expensive viaducts in their determination to grab a piece of the action.

Later in the 19th century these railway companies, some of them ostentatiously rich, began to attract the attention of large predatory rail companies. The London and North Western Railway and Midland Railway, blown well off their usual courses, muscled in to the Newport and Swansea valleys through shrewd acquisitions. Curiously the Great Western Railway was content mainly to co-exist alongside the small valley companies with its busy east-to-west main line and a few valleys branches, but it was natural for the bulk of the valley routes to pass into its care when Britain's railways were grouped under four principal owners in 1922.

It was perhaps because those independent lines had lasted so long that the GWR did little to remodel the railways in the valleys. The GWR had survived since the days of Brunel through rational and ruthless management but the railways in the valleys were largely left to continue according to their pregrouping boundaries throughout the GWR's period of control. This was particularly noticeable in the passenger services. The Afan Valley, for instance, retained two independent routes at its top end even though it was relatively thinly developed with collieries and housing. Before the grouping the GWR was running passenger trains to Abergwynfi via a tunnel from the Llynfi Valley. The Rhondda and Swansea Bay Railway also ran passenger trains, from Treherbert down to Swansea via Blaenrhondda tunnel. The two routes came together at Cymmer, yet the GWR made no attempt to rationalise the services or infrastructure. When British Railways took over the services in 1947, the tiny village of Cymmer still possessed a pair of two-platform stations and two signalboxes standing back to back like sulking lovers who had yet to make up for a tiff which had occured decades earlier.

The passenger rail system in the valleys had started life with a congenital defect. That defect was invisible and irrelevant at first, when the pattern of rail passenger services was an influential

Long rakes of coal wagons hauled by 0-6-2T locos were the lifeblood of the valleys during the coal boom. The tradition was about to end in February 1964 as ex-GWR 56xx Class loco. No. 6685 shunted at Trelewis, near Nelson. Steam was about to vanish from the Western Region, and most of the local collieries followed.

Peter Clark

factor in the development of new villages for mineworkers and their families. The first signs of the defect appeared when the railways were in their prime and moving into middle age. By then the First World War had turned European society inside out, the trade union movement was strong in South Wales and people's expectations had begun to change. Working families had better pay and more spare time. They were better educated, and became less satisfied at living out their lives in the same place and in the same manner as their forebears. The GWR failed to pick up on that social change, or at least failed to act on it, and continued to run the passenger trains in the valleys just as the Taff Vale Railway, Rhymney Railway et al had done in a previous era. But instead of having their lives dictated by the rail services, the people wanted to dictate the rail services to suit themselves. When the rail companies remained obdurate – because the passenger business was trifling alongside the vast freight revenues – the people turned to road transport, which didn't take the high-handed approach of the railways.

Under the GWR the chance to perform surgery to correct the genetic problem was missed. British Railways also had that opportunity, and indeed carried out some treatment in 1953, but by the time the valley railways reached maturity the cancer was so deep-rooted that it caused the loss of several limbs and came to pose a threat to the very existence of passenger rail services in the valleys.

Just as a fine oak tree which has grown over a century or more may die in a much shorter time, so too could the railways in the valleys which, as late as the 1930s, had looked unassailable.

The railway inherited by British Railways was a different kettle of fish from the lucrative operation of the Taff Vale Railway and GWR. The national rail network was losing money hand over fist and in South Wales passenger services could no longer hitch a free ride on the back of highly profitable freight trains.

The coal industry was nationalised too, and in the 1950s and 60s many collieries closed while a favoured few extended their underground tentacles ever further outwards from the mineshafts. The early mining redundancies did not have such a profound effect on the local economy as later ones. This was a boom time for Great Britain. Families affected by mining redundancies could often find work in other industries, in offices or in the relatively new mass-market for leisure activities. Some American firms set up satellite factories in South Wales to take advantage of the industrial infrastructure and the semi-skilled labour available. Depopulation rather than rising unemployment was the trend in some valleys, notably the Rhondda.

If anything, the early decline of mining was a boon to the passenger railway because fewer freight trains made for more reliable passenger services. While there was less demand for miners' trains, laid on to ferry miners to rickety wooden platforms serving individual collieries, the demand for travel to places like the Trefforest Trading Estate and Cardiff grew. The great coal routes from Pontypridd and Caerphilly became valued as commuter routes, emulating the patterns previously set on the lines from Barry, Penarth and Coryton to the city.

It was the increase in car ownership rather than the decline of mining which was to harm the railways' passenger custom. Cars provided a more effective way than the trains of reaching new industrial units at places like the Trefforest Trading Estate. The pit-head had provided a single point of entry and exit for workers clocking on and off, a feature which was well suited to rail services. On the new industrial estates, by contrast, workplaces were scattered and a private car – or a bus service – could cut out a long walk for many workers. The Trefforest estate had its own station, but it lay at the north end of the two-mile-long site and on the opposite side of the river Taff. Rail custom here declined to a point where only a peak-period service was needed.

1953 – A Steam Revolution

In the early 1950s, passenger trains in the valleys were examined objectively for the first time in their history. The trains were losing popularity to the buses and cars, which were more convenient to use than a set of rail services which still pined after Victorian travel patterns. British Railways looked long and hard at the problems and came up with a comprehensive change which was ahead of its time in respect of services outside the former Southern Railway territory.

The biggest innovation introduced in autumn 1953 was a regular interval pattern for the chief valleys services. For 16 hours each day, the main routes had services at the same minutes past each hour. This was easy for people to remember. The hourly services from Treherbert and Merthyr were dovetailed south of Pontypridd to give an even 30-minute spacing between trains. The managers drew back from comprehensive change, however, and the persistence of odd timings on the Newport to Brecon and Aberdare to Pontypool lines caused the Rhymney line trains to vary from the rigid hourly pattern when connections had to be made at Bargoed and Hengoed.

For the first time, the local management acknowledged the demand in the valleys for mass leisure travel to a wider variety of destinations than just the seaside, although the beach resort at Barry Island was given a half-hourly through service from Pontypridd by the extension of all Treherbert and Merthyr trains. Gaps in the train service during the day were abolished so the service was convenient for shopping or visiting friends. Equally important was the introduction of cheap day return tickets in an attempt to attract passengers to trains which were running with spare seats throughout the day.

Perhaps the most futuristic aspect of this revamping was the publicity which accompanied it. Timetable leaflets were produced and the system map colour-coded the various through services. The new cheap fares were advertised on poster hoardings in big bold letters that attracted passers by.

"That style of advertising continued in the valleys for nearly 40 years," says John Davies. "I wanted to keep it because it was direct and could be seen from a distance. Burying the information on cheap fares in a box at the foot of the timetable posters wouldn't have the same effect. It took the formation of Regional Railways and an obsession with corporate policy to sweep that all away. The fact that something has been there for years doesn't mean it's not always valid."

The most remarkable achievement of the 1953 change was the co-incidence of so many initiatives – a leap that was never repeated even in the service revolution of the 1980s. Along with the innovations already described, the trains themselves were formed into fixed five-coach formations of non-corridor stock and 10 new Standard Class 3MT 2-6-2T locomotives drafted in to cover the services between Barry and Treherbert and Merthyr. They had to be modified with rails atop the bunkers so they could run a complete out-and-back working on the Barry to Treherbert route without stopping for more coal. Former GWR 2-6-2T locos of the 41xx series handled many of the Rhymney Valley services. The new service made more efficient use of rolling stock. Gains of up to 40% were achieved and antiquated rolling stock from the days of the Taff Vale Railway was despatched to the scrap yards or kept for occasional strengthening of the five-coach trains.

"The scale of the change was cataclysmic, in the context of the times," says John. "It involved not only timetables and trains but advertising and fares. In terms of its impact on the culture of the railway, 1953 was more significant than 1983. Before 1953 the idea of managing resources was completely alien, but when we came back to it in 1983 we could say this had all happened 30 years previously."

Wonderful and extensive though this change was, British Railways failed to carry it through to its logical extent in subsequent years. The 1953 reshaping had achieved its aims of cutting costs and increasing revenue but, instead of using that achievement as a reason for more of the same, the management saw it as a reason to be content with a job well done. The culture of continually honing a rail service to match its economic and social environment was still absent, and would remain so for three more decades.

The positive changes in the remainder of the 1950s were chiefly dieselisation, development of better services for commuters in the morning and evening peaks, and weeding out long miles of duplicate trackwork which had largely been unnecessary since the

POST WAR CHANGES

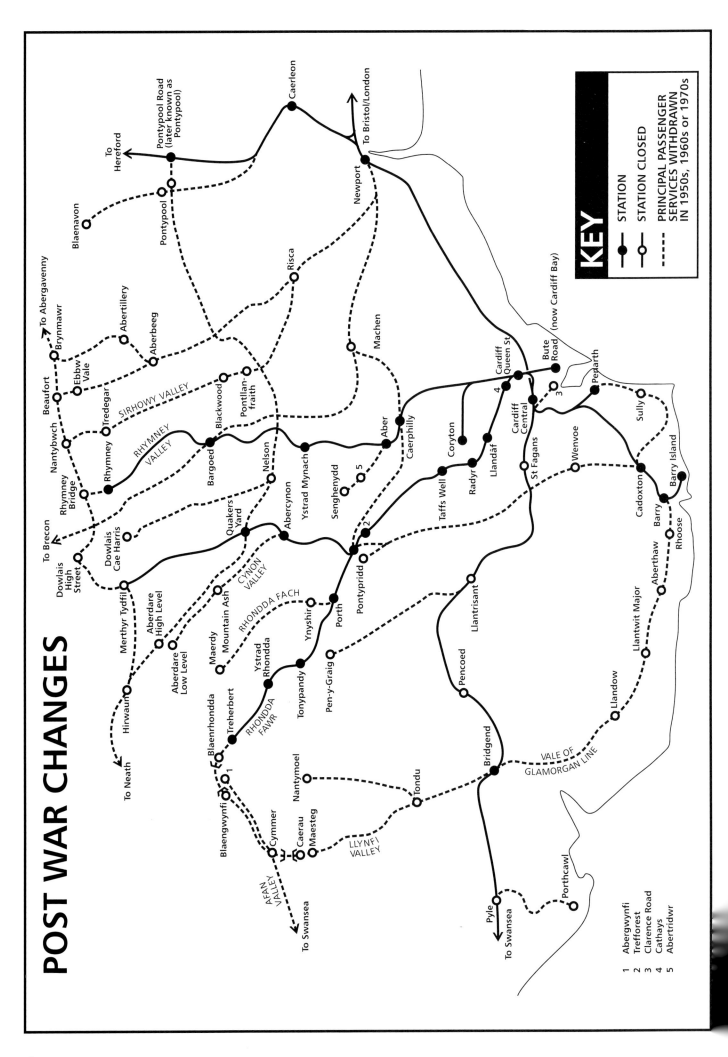

KEY

●—●	STATION
○—○	STATION CLOSED
- - -	PRINCIPAL PASSENGER SERVICES WITHDRAWN IN 1950s, 1960s OR 1970s

1 Abergwynfi
2 Trefforest
3 Clarence Road
4 Cathays
5 Abertridwr

end of competition between the pregrouping companies in the valleys. The negative aspect of the mid and late 1950s was that the valley services were not scrutinised objectively. In this respect they were typical of the whole of British Railways which, partly through government constraints, was piling up problems for the near future by its inability or unwillingness to modernise its operations. It had embarked on what it euphemistically called a Modernisation Plan, but that chiefly consisted of replacing steam traction with diesel and replacing thousands of wooden-body wagons with almost identical wagons built from steel. The Modernisation Plan of 1955 failed to address the fundamental issues of the railway Britain would need for the future and British Railways went deeper and deeper into the red.

The Modernisation Plan was the last time Welsh railways would have adequate funding for upgrading and renewal, something they had enjoyed and perhaps taken for granted in their first century of existence. In 1957 new diesel multiple units (DMUs) came pouring in to South Wales, first taking over the valley services radiating from Newport. The Cardiff valleys followed in 1958.

The DMUs were put to work on the steam timetable of 1953. They covered all duties except a few peak workings and some of the quieter routes, such as Cardiff to Pontypridd via St Fagans. The DMUs, later designated Class 116, were excellent trains and were well received by the public. They didn't cut any time off the journeys between stations but saved time over complete diagrams because they didn't need to stop to take on fresh supplies of water. Most services were handled by three-car sets but on the core Treherbert and Rhymney services six-car formations were the norm. It is a reflection of the profligacy of the 1950s that those six-car trains gave increased capacity over the five-coach steam-hauled rakes at a time when rail's market share was declining.

The trains represented a massive investment but British Railways' laissez faire attitude was to cost not only the railways but the whole economy of the valleys dearly. When the ruthless financial hurricane of the 1960s blustered into South Wales the passenger services in the valleys were defenceless, and within a few years some of the diesel trains which had looked so promising were being transferred to other parts of Britain.

The Defeatism of the 1960s

It would be unfair to pin on Dr Richard Beeching, the first chairman of the British Railways Board the entire blame for line closures in the valleys in the 1960s. In many cases he failed to see the wood for the trees but the government of the day had decided that correcting British Railways' bank balance, after more than a decade of neglect, was suddenly a matter of the utmost urgency. Beeching had to make so many changes is such a short space of time that he had little time for analysing the potential of local passenger services. Decisions on the future of hundreds of services had to be made rapidly and by reference to a traffic survey conducted over a single week in April 1961 rather than to the services' potential for growth under a different management style or in Britain's developing post-war social framework. Snap decisions were needed on the future of priceless railway infrastructure, much of which would be expensive or impossible to restore should the need arise in future.

Although some of the most hopeless passenger services in the valleys had been pruned in the mid 1950s, others remained intact along with miles of duplicate pre-grouping railway line. Then, in the period before Beeching's reshaping report was published, BR managers attempted an appallingly cack-handed reshaping of their services in South Wales.

In 1962 some of the local services feeding into Newport were withdrawn. The chief problem was not lack of use but that the tracks were needed for intensive freight traffic, which served the steelworks at Ebbw Vale and several prolific collieries. At this time Ebbw Vale steelworks still had its blast furnaces but the local supplies of iron ore had long since run out. BR's most powerful steam locomotives struggled against the gradient to carry the iron ore from Newport docks to the top of the valley at Ebbw Vale, nearly 1,000ft above sea level.

Companies like the Taff Vale Railway had enjoyed the convenient circumstance wherein the heavy trains went downhill to the sea and the engines had an easy task returning the empty wagons against the gradient to the collieries. The 0-6-2T became the standard design for most companies, with a pony truck to lead the engine on the relatively fast descents. These engines were small in relation to the volume of coal being moved in the valleys in the decades before and after the turn of the century, and the railway companies benefited from energy savings as well as the lower costs of building or buying small engines.

Ebbw Vale presented a different problem at the start of the 1960s. The heavy ore trains were slow movers and had to be sidelined into loops on the way up the valley to allow the much faster DMUs to pass. Each stop brought delay followed by another burst of energy to restart the reluctant hopper wagons. This practice also contributed to delays in the passenger service. The solution adopted was to strip out Ebbw Vale's passenger service, rather than invest in appropriate infrastructure. Some managers of the period believe another factor behind the withdrawals was that local passenger services shuttling in and out of Newport station would have complicated the designs for multiple-aspect signalling which were then being prepared for the main line through Newport. Main-line and freight traffic brought in far more income than the passenger trains from Ebbw Vale and Brynmawr but solutions must have been possible for satisfactory retention of passenger services for such a large catchment population. Sadly, defeatism had already set in at the BR management offices.

A contributory factor in the case of Ebbw Vale was that it was still being served, after dieselisation, by a branch service. A shuttle train connected at Aberbeeg with services on the Brynmawr to Newport corridor, which was more heavily populated. If the problem of integrating freight and passenger services had been looked at more positively, Ebbw Vale would have been given through services as well in an attempt to make them more popular and to give a half-hourly frequency lower in the valley, as had been achieved south of Pontypridd in 1953. Instead, the laziest option of all was taken, and the Brynmawr and Ebbw Vale lines lost their passenger trains in April 1962.

The Sirhowy Valley line, which left the Brynmawr line at Risca, suffered even more through BR's ignorance of the changing market for passenger travel and had its through services reduced. The line from the large town of Tredegar through Blackwood and Pontllanfraith to Risca had been mostly acquired by the London and North Western Railway and by the 1930s the London Midland and Scottish Railway was running 11 trains a day through from Tredegar to Newport. By 1958, however, most of the Tredegar trains terminated at Risca, causing an inconvenient change for passengers and depriving the town of Risca of extra services to and from Newport.

In the 1950s, or earlier, an innovative management alert to trends in employment and recreation might have espied the potential of the viaduct across the Rhymney Valley at Maesycwmmer, near Ystrad Mynach. All the infrastructure was in place to run a new service between Tredegar and Cardiff via Caerphilly, linking several important towns with each other and with the Welsh capital. By then Cardiff was becoming established as a place of mass employment in offices, shops, banks, steelworks, docks and a variety of other industries, and has continued to dominate the employment scene of South Wales ever since. The Tredegar branch served Tredegar and Blackwood well. The latter town's station was adjacent to the Woolworth's store – the perfect indicator of the centre of any town in those days!

The Tredegar service withered on the vine till its withdrawal in 1960. In the 1990s the residents of Tredegar have an inadequate transport infrastructure, a bus service that takes well over an hour to reach Cardiff and an unemployment rate of around 20%. Further down the valley the people of Blackwood are tangled in a vitriolic debate about a bypass to relieve traffic congestion in the town at the expense of a worsened environment for many residents.

Ignorance, or a deliberate overlooking, of the tributary effect of local rail services was a feature of the Beeching cuts. When

Beeching and his lackeys cast their jaundiced eyes over the valleys services they found what seemed to be obvious candidates for closure. They were obvious candidates not because they didn't serve places of importance but because they were still operating along the pre-grouping patterns which had long since become irrelevant to the majority of the population. Services run as self-contained branch lines were bound to look hopelessly uneconomic to anyone who refused to take into account the custom they contributed to the core rail services. All the services which relied on connections in the Cardiff alleys were closed, while all the services which ran through to Cardiff were allowed to continue.

The arbitrary way of the Beeching cuts has left a legacy of anomalies and absurdities around Britain, and South Wales has its share. Significant towns like Llantrisant and Caerleon lost their rail services simply because they had the misfortune to lie beside main lines, from which all local services were stripped. Cefn-Onn halt, at the southern end of Caerphilly Tunnel, served a park and a smattering of farmhouses but was allowed to remain open simply because it was not on a main line. Llantrisant station (under the new name Pontyclun) was successfully reopened in 1992 but Caerleon, now host to a university college and hospital as well as a large population and Wales' most significant Roman tourist attraction, still has no station.

There are physical reasons for the valleys to have come to depend increasingly on the coastal towns and cities of South Wales for employment. The valleys are narrow and cramped. The only flat expanses of ground for new factories have been the sites of former colleries or spoil heaps. At the height of the coal boom, thousands of people earned their crust in the valleys but the majority of them worked underground. There simply is not the space on the surface for that many people to be employed in new activities there. The coastal belt, by contrast, has vast acres of flat land. The ports are conveniently close for import and export of materials - a prime factor in the resiting of South Wales's blast furnaces at Port Talbot and Llanwern. The towns and cities are more compact than the valleys and have always been one step ahead in telecommunications. They are also home to a variety of institutions, banks and other organisations which have attracted other office-based activities which want to be close by. The influence of rail and road transport corridors running from east to west may be over-stated but nevertheless the proximity of the M4 and South Wales main line favours sites on the coastal zone.

Although efforts have been made to provide alternative employment within the valleys, the modern role of the valley towns is principally as dormitories for people working in Cardiff. This has created a demand for travel on a north-south axis, a demand that fuelled the railways' renaissance in the 1980s.

This trend in commuting was already established by the late 1950s but BR largely overlooked it. The Senghenydd service continued as it had operated in the days when there was little reason to commute from Senghenydd to Cardiff. The Senghenydd branch served a short and densely-populated side valley north of Caerphilly. Although DMUs worked it from 1958, the service continued to terminate at Caerphilly, forcing Cardiff-bound passengers to change trains or, increasingly, take a more convenient form of transport. A through service to Cardiff might have survived until today, helping to turn Abertridwr and Senghenydd into attractive dormitory towns for commuters by facilitating travel to and from the capital for the former mining families and their descendants.

The Senghenydd to Cardiff and Tredegar to Cardiff services would have complemented the hourly core service between Rhymney and Cardiff. They would have provided a more frequent service for the lower and middle sections of the Rhymney Valley. Such a pattern of services emerged in the 1980s but with trains terminating at Caerphilly and Ystrad Mynach or Bargoed, instead of continuing to separate destinations.

The line between Abercynon and Aberdare also continued to be worked largely as an isolated section after the 1953 change and after dieselisation. The population within a convenient walking distance from stations on the line was greater than that surrounding the neighbouring Merthyr line. However, the Merthyr line was built earlier, Merthyr having been one of the earliest industrial towns in South Wales and the principal target of the infant Taff Vale Railway. When the Aberdare line opened, the relatively unimportant passenger services happily turned round at Abercynon, where the relatively few passengers transferred to and from trains on the main line to and from Merthyr. As time wore on, the change at Abercynon became more and more influential. After the 1953 change roughly two-thirds of the Aberdare trains terminated at Abercynon and only a fifth ran through to Cardiff. Changing at Abercynon would have been a nuisance to the many passengers making the short journey to Pontypridd from stations on the Aberdare line. The isolation of the service did nothing to help passenger numbers or to make the service watertight before Beeching. Its withdrawal, as with the Ebbw Vale service, conveniently removed an obstacle in the way of the intensive freight service on the same tracks.

It was not until the mid-1980s that the lesson was learned. Fortunately the Aberdare line had stayed open for freight traffic and when it was reopened to passengers in 1988 John Davies made it a matter of cast-iron policy that every train from Aberdare must run through to Cardiff. The new Aberdare line was a soaraway success; had the recession and other financial hardships not intervened, the service could well have been extended and its frequency doubled in the early 1990s.

Publication of Beeching's reshaping report was met with dismay in Senghenydd and Abertridwr. Here, members of the Aber Valley Anti-Railway Closure Committee hold aloft their placards for the Western Mail's photographer outside City Hall, Cardiff, on 30th August 1963. Had Beeching and his subordinates attempted to run all trains direct from Senghenydd to Cardiff they might have reversed the line's fortunes. Instead, passenger services were withdrawn in June 1964 and the line closed outright in 1977. *Western Mail and Echo Ltd*

The most farcical situation to be perpetuated in the 1960s from pre-grouping times centred on the Afan Valley. After DMUs started working in the valley the service was still split along pre-grouping boundaries, with no attempt to co-ordinate trains on the two lines at Cymmer. The Rhondda and Swansea Bay service was withdrawn in 1962 south of Cymmer, but its northern stub had to be retained because of the inadequacy of the road alternative to Blaenrhondda Tunnel. The road over the exposed ridgetop was often impassable in winter. The vagaries of the railway closure proposal therefore forced BR to rationalise in the Afan Valley in a logical way, for once; the former GWR service from Bridgend to Abergwynfi was diverted to run through the tunnel to Treherbert.

Treherbert itself remained the terminus not only for the Blaenrhondda tunnel trains but also for the hourly services from Cardiff. That division dated back to pre-grouping times when the line north of Treherbert was worked by the Rhondda and Swansea Bay Railway. Services from Cardiff could logically have continued to Blaenrhondda, at the top of the Rhondda Valley but the old division outlived successive railway managements. The track from Treherbert to Blaenrhondda was lifted after the demise of the Treherbert to Bridgend service. In the 1980s, Mid Glamorgan County Council and BR investigated the feasibilty of relaying the rails to Blaenrhondda but the cost proved prohibitive. Running on to Blaenrhondda would have adversely affected the turnaround time of trains, and this was almost certainly the reason for not extending them in the 1960s.

Back in the Afan Valley, the newly created Treherbert to Bridgend service, which ran roughly every two hours, was worked by a single power car. A six-car formation had to be sent all the way from Treherbert to Bridgend (nearly 18 miles) twice a day to cater for school children travelling less than four miles between Caerau and Llangynwyd. In 1968 a section of Blaenrhondda Tunnel collapsed so the Afan Valley had to be serviced by forwarding DMUs from Cardiff to Bridgend. Still nobody took the logical step of reducing or cutting out altogether the rail service north of Caerau to concentrate resources on providing an attractive hourly service between Maesteg and Bridgend. The Maesteg line had a Cinderella service, perhaps because of the dead wood attached to it. A closure proposal was inevitable and worked its way through the system as a proposal for closure of the whole service rather than the section north of Maesteg or Caerau. Maesteg had to wait 22 years before the option which had been staring BR in the face since 1953 – provision of hourly trains between Maesteg and Cardiff via Bridgend – was taken up. This time the service was tailored to the needs of the population and was an instant success.

Another shortcoming of the 1960s was the absence of any notion that rail services could influence future developments and benefit from others. A Tredegar to Cardiff service was not considered because Tredegar people always travelled to Newport. BR managers apparently never stopped to think why there were so many more people travelling to Cardiff from Rhymney, two miles away in the adjacent valley. They never considered that providing through trains from Tredegar to Cardiff might in itself develop a market for travel between those places. The loop line from Penarth to Cadoxton via Sully was a fairly obvious candidate for closure in the 1960s but shortly after its disappearance the area it had served – a pretty area near the sea and not far from Cardiff – experienced a population explosion. The Sully service, like the Llantwit Major service, could well have had a useful function had it managed to survive a few years longer.

There were numerous services in the valleys which could not be justified in modern economic terms. Sadly the baby was thrown out with the bathwater, and significant towns like Aberdare and Tredegar lost their rail services along with the smaller settlements. The core valley services which survived Beeching with ease were also damaged in the 1960s. Not only did they lose contributory custom from the abandoned branch services but a decade of cutbacks had instilled in BR a deepseated feeling of defeatism. From then on BR's solution to practically any challenge was to withdraw a little further into its shell and, for good measure, put up fares at the same time.

Stagnation

The railways had undergone a chain reaction in the 19th century where one expansion triggered the next. The same happened in reverse from the 1950s when BR snagged a strand of wool and its rail services began to unravel. When the 1970s came, nobody knew how to tie the knot which would stop the unravelling process. All the local managers could apparently do was keep tugging the wool. By the end of the 1970s (the most unremarkable decade in the history of railways in the valleys) so much fabric had been unravelled that there was hardly anything left.

The early 1980s was the nadir for the services. By then more than half of the impressive fleet of DMUs delivered in the late 1950s had been transferred from South Wales, a large contingent having left to operate the Birmingham Cross-City service in 1976. It was not for want of rolling stock that the valleys services reached their poor condition in 1980. BR's managers in Cardiff had had all the trains they needed, all the tracks they needed and all the demand they needed to run a substantial network of local services focused on Cardiff. What had been lacking, however, was an understanding of the market and the energy required to alter the system's many shortcomings.

The valleys routes entered the 1980s still running to the pattern set in 1953, although the knee-jerk school of management had made a few changes in between. These included cutting back Barry Island's half-hourly service throughout the year to hourly in winter and, even more unhelpfully, removing two of Merthyr's hourly services in the middle of the day and reversing the trains at Pontypridd and Abercynon instead. The general stagnation, in tandem with numerous other factors, brought the valleys services to their knees in 1980 when the ultimate disgrace came - a proposal underwritten by Mid Glamorgan County Council to close the flagship Treherbert line above Porth and use the trackbed for a new road. Plans were also hatched to close the line between Pontypridd and Merthyr, and to replace the trains above a new Bargoed Central station with rail-feeder buses sponsored by the council. Some railway workers were also councillors, and in 1981 the valley services were hit by a local strike. The strong link between the rail unions and the council helped to stave off the closure plans for the Merthyr and Rhondda lines. However, the Rhymney line closure remained a live issue, to the consternation of vociferous local residents.

The last colliery in the Rhondda Fawr valley closed in 1981 and a proposal for the railway to be singled had been progressing since 1979 because of the poor condition of one of the tracks. Had the second track been left in place for just a year or two longer, the Treherbert line could have been enjoying three or four peak-period services per hour within 10 years and would certainly have benefitted from more reliable operation.

Meanwhile, the Rhymney Valley tracks saw their first investment for many years when a new crossover between the main running lines was installed at Ystrad Mynach. This, however, was simply to allow the trains which terminated at Bargoed every hour to be turned round short at Ystrad Mynach instead.

1982 was marked by a national rail strike which inflicted yet more damage on the ailing valley services. In response, BR devised a timetable with yet more pointless cutbacks. Barry Island, which has a significant resident population, was then served every two hours in winter and the intervening services stopped short at Barry station. Worse still, the upper Rhymney Valley was to lose its through service to Cardiff and be served by a single power car shuttling between Bargoed and Rhymney. Passengers had to change trains at Bargoed, and the *coup de grace* was that even the connections at Bargoed were not arranged conveniently. There was a 15-minute wait for passengers in one direction.

The valleys services had managed to eke out the 1970s without sustaining severe damage, but in the early 1980s cutbacks were appearing at an accelerating rate and the valleys services looked on the brink of imploding. It was into this scenario that John Davies stepped in autumn 1982 as the new passenger manager for South Wales.

THE TAFF MAIN LINE

Above left: The vast island platform at Pontypridd was once the focal point of the Taff Vale Railway in the valleys, but in April 1988 only one of its seven platform faces remained in use. The track for trains to Cardiff had curved along the right of the platform in this view, but that line was not reinstated when the time came to increase Pontypridd's platform capacity in 1991 because it would have required an expensive junction to the north of the station. Instead, a new platform was created to the left of the layout, where the BR lorries are standing.   *Stephen Miles*

Above right: The huge canopy at Pontypridd remains invincible not only because of its listed status but because of its solid construction.   *Stephen Miles*

Left: By March 1989 the single-platform bottleneck at Pontypridd was so severe that when a half-hourly service to Merthyr was introduced on Saturdays the extra trains had to run non-stop through the station on the freight lines. Passengers were annoyed at trains, like the one shown here, missing the most important stop in the valley and the anxiety with which this enhanced service was met caused it to be abandoned shortly afterwards.   *Stephen Miles*

Left: Pontypridd's new platform on the up freight line is under construction in April 1991 as an Aberdare to Barry Island service approaches the operational platform face. Constructing the new platform entailed craning a wide footbridge into position and shifting the bridge parapet on the left to create space for the platform. The train is passing one of the numerous bay platforms which were installed for the branch services which formerly terminated at Pontypridd.
Stephen Miles

Right: A northbound Sprinter passes the A470 dual carriageway as it arrives at Taffs Well on a wintry January day in 1991. The A470 provides the competition to the railway on this corridor, yet its proximity to the railway here has contributed to the healthy patronage of Taffs Well's station car park. Two relics of South Wales's coal boom are visible in this picture. To the right of the Sprinter are the remains of the four tracks once needed to cope with the volume of traffic on the Taff Vale Railway's artery to Cardiff Docks, and towering above the scene is a brick pillar which once carried the Barry Railway's Walnut Tree viaduct over the Taff Gorge – part of an expensive attempt to tap into Cardiff's lucrative coal-export trade. *Stephen Miles*

Right: A southbound Sprinter rolls past Llandaf's Taff Vale Railway signal box as it approaches Llandaf station. In 1987 and 1988, Llandaf was served only by the Rhondda trains as the Merthyr trains were routed via the City Line. Llandaf clearly merited a 15-minute frequency and the Merthyr, Aberdare and Rhondda trains were all sent through Llandaf from 1989. *Stephen Miles*

Below: Taffs Well was the original turnback point for trains on the City Line. Trains would run into the stub of the branch to Nantgarw colliery, visible behind this Treherbert to Barry Island service, before heading back towards Danescourt. This manouevre was possible because the engineers had worked at breakneck speed to reposition two signals on the down line from Pontypridd. *Stephen Miles*

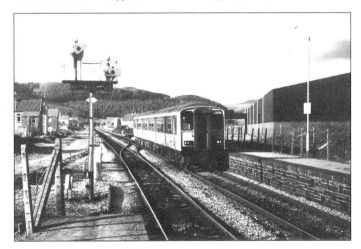

Above: The complex trackwork and signalling at Radyr is a legacy of the days when Radyr was home to a bustling freight yard but, in 1996, is in the process of being radically reshaped. In 1988, when this picture was taken, the freight lines on the right were in use as headshunts for the yard. *Stephen Miles*

Left: By today, after three county councils have funded prolific programmes of new stations, it is easy perhaps to forget the revolutionary nature of this scene in summer 1983 - the construction of the first new station in South Wales for decades. Cathays station, near central Cardiff, was an immediate success because of its location close to the university college, the civic buildings of Cathays Park and the dense terraced housing of Cathays. *Western Mail and Echo Ltd*

CHAPTER 2

SWASHBUCKLING TIMES
Tackling The Problems Of 1983

Any business venture needs an element of luck to succeed and in autumn 1982, when John Davies became passenger manager for the Western Region's Cardiff division, it was high time for the valleys' crumbling passenger railway to throw a double six.

The first dice to come rolling onto the game board was a team of young managers with fresh ideas of how a railway should be run. Besides John Davies, several other capable managers took up posts in Cardiff at the same time. Among these were Keith Galley, marketing manager, and Stuart Davies, services manager. Alan Beardsworth continued to work his customary magic as advertising and publicity manager.

The second six to roll out of the shaking pot was Frank Markham, a somewhat unorthodox divisional manager who saw his role as an enabler rather than a director. Paradoxically, it was by taking a back seat that this man was to became one of the most crucial figures in the revitalising of the valleys services.

John Davies moved to Cardiff from East Anglia, where he had been in charge of passenger marketing for the Eastern Region's Norwich division. In Norwich he had been champing at the bit to make improvements to the local services that radiated across Norfolk and Suffolk from Norwich and Ipswich. Many features, good and bad, of those services were to influence John's subsequent initiatives in the South Wales valleys but in East Anglia he found he was barred from carrying out even simple changes which would have assisted the marketing strategies he was attempting to operate.

"When I moved from freight marketing on the Western Region to marketing manager at Norwich I found a totally different culture," says John. "The Eastern Region was autocratic and bureaucratic at the same time. The people at the top proposed, and you disposed."

The foundation stone for the valleys' rail revolution was that the management in all departments would be fluid enough to be able to respond with instant changes as the need arose. Efforts would be made to keep the staff on side, as far as that was realistic, and the management would act on feedback which came from the staff, who had their ears to the ground.

There was a lesson to be learned from the rigid, bureaucratic way the Eastern Region managed its timetable changes. The times were reviewed every three years in each division. One year would be the turn of Norwich and Doncaster divisions, the next would be Newcastle and Leeds, the third year would be Kings Cross and so on. Only in exceptional circumstances was anything changed during a three-year period.

While at Norwich John Davies had asked for amendments to the services during a three-year period to satisfy demands he had spotted in the East Anglian market. "I would say, 'Look, this isn't satisfactory and, believe me, it needs some alterations.' 'Not for you to decide, sonny,' the chap in York would say. 'That's our business. You keep out of it. You just sell the services.' But you can't sell a service which isn't doing what the market wants it to do. Things got to the stage where the man at York left a message with the divisional manager in Norwich one day saying, 'This man's interfering. Tell him to keep his nose out.' The divisional manager hated the bureaucracy at York and told them to get lost, but I couldn't do anything because the control was absolute. When I came to Cardiff I made damn sure that I would drive alterations rather than be driven."

The Western Region never attempted to go as long as three years at a stretch without amending timetables, but John was

determined to have the freedom to change services quickly whenever adjustments were needed. This freedom was to come in useful in autumn 1987, when fundamental alterations had to be made to a new valleys timetable.

Some positive aspects of the East Anglian services were to bear fruit when applied in Wales. The ticketing on local services was simple and easy to understand and operate; only single tickets were issued, by guards using bus-type ticket machines. There were no ticket barriers at stations and the PayTrain concept was well publicised and widely understood. The Eastern Region used its rolling stock efficiently, and this had a bearing on the way John tackled the services in West Wales in particular. In 1982 the trains west of Swansea were costing three times more to operate than the revenue they brought in. The DMUs running the valleys services at the time were less wasteful.

The most significant lesson from East Anglia, however, was none of these but a warning about management structures. When John rolled up his sleeves in Cardiff his first action was to hammer in a few fenceposts around his territory.

"The first thing was to say to Paddington headquarters that we wanted the freedom to do our own thing," says John.

The valleys services were in desperately poor shape, crying out for some positive action. But John's division stretched from Craven Arms to Fishguard, encompassing the Cardiff to Gloucester line via Chepstow as well as InterCity services in South Wales. Within that territory there was all manner of mess. Ailing though the valleys services were, the longer routes had to take priority in the intensive-care beds and the valleys had to grin and bear the pain. The early remedies prescribed by John and his new team established the style which would soon be used to great effect in the valleys.

"Coach deregulation was playing havoc with the business in West Wales and on the InterCity trains between Swansea and London. There was a lot of pressure on InterCity: there was downwards pressure on costs, the service was too lavish, and there were disputes with the Bristol division about trains serving Bristol Parkway," says John.

"The first clash with Paddington was over fares policy, which at that time was in some disarray. They had been setting the fares centrally. They were a problem not only in the valleys but also on the main line. The peak fares were too expensive, so many people were travelling by other ways. Trains came in to Cardiff in the morning from Swansea and Newport with plenty of spare capacity. They were operating peak fares even though they were far from having a capacity problem on InterCity in South Wales."

"I wanted to have just one fare to apply all day. We had to take on Paddington and the national accounts office in Croydon who were wary of new ticketing arrangements. When we took this on we didn't realise how many vested interests would try to stop us. They wanted their own control. They'd had control for years, they didn't think the local managers know what they were talking about, and they wanted a tidy fare structure that looked good on paper. The fact that the fares were too expensive didn't matter."

Remote control also gave rise to fares anomalies which were not corrected and got amplified by each fares increase. One anomaly was that a weekly season ticket from Merthyr to Cardiff cost more than five peak day returns. The season ticket wasn't selling because six-day working weeks had long since disappeared.

Another problem for the railways arose from the deregulation of road coaches in 1980, a change which allowed bus operators to introduce new services without registering them provided the routes exceeded a certain benchmark distance. New competitors moved in to South Wales in an attempt to poach custom from National Express.

"National Welsh and South Wales Transport woke up from the slumber of the National Bus Company and saw that they were able to introduce coaches on long-distance routes," says John. "They were able to convert a series of short-distance express buses into a long route from Milford Haven to Bristol, on which there was a coach every hour. 'Express West', as the service was known, was doing excellent business. For a while they were even duplicating and triplicating buses on some services. National Express introduced its Rapide coaches on the London route at the same time."

Fighting had broken out in the ranks of the bus industry, although nowhere near as fiercely as it would when all bus services were deregulated in 1986. But the bus companies were not the only ones getting bruised. Usage of InterCity services from Swansea and Cardiff to Bristol Parkway and London had fallen, and custom on the West Wales lines had plummeted.

"The first thing we did was to tackle the coach competition to the west of Cardiff. We put in what became known as 'corridor fares'. Under Keith Galley's guidance we introduced cheap fares in stages, taking on one express coach route at a time. We started with Swansea–Cardiff, then went on to Carmarthen–Swansea, then West Wales. At each stage there were squeals from the bus companies.

"National Welsh decided to introduce a non-stop commuter bus from Bridgend to Cardiff. Members of National Welsh staff came to Bridgend railway station to hand out leaflets advertising the service. On the second day they did it we threw them off, because the station was private property and we had control of the advertising. Our public relations officer, Neil Sprinks, had made sure the press were alerted, and the South Wales Echo was at Bridgend station to witness the National Welsh staff being thrown off!

"Then we went down the hill to the bus station, which was public property, and gave out our own flyers. We'd reduced the rail fares to compete with the bus. We stood at the bus station and told people to use the train. They couldn't chuck us out because it was on a public highway. Cautious voices higher up in BR were telling us not to mess around with things like that. But we got away with it and National Welsh did not. That was the kind of swashbuckling that went on."

Motivation

Although bravado was an excellent tool for tackling backward senior managers and competitors outside the railway, it was not the right device to force changes in the attitudes of the staff who ran the valleys services. The 1980s had already seen two rail strikes in the valleys, both of which did immense damage to custom. Even the most watertight business plan for revival would end in catastrophe if its implementation resulted in the valley services being stopped through their third strike in as many years.

"We could see the business ebbing away," says John. "We saw the competitors having a field day – buses and coaches at that time. Roads in the valleys were being improved, the rail fares were too high and services were, in most cases, of poor quality and poor frequency.

"The message I was giving the lieutenants, or those who would listen, was that we would have no railway within a few years if we didn't change. Some people said we were being subsidised by the government so there was no need to bother changing anything - the subsidy was to cover the kind of shortfalls I was pointing out to them. On the other hand, the younger people could see that we had to do something, and do it fast. They also saw that we had to do it sensibly and take the staff with us, because we couldn't afford a series of strikes."

Complete closure was not an imminent threat to the valleys services, except possibly in the upper Rhymney Valley. Although usage had declined badly, the trains were still important to significant numbers of people. People had learnt from the Beeching cuts and would fight closure proposals tooth and nail. Mid Glamorgan County Council might have dreamed of a swanky new road along the trackbed of the Rhondda line but as long as a handful of people could prove in a closure hearing that they would suffer hardship from complete withdrawal of trains, then the railway would stay. A more likely outcome had the services declined further would have been a wholesale reduction in services in the valleys, leaving some parts with trains in the peak periods only.

Complete closure of services, however, was the picture often painted by management in an attempt to influence the staff when the time came to implement radical changes.

The image John wanted to portray, of a manager bent on improving the railways, was not helped by the May 1983 timetable change, over which he presided or at least appeared to preside. The groundwork for the new timetable had been accomplished before John arrived in Cardiff. With so many other services needing urgent attention in South Wales, there simply was not the time to reverse the cuts that were already working their way through the pipeline.

"We had to tell the staff, 'Carry on, do the best you can for now'. There was a faction in the valleys that said, 'Don't bother to do anything with the services because, whatever you do, the DMUs will let you down'. If it wasn't for those negative thinkers at Canton depot we could have had a much better service. I said, 'These DMUs are all we've got at the moment, so get on with it'."

It transpired that the DMUs' unreliability was over-stated because the trains were sometimes used as scapegoats when other operational problems arose.

"If there wasn't a spare driver to cover a working, the train would be cancelled and the control would put it down to DMU failure. I knew, without much evidence to support it initially, that there was a lot of covering-up going on. Some of the supervisors didn't see why they should go to the trouble of putting it right. They were working their way to retirement and didn't want to rock the boat."

"I found out a couple of years later, to my shame, that they were booking two guards on every Sunday train to give them a little extra money. They denied this when I asked them, so I asked for a statement of guards' returns on Sundays. Most trains took two or three pounds in fares. I asked the supervisors why they needed two guards per train, and they said, 'If you stop that they'll refuse to co-operate.' I told them, 'Manage, for a change, instead of finding bogus ways to boost people's incomes'."

Motivating the staff was one of the biggest challenges facing John and his team, a challenge which applied to some extent to all the changes they wanted to make across South Wales. One day John carried out some impromptu passenger counts on the trains at Carmarthen and on the competing Express West coaches, which ran past the front of the station in those days. The results were startling, and soon John returned to the same spot with a supervisor in tow.

"The train was a locomotive and five coaches. It had 30 passengers. The bus also had 30 passengers. I turned to the supervisor and said, 'Now you see the extent of the problem. If someone from the Department of Transport gets shirty and starts asking why so much is being spent on the railways then finds out that a five-coach train is carrying the same number of passengers as a bus which runs at a fifth of the cost, they'll suggest withdrawing the trains'."

The supervisor was impressed by this argument. From then on there was an acceptance at last that change was essential to the future of rail services in South Wales.

Correcting Timetable Madness

When action had been taken to rerail the other services in South Wales, John and his team at Brunel House turned their attentions to the services which passed through the station outside their office windows, Cardiff Queen Street. The fares structure in the valleys stuck out like a sore thumb, but the first task was to examine the system carefully to discover what needed to be tackled as a priority.

This investigation threw a new light on the most recent timetable changes, all of which proved to be counter-productive. In 1982

Merthyr service had been cut to two-hourly for part of the day by dint of turning round some trains at Pontypridd and Abercynon. This meant passengers could not rely on a train every hour into Cardiff or Pontypridd or back up the valley. A patchy service of this sort was on course to take a hammering once the new A470 dual carriageway, then under construction, was completed.

Barry Island, Bargoed and Ystrad Mynach also competed for the prize for the most pointless and counter-productive change in the early 1980s. The half-hourly service to Barry Island was reduced to hourly in the 1970s. In 1982 Barry Island's service was reduced again, possibly by managers who saw Barry Island purely as a beach resort and overlooked the local population. In 1982, Barry Island was prescribed a train every two hours between September/October and May.

Barry Island has long since ceased to be an island and the railway reaches it by a low half-mile viaduct across a patch of flat land that at one time was washed with seawater. The main route through Barry, even after the disappearance of passenger services through he Vale of Glamorgan, was straight on towards Llantwit Major. Passenger trains which terminated at Barry needed to switch to the other track to return to Cardiff, and the trackwork and signalling was such that the DMUs had to proceed nearly half way along the short Barry Island branch to clear the points which would lead them back into Barry station on the Cardiff-bound track. The cutbacks saved no time and almost no fuel, but denied Barry Island a proper service even though the trains almost reached its platform ramps every hour.

A feature of the new timetable in May 1983 was the isolation of the service at the top of the Rhymney Valley. This move was so blatantly counter-productive that it is difficult not to suspect an ulterior motive. The 1960s had shown how services isolated within valleys, such as the Aberdare and Senghenydd branches, were crippled and vulnerable to attacks by Beeching's foraging axe-men. The 1980s and 1990s later showed how BR was able to circumvent the 1963 Railways Act by manipulating usage of trains in advance of closure proposals.

Mid Glamorgan County Council had already drawn up plans for closure of the line between Bargoed and Rhymney and intended the closure to form part of the project for a new, centrally located station for Bargoed.

The May 1983 timetable brought a single power car to the top of the valley to provide a two-hourly shuttle service between Bargoed and Rhymney. The idea was ostensibly to save power-car mileage, since only one powered vehicle would ply the northern end of the line instead of the two in each standard three-car DMU set. The platforms and tracks had been reduced at Bargoed – once a busy interchange where the Cardiff–Rhymney and Newport–Brecon lines crossed – and the single car shuttle could not occupy the sole remaining platform road while the Cardiff train arrived

and departed. Consequently, there was a 15 minute wait for passengers travelling through Bargoed in one direction.

On top of the huge disincentive to travellers, the change actually cost more in pure financial terms than it saved. No facilities were laid on for train crew to take their breaks at Bargoed, so each shift on the shuttle had to be staffed by two drivers and a conductor. These high labour costs negated any savings that were meant to come from reducing power-car mileage.

"As an economic solution to the problem of declining traffic it was a disaster," says John.

The final nonsense was more subtle but conspiracy theorists may wish to believe it was linked to plans - which came close to being put into practice - to single-track the line between Ystrad Mynach and Bargoed. In the early 1980s a connection was installed at Ystrad Mynach to allow trains to reverse there and set off back to Cardiff along the appropriate track. Bargoed's hourly service was cut to two-hourly, the intermediate trains being turned round short at Ystrad Mynach. However, the rest of the timetable remained unchanged. Every two hours a train would wait with its engines idling at Ystrad Mynach for the period it would previously have used to reach Bargoed, reverse and come back to Ystrad Mynach.

It was Ian Walmsley, the DMU engineer at Cardiff Canton, who alerted John Davies to the folly of this situation.

"Ian Walmsley was quite an enthusiast of the DMUs and he went to extremes to look after them. In 1983 we didn't have the luxury to wait for the possibility of new rolling stock. We had to improve the business with what we had, even though the trains leaked oil badly and were frequently late coming off maintenance," says John.

"Ian pointed out to us that the DMUs which stood at Ystrad Mynach came back to the depot with coked-up engines. The idling was actually damaging the engines. They had to have more maintenance because of idling than they would need if they'd been running for that extra time. The drivers wouldn't switch off their engines because they were afraid they wouldn't be able to start them up again!

"The timetable had been botched up. Ian Walmsley said we should change the timetable so the DMUs had no idling at Ystrad Mynach. When we made that change the reliability of services improved."

The October timetable therefore brought three significant changes, all of them ironing out ill-conceived cutbacks. All trains on the Barry line ran through to Barry Island, Bargoed got its hourly service back and passengers from north of Bargoed could relish the luxury of through trains again. (They did not, however, believe that the sword of Damocles hanging over their line had been taken away, and at meeting after meeting John had to face

The futility of cutting Barry Island's service to two hourly in the 1970s is illustrated by this view of the entire Barry Island branch. Trains had to proceed about as far as the Sprinter in this view in order to reverse at Barry, so hardly anything was gained - and much was lost - by not sending every train the extra few hundred yards to Barry Island station, which is behind the signal arm on the left of this picture. *Stephen Miles*

the wrath of local community leaders.) Rectifying the two hour gaps on the Merthyr line had to wait a little longer.

Timetables were also altered slightly to coincide with the first significant investment in the valleys system since dieselisation in 1958 - the opening of Cathays station. A station in central Cardiff, close to the university college, Welsh Office and other institutions, had been planned by South Glamorgan County Council for several years. No new stations had been constructed in South Wales since the demise of the Great Western Railway and one Conservative councillor attacked the planned expenditure of £83,000 on Cathays station which, he predicted, would be an unwanted platform. In the event, Cathays reached its five-year target of usage in its first three months.

This unexpectedly warm welcome was partly due to the new culture on the local railways which coincided with the opening of Cathays station and was helped by some judicious timetable planning back in early 1983. The Cathays Park area of Cardiff is a significant employment zone for white-collar workers and Stuart Davies decided in advance that Cathays station, on the line from Cardiff to Pontypridd, should be served by as many trains as possible from Cardiff's commuter land, the area served by the Barry and Penarth trains. Consequently, the October 1983 timetable established as a principle that Rhymney-line trains would mostly start at Cardiff Bute Road or Cardiff Central while the Barry and Penarth services would run to Pontypridd and beyond via Cathays. This arrangement also had the happy bonus of providing frequent through trains between the campus of the University of Wales College of Cardiff and the Polytechnic of Wales at Trefforest. The trains became popular with students who needed to attend events or use research facilities at one campus or the other.

Amendments to the timetable in October 1983 and the opening of the new station were, however, overshadowed by John Davies's first spectacular action to attract fresh custom to the valley trains. John and his eager new team of managers had cut their teeth solving problems in West Wales and on the InterCity route in South Wales. They had established a degree of autonomy from Paddington headquarters and had tested some bold ideas. Now they were confident enough to take on the biggest problem of all – the fares structure in the valleys.

Fare Reductions

By 1983 poverty was rife in the valleys. All the collieries in the Rhondda Fawr valley had closed, as had many others across the South Wales coalfield, and thousands of former mining families found themselves having to rely on state benefits.

It was partly because of this background that cutting fares was the quickest way to attract new passengers to the trains in the valleys. Unemployed people were not short of time so train frequency was not such an important consideration as elsewhere. They were short of money, however. The high fares being charged in the valleys were way out of step with the economic transformation that had taken place there fairly suddenly. The fares structure itself was unnecessarily complicated and took little account of the geography of the valleys.

"Keith Galley and I went to talk to the staff. Everybody was agreed that the fares were wrong, but we didn't know quite how," recalls John Davies.

He secured three management trainees from Western Region headquarters and gave them a month to investigate fares in the valleys and come up with suggestions for tackling the problems. Time was quickly running out for all-day, all-week services in the valleys and John was determined to make changes in October 1983.

"Those trainees had the hardest month's work they've ever had," says John. "They came back recommending a new fares structure, taking into account peak and off-peak flows. They looked at the effect of reducing fares by different amounts in different places. We told them fares changes had to earn at least enough money to cover the reduction by attracting extra passengers. That was a tall order, and they came up with a good plan. Even though it was substantially changed a few months later, it was excellent as a starting point."

One element of their research which was thrown out was their recommendation of a zonal fares structure, like that in London. Keith Galley told the trainees, "A zonal fares system is only of interest to the people who invent it. To the customer, the only relevant fare is the fare from A to B which he uses. The fact that it relates to various other fares in the network is of no interest. The system also creates big steps between the zones, which is hard luck on people who happen to be travelling from the edge of one zone into the next one. It creates cheaper fares for some people, but others find they're being ripped off and they shout about it and at the end of the day you've achieved nothing."

The valleys system was compact enough for each passenger flow to be priced individually. This could take into account the varying social circumstances and affluence of people in various places served by the system, it could take into account rail's advantages and disadvantages in certain locations, it could acknowledge patterns of travel to and from the larger towns in the valleys, and it could be varied according to the spare capacity on trains in certain corridors.

When the trainees presented their research they offered a low risk option and a high-risk option. The low-risk choice involved putting a sensible fares structure in place and selectively reducing fares on the principal corridors. The high-risk option involved slashing the fares by large amounts all round the system, at the same time as introducing a sensible fares structure tailored to the needs of the valleys. John and his colleagues asked the trainees which option they would choose if they were middle managers whose careers depended on not making damaging business decisions. Two of them opted for the high-risk choice. The other clearly didn't know John Davies very well.

One of the basic elements of the new fares structure which was then devised was an incentive for people to use the trains within the valleys. The trains' key earnings were from the tops of the valleys to Cardiff. Only small reductions were needed to those core fares but the fares for journeys wholly within the valleys could be reduced dramatically at no great loss to BR, filling half-empty trains and generating masses of publicity and goodwill into the bargain. Accordingly, the fares which saw some of the most drastic reductions were fares from stations on the Treherbert and Merthyr lines to Pontypridd, an important local hub and market town. The return fare from Treherbert to Pontypridd was cut from £2 to £1, with no peak restrictions.

To protect the core revenue, Heath and Llandaf were designated boundaries for peak fares. Anyone travelling from the valleys to a station south of Heath or Llandaf in the morning peak had to pay a peak-period fare. Anyone travelling to a destination north of those stations paid a much lower fare, a fare that was constant at any time of day.

Another important feature of the new fares structure was a huge cut in fares in the upper Rhymney Valley. John deliberately made train travel from Rhymney to Cardiff cheaper than the parallel journey to Cardiff from the heads of the other valleys still served by rail.

"The competitive situation there was so bad we were prepared to try anything," says John. "We desperately needed more passengers at the top of the Rhymney Valley."

The new fares came into force throughout the valleys system with the October 1983 timetable change. There wasn't enough time to experiment on one line at a time. The situation called for all or nothing. Every station saw its fares reduced, to a greater or lesser degree, and everywhere there was a phenomenal reaction. The fact that the fares cut was comprehensive generated much greater publicity than would have been forthcoming had just one line's fares been reduced at a time.

"There had been an experiment in Sweden some years previously. They had major reductions in fares and got more passengers onto the trains. I decided that if this was going to work in the valleys it would have to be dramatic. I didn't want people to think, 'That's nice. I'll think about using the train some day.' They had to say, 'We will use the train!' If they didn't react like that we would have failed," says John.

"The strategy hit the headlines. It was front-page news for the South Wales Echo. Railways just weren't known for this sort of thing. There was so much publicity that it got people saying, 'One pound! That's cheap.' Before we had all this publicity people wouldn't even bother to ask what the fare was. They assumed it was too expensive."

The best testament to the mood of the time and the effect of the publicity is the record of Caerphilly station. Caerphilly is a relatively affluent town close to Cardiff but separated from it by a mountain. The railway tunnels in a straight line through the mountain while the roads make a time-consuming detour over or around the mountain. To some extent the railway had a captive market in Caerphilly, so the off-peak fares were not reduced. The general euphoria was such that off-peak ridership from Caerphilly shot up in line with that from the places which had seen reductions in off-peak fares.

"People who hadn't used the train previously wouldn't have known that the fares were the same before. The publicity got them to ask at about the fares and they thought they were pretty cheap."

The publicity and the good reception created a buzz on the trains. Even the most cynical members of staff had to admit the results were spectacular. But the great experiment wasn't over yet; John planned to strike again while the iron was hot.

"When the Great Northern line out of London King's Cross was electrified they had a week of half-price fares on top of a structure where the fares had already been reduced. They got thousands of people onto the trains, people who thought they would try it out just because it was so cheap," says John.

"When we reduced our fares we wanted to make sure everybody knew about it. Three weeks afterwards was half term week, when the local schools would be closed for the holiday. The trains on our main valley routes were already packed, but we decided to halve the fares for the week. We advertised it as 'Half-price for half-term'. We paid for advertisements and got an awful lot of good editorial coverage in the media."

"People said we were daft to reduce prices when the trains were already well filled. We felt – quite rightly as it turned out – that people would put up with cramped travelling conditions because the fares were so cheap. We had very few complaints and the trains were packed to the gunnels. We had the best response I've ever known from railway staff. They were initially very sceptical. It was a big culture shock, and when they realised we meant business they pulled the stops out. They were so thrilled to see all these people on the trains that they went to Herculean efforts to keep things going and put on a good show. We still had slackers but the majority worked hard at it. I think the shock therapy did the trick!"

The fares reduction was an eminent success. Within two months of the change, ridership on the valleys system had increased by 40%. The top end of the Rhymney Valley – which was supposedly incapable of sustaining a train service – saw a threefold increase in passengers, who were thankful not only for cheaper fares but for the restoration of their through trains to Cardiff. By Christmas 1983 the official results came through the system. They showed that the increases in South Glamorgan – chiefly the Coryton, Penarth and Barry lines – were lower than in the valleys, confirming the need for a different strategy there.

"We knew we'd gained an increase in passengers but we didn't think it would be as much as 40% overall. We actually had an increase in revenue, despite the fares reductions and the half-price week," says John.

"The whole thing shook the valleys. It was a change of seismic proportions, as far as the railway was concerned. Most commentators were with us. The people who were against us tended to be some of the hierarchy in BR, who said, 'It hasn't worked before so it's not going to work now'."

Such a widescale change inevitably threw up a few fares anomalies. Because the valleys were now being managed like a homely Welsh farmstead instead of a Stalinist collective farm, all these anomalies could be abolished almost as soon as they were spotted. For one thing, the policy of not applying peak fares for journeys down the valleys as far as Llandaf or Heath meant that it was cheaper in some cases for Cardiff-bound commuters to buy a cheap day return to Llandaf plus a peak return from Llandaf to Cardiff than to buy one peak return for the whole journey.

"Where we found people re-booking in significant numbers we corrected the anomalies straight away. We didn't wait till the next general fares revision. It was much easier to change fares then than it is now, because you didn't have to change computer software. You just had to make sure that all the conductors and station staff had got the instructions."

The booking clerk at Porth station, a railman of many years' experience called Cliff, alerted the management to a fare which had been cut too far by the mechanics of the new fares structure. Porth to Pontypridd, a popular destination, cost just 40p return. It was £1 before the change. Cliff was delighted with the reduction as a principle but said BR was throwing money away at Porth. The fare was quickly increased to 60p, a change which hardly affected the brisk trade there.

Some years later, John attempted to correct an anomaly he had deliberately introduced in 1983 - the extra-cheap fares in the upper Rhymney Valley. "We decided that it would be sensible to have the same fare from the tops of all the valleys so that we could

Passengers besiege a six-car evening train to Rhymney at Queen Street station in 1985. Scenes like this were commonplace after the 1983 fares cut and they convinced John Davies that more frequent trains were needed to keep the cramped platforms at Queen Street relatively clear.
Western Mail and Echo Ltd

advertise the same maximum fares everywhere. Our attempt to raise the Rhymney fare by more than the increase applying to the heads of the other valleys was found out by the busybodies who made it their business to spot these things!"

This is a reference to the eagle-eyed members of the Glamorgan Rail Users' Federation, a voluntary group set up to defend the valleys services when they were at their lowest ebb.

"Our cover was blown. We were following a basic principle in retailing: you lower the price to get far more people buying, then you increase it gradually and nobody notices. It's the same principle that's used in the shops. Apparently when it's done on the railways it's unethical, but when other firms do it it's commercial practice!"

As part of the change to the new fares structure, conductors in the valleys were equipped with Setright ticket machines.

"The sweeping changes we were making to the fares structure, coupled with discount offers, made monitoring of tickets difficult," says John. "We soon heard from Harry Carradice at the Central Fares Office in Croydon. He was a powerful man who ruled with an iron rod. He was protecting income, and in a way he was right. He wanted to ensure that the railway wouldn't lose any income as a result of innovations in ticket sales.

"I'd never met Harry at the time we were going through these arguments. Some years later I met him. He was a super chap, and we had a good laugh about 1983. I said, 'I had the last laugh. It all worked out all right for me. It could have gone the other way and I don't know what would have happened!' It was nice to know that he didn't hold it against me."

There were plenty of other doubting Thomases to convince before the fares reduction went ahead. One senior manager asked John if he had a contingency plan, in case the whole thing flopped. John replied that he had but the manager didn't ask what that plan was - a stroke of good fortune since John had no plans of the sort! Failure was unthinkable.

It is easy to see what made the BR hierarchy uneasy about the changes proposed by John. The future of a whole group of passenger services was being gambled by a manager who had little experience of changing services at all, let alone turning them upside down in one go. His ideas often appeared to be running counter to established practices on the railways and he seemed to care little for the advice of more experienced people who had seen decades of service in BR. Most alarmingly of all, he appeared to be acting chiefly on hunches.

The people who thought such things, however, overlooked one crucial factor – a factor that was to make the whole valleys revolution proceed with scarcely a falter. That factor was his knowledge of the market in South Wales. John was born and bred in industrial South Wales. Whether being a Welshman made him more eager than most to see the valley trains full of passengers again is difficult to prove either way, but the fact that he had seen those railways functioning in better times ought to have fired his determination to see a better deal not only for the railways and their staff but also for the deprived people in the valleys. Those people might not have had jobs or decent houses but one thing John wanted them to have was a rail service that matched their pockets and their travel needs. After all the people of industrial South Wales were John's former schoolmates, his friends and his relatives.

John's understanding of the valleys is illustrated by one episode concerning Peter Owen, an advertising manager from BR's Central Advertising Services. He was also Welsh but came from Chepstow - a town on the English border which has closer ties with the agrarian lifestyles of Monmouthshire and Gloucestershire than with the heavy industry of the valleys and the South Wales coastal belt.

"We engaged CAS to do the advertising campaign for our new fares," says John. "We asked them for a sample of what they could do. We liked it and we engaged them instead of the Western Region advertising people in Paddington. There was a hell of a row, but we told Paddington that CAS were doing far sharper advertisements than they were. Our campaign was sharply focused, concentrating on key things. It was simple to understand. CAS told us to go for the selling message even if the advertisements didn't tell the whole story – tell the public something big was happening without worrying about the finer detail.

"Peter Owen said we had a big problem in the upper Rhymney Valley because nobody on BR had been able to sell a two-hourly local service successfully. I said, 'People have a strong affinity to rail travel there. If you do something, they'll respond.' He disagreed but we told him to go ahead.

"It turned out that we were right, but he wasn't upset. It shows that you can't always apply national solutions to a local area. You've got to understand the market. I've said repeatedly over the years that the valleys is a unique local market. It's got characteristics that few other markets have. You can do as much generalised research as you like but nothing beats getting out there and finding out what makes the public tick. That was a problem with some of my predecessors – they relied on figures that came up in research rather than getting close to the market."

Before any change could be made there were always numerous people, above and below John in the echelons, who had to be persuaded of the value of the change. But there was one man who understood, appreciated and trusted John's unusual approach – divisional manager Frank Markham. By sheer good fortune he was in the crucial buffer zone between John and Western Region headquarters at Paddington. As long as he was willing to give John and his colleagues the few extra inches of tether they required, there was little that Paddington could do to stop the changes John proposed.

"Frank Markham was happy for us to do what we wanted as long as it was legitimate. I went to him a number of times to ask what he thought of my proposals. 'If you think it will work,' he would say, 'Give it a go. If it fails, then better luck next time.' Before him the attitude had been, 'Don't try it because if you fail you're out on your backside.' "

"I've rarely worked with such a good guy. He was a bit of a loner and a lot of people didn't like him because he had this unconventional style of managing. He didn't direct from the top like his predecessor, who was an autocratic type. Frank Markham came to Cardiff with not a good reputation. He'd been marketing manager at Bristol and had some rather un-railwaylike ideas. Everybody looked at him with great suspicion when he was elevated to divisional manager at Cardiff, and thought he would be difficult to work with. I didn't find that, and neither did David Warne, the operations manager. Frank Markham was a man I greatly admired. He gave me the freedom to do my own thing. Without him it would have been much more difficult to do what we did."

That fateful year in the history of the valley trains, 1983, had begun with despair and more cutbacks. In January John Davies held out little hope for them and couldn't fathom where to start rectifying the problems, if that was indeed possible.

By the end of 1983 the worst of the cutbacks had been reversed, the valley routes had an important new station in Cardiff, they had a new ticketing structure, much cheaper fares, and - most encouraging of all - 40 per cent more passengers.

"We had been lucky getting it right first time," says John. "Although there were still huge problems to be tackled, this initial success gave us the heart to carry on."

THE MERTHYR LINE

Above: The rather shabby terminus at Merthyr was biding its time in 1989 while the details of a proposal to redevelop the site for shopping were being discussed. The station, once also serving routes to Abergavenny, Hirwaun and Pontsticill, was closed in 1996 and replaced by a new single platform a little further from the town centre to release the old site for property development.

Left: Merthyr's bus and rail stations are not adjacent, so Mid Glamorgan County Council created this space at the forecourt of the railway station for Silverline's buses to Brecon to connect with trains. The interchange is neatly illustrated in this 1990 view.

Below: A special train, the Western Requiem, passes Black Lion loop in 1977 as it returns to Cardiff from Merthyr behind loco No. D 1010 WESTERN CAMPAIGNER. The loop and signal box were retained chiefly to serve the sidings of Merthyr Vale colliery but they allowed a half houfly passenger service to run in the morning and evening peaks. After the colliery had closed the loop was removed, confining the Merthyr line to an hourly service.   *Stephen Miles (3)*

Right: Although Regional Railways was in charge of the Valley Lines in April 1991, the popular local branding is still evident on the station sign at Merthyr station. Opposite the service train is a Class 37 locomotive, aptly named Taff Merthyr, which had arrived with an inspection saloon carrying civic guests as part of the celebrations to mark the Taff Vale Railway's 150th anniversary.

Left: This 1986 aerial view of Abercynon clearly shows the lack of a connection between the Merthyr and Aberdare lines at the north end of the platform, a situation which necessitated construction of a second Abercynon station on the Aberdare branch in 1988. Building a new platform was considerably cheaper than remodelling the junction. The track between the platform and the old engine shed is a long sand drag, to halt any train that might run away on the steeply graded track towards Merthyr.

Right: Another element of the TVR 150 celebration in 1991 was an hourly service to Merthyr on a wet Sunday to connect with a vintage vehicle display in Merthyr. Extra services were provided by a rake of coaches topped and tailed by Class 37 locos. Here the driver of the rear loco is surrendering to the Abercynon signalman the token for the single line between Black Lion and Abercynon as the unusual train heads back towards Cardiff Bute Road.

Left: A Merthyr to Penarth service glides past Pontypridd Junction signal box in 1991. The Rhondda line is visible in the foreground. Two years later the ground between the two routes was excavated and a concrete box pushed underneath the tracks to take the Pontypridd inner relief road. Remarkably, the trains kept running while the bridge was constructed beneath the tracks. *Stephen Miles (4)*

CHAPTER 3

THE PEOPLE'S RAILWAY
The Marketing Revolution

The rail passenger system in the valleys leapt into 1984 rejuvenated like a patient after a successful heart-transplant. A fares structure tailored to the needs and pockets of the local people was the new heart, and it had instantly begun pumping the healthy blood corpuscles of extra passengers and extra income around the system.

It is in 1984 that the story of the rail renaissance in the valleys takes a different turn from previous successful attempts to increase patronage of rail services, in South Wales and wider afield. Where many managers would have sat back, congratulated themselves on achieving a rapid 40% increase in usage and turned their attentions to other matters, John Davies and his colleagues in Cardiff viewed their success merely as an indicator of how much more could, and should, be done in the valleys.

The scope for improvement manifested itself not so much in an inefficient use of resources (which had partly driven the 1953 timetable restructuring) as in a perception that the trains were not serving their market as best they could. However, deciding what this unique market needed and finding ways to meet the demand from limited resources was far more difficult than making changes that were led by operational needs. The way John Davies tackled this problem characterises the valleys' rail renaissance more than any other feature. He followed the maxim: if in doubt, study the market. From now on, the people themselves would be the prime motivation behind improvements to the rail services.

John's hunch about fares had been verified by the experiment of 1983 and now he had a notion that a different way must be found to answer the needs of the people who lived south of Cardiff, along the Barry and Penarth lines.

"We didn't have as much success on the Barry and Penarth lines as we had elsewhere with the new fares structure," he says. "It proved that cutting fares was not the universal panacea. On the Barry and Penarth lines we even lost money, because we didn't attract enough extra passengers to cover the drop in income which resulted from lower fares. When we analysed the situation there we realised that an hourly service wasn't enough to attract people. Because they lived fairly close to Cardiff they expected to walk on to services without having to refer to timetables."

This was an acknowledgement that the social make-up of the area south of Cardiff was completely different from that in the valleys. The residents of Penarth, Dinas Powys and other places served by the railway were generally middle class and employed in white-collar work. In the valleys, characterised by unemployment, money was scarce but time was less of a problem; south of Cardiff money was not too short but time was of the essence. The people of the valleys were more used to accepting whatever they were given, notwithstanding the erstwhile strength of the trade-union movement there; on the Barry and Penarth corridors, the people were used to influencing the provision of services and facilities. They had the political leverage to get what they wanted in many cases, and they had the money to be able to vote with their feet if anything fell short of their expectations.

"We didn't know frequency was the key to this yet, so we tested the market," says John.

In February 1984 the number of trains on the Penarth branch was doubled, giving the town a half-hourly service to and from Cardiff throughout the day. To run this month-long experiment an extra train shuttled between Cardiff Queen Street and Penarth every hour, supplementing the traditional service which ran through to Penarth from the valleys.

"We would do a check on the income returns and if they showed an upturn we would continue the experiment. If they continued to rise, we would make the half-hourly service permanent. We wondered if a month would be long enough to indicate a meaningful response from the market, but as it turned out things began to change immediately. We had problems with staff who couldn't see the point of doubling the frequency. There was a lot of apathy, and some thought it was a management trick. I remember having a row with a conductor who said he would rather be sitting in the messroom at Canton. He had been taken off a spare roster to crew the extra service to Penarth and thought he was wasting his time going on the train. The Penarth experiment showed an immediate increase – not tremendous but enough to convince us that we should give it longer."

By this time the management had already devised a plan to double train frequency on the Barry line, which had lost its half-hourly service in the 1960s. The fact that the machinery of the Great Britain train timetable had ground past the point of no return for the May 1984 edition meant little to this group of managers who knew they had unearthed the key to better patronage on the Barry line.

"We made last-minute adjustments to the timetable. We used to produce a staff timetable, which I regret to say we never marketed to the public. It was a booklet consisting only of table 130 from the national rail timetable. If we made late alterations we could print them in there. The local people knew, even if the national timetable was inaccurate. We rode the criticisms of that."

In June 1984 Barry regained its half-hourly service, which it welcomed with open arms. Meanwhile, the fact that the Penarth shuttle train was spending a large part of its day idling at Queen Street had not escaped John's notice, and neither had the needs of another well-to-do market in the area - the catchment of the Coryton line. This stub of the old Cardiff Railway served the semi-detached houses and tree-lined avenues of north Cardiff. The Coryton services were tailored to the needs of commuters; there were trains in the peak periods and some around lunchtime. An infrequent service on such a short route would not appeal to many people - who had cars, taxis and frequent buses as alternatives.

"In May 1984 we experimented by running the Penarth shuttle up to the Coryton line, to give a more frequent service off-peak at no extra cost to us," says John. "But we couldn't get a train to run from Penarth, turn round at Coryton and get back to Penarth in an hour."

In the event the extra trains ran as far as Rhiwbina only. The main sacrifice was the demand from Coryton station; Whitchurch, the other station which was not served by the off-peak train, generated relatively little custom for the railway.

"In commercial terms it didn't make sense, but in terms of using marginal resources it did."

The experiment failed for the most bizarre of reasons. News that off-peak trains would run as far as Rhiwbina had sparked a fierce debate. It was alleged that the management was planning to close the western end of the branch, even though that section had the same service as before. The Rhiwbina shuttle did nothing to undermine that service; if anything it could have strengthened the branch's position by proving a need for off-peak services. Following protests by self-appointed rail watchdogs, the public was already sceptical when the service enhancement was instituted.

"When the rail supporters cry foul, the general public you're trying to attract think the service can't be any good because the rail supporters are saying it's no good. In this case, there was a substantial improvement in services," says John.

"This, I'm afraid, often typifies the so-called rail supporters who sometimes destroy the case they are trying to promote through injudicious lobbying. Sometimes they get it right, of course, and I was genuinely pleased with the support we got over the years from the Glamorgan Rail Users' Federation."

Among the many interested observers was South Glamorgan County Council. Buoyed by the extraordinary success of the new station it had funded at Cathays and pleased with the half-hourly services now running permanently on the Penarth and Barry routes, the council asked BR to lay on an hourly off-peak service over the full extent of the Coryton branch in 1985. Such a service would require an extra off-peak DMU diagram and BR could see no way the carryings on the Coryton line, especially after the failure of the Rhiwbina shuttle, would pay for the costs incurred. South Glamorgan was insistent, however, and offered to cover any shortfall in the experimental service up to a maximum of £17,000 for the first six months.

"We agreed to put an hourly service in and we did it as cheaply as possible using a single power car. We started on Saturdays from October 1984. The single car was frequently bursting to the seams, although the loadings wouldn't have justified a three-car DMU."

At the end of the six-month experiment BR turned to the council to extract its pound of flesh - a pound which had become an ounce.

"The £17,000 mooted at the outset became £1,700. That's all the loss was. We were delighted to have been proved wrong. After the first six months we said we would carry on the hourly service, and after that we never needed to ask the county council for money."

That remains the only time a county council in South Wales has ever provided revenue support for a rail service. After it, the county councils in South and Mid Glamorgan adopted a policy of funding capital improvements rather than underwriting losses which BR might accrue on services.

"The county council underwrote a test-marketing exercise on the Coryton line. It would be difficult for a local authority to do that now because the costs attributed to rail operation are higher. In the mid-1980s we were naive in believing that we were covering our true marginal costs, and perhaps that naivete helped us," says John. "After privatisation we may see more test-marketing, but in recent years there has been a great reluctance by the railway authorities to experiment with anything of that sort."

The railway authorities were also sceptical in the mid-1980s.

"We were hesitant but we did it because we had Frank Markham as divisional manager. We had somebody there to act as a sponge between us and higher authority. People thought I was crazy test-marketing on the railway. Although test-marketing was a common procedure in retail, it was unknown on the railways in South Wales when we tried it on the Penarth line."

"It had been tried elsewhere on BR. An all-purpose railcard, a citizens' railcard for people of all ages, was test-marketed in the Stoke-on-Trent division. It wasn't too attractive so the railcard scheme was not introduced across the network. I was responsible for test-marketing Saver-type tickets in the early 1980s, on InterCity trains from Norwich and Cambridge. Those ticket types were generally successful and they were established across the network. Test-marketing was happening on other consumer products all over the place. Supermarkets would try a product in a local area and apply it everywhere if it worked."

By May 1985 all the local services contained within South Glamorgan had been greatly improved, primarily by BR management second-guessing what the market needed; improvements to the Penarth and Barry lines involved simply answering the latent demand for more frequent, regular services. Tackling the complexities of the valleys market would be more difficult, but the South Glamorgan experience gave John Davies and his colleagues courage in their conviction that new services should take the market as their starting point rather than the resources available.

Timetable Changes

When the time came in 1984 for an objective appraisal of the valleys timetable an obvious priority was to ensure that any changes would not disrupt the travelling habits of established customers. The local services were important, for example, to children attending several schools, notably two private schools in central Cardiff and a comprehensive school in Merthyr Vale. Changing the times of trains just a few minutes either way could make these children late for morning assembly or force them to leave lessons early at the end of the day.

The basic valleys timetable had seen little change since 1953, other than some ham-fisted pruning. The basic patterns of travel had changed relatively slowly, compared with the rate at which they were changing in the 1980s. Although in the mid-1980s there was still a large demand for travel to and from Cardiff at the traditional peak periods, there was also demand at the shoulders of the peaks because of the increase in flexi-time and part-time working. The employment scene within the valleys had recently been turned on its head; there were no collieries functioning in the Rhondda Fawr valley and people who found alternative employment in the numerous new factories soon discovered that cars often provided a more practical way to commute than trains.

Against the background of this shifting market, John Davies thought twice about reversing cutbacks which were made to cut costs and no other reason - chiefly the withdrawal of two trains in the afternoon on the Merthyr line and the halving of Rhymney's hourly frequency. Simply restoring the services to their post-1953 form might not serve the new market in the best way. Once again the people provided the answer.

"I spent one afternoon at Pontypridd, watching and listening," says John. "I saw a lot of people coming to the station with their shopping bags who saw there was no train to Merthyr for over an hour and said, 'Oh well, we'll get a taxi.' I thought, 'Taxi to Merthyr? For God's sake, what are we doing?' We were throwing custom away."

Worse still was the fact that the trains had nothing better to do than take the shoppers home. One of the afternoon trains which had been stopped from running through to Merthyr spent a while out of use in Pontypridd station before returning to Cardiff. The other turned round at Abercynon and came straight back, throwing the even half-hourly spacing south of Pontypridd into disarray. By further observation, John found that this, too, was harming customers.

"There would be two trains 10 minutes apart then nothing for another 50 minutes. It happened at a very bad time in the afternoon, particularly for the students at Trefforest. People would turn up for a train thinking one would arrive within 30 minutes but then they'd find they had to wait up to 50 minutes for the next one. I went to Frank Markham and told him this was nonsense and that we should restore those two trains to Merthyr. 'Well get on with it,' he said. 'If it doesn't work, don't worry. Try something else'."

It did work. The Merthyr gaps were filled on Saturdays first, and on weekdays later. Business started climbing on the route immediately, helped along by a careful marketing campaign.

"We did a promotion along the Merthyr line to tell people there was an hourly service to Cardiff and Pontypridd. It wasn't saying we'd reintroduced these trains but simply advertised the sort of service people would warm to."

The message was limited to outlining train frequency, journey time and cost, with a telephone number for further details. The municipally owned bus firm, Merthyr Tydfil Transport, resolved to make an incisive response to the railway's marketing campaign.

"It took two years for them to get the necessary changes through the council committees, and by that time the customers had gone elsewhere!" says John.

Testing the new all-day services to Merthyr and Coryton on Saturdays initially resulted in the Saturday timetable taking its first steps towards autonomy in October 1984. Traditionally, the Saturday service had been the same as the weekday service. Where extra trains were needed, these were simply slotted in between the trains which ran throughout the week.

When the valleys timetables were reviewed it was clear that there was great demand for off-peak day-return travel on Saturdays, a demand which was not entirely being met by the pattern of the weekday timetable which was constructed around commut-

The Valley Lines' trump card has always been its penetration of Cardiff city centre. This 1991 view shows a train departing from Queen Street station surrounded by shops and office blocks. Developments like the Capitol centre, on the right, helped to transform Cardiff's attractiveness to shoppers. *John Davies*

ers' needs. Once the Saturday service had been modified to meet the people's needs, traffic grew to such an extent that the valleys system became the only one in Britain (with the possible exception of the West Midlands) where Saturdays were busier than weekdays.

Various factors may have influenced this situation, chief among them the location of Cardiff's two main stations. In a city like Manchester the principal stations were a few minutes' walk from the main retail areas, a distance which was enough to be a disincentive to people returning with several bags of shopping after spending the best part of the day on their feet. Cardiff Central and Queen Street were perfectly situated for Cardiff's shops, which stretched between the two stations. Indeed, clever shoppers from the valleys would alight at Queen Street and work their way through the shops towards Central, where they were guaranteed a seat on the homeward-bound train before the crush at Queen Street.

Even in the 1970s Cardiff exerted a strong pull on the valleys, at a time when its retail area had become run-down and lost much of its appeal as a place for recreational shopping. In the 1980s the city centre became a brighter, cleaner and livelier place, and consequently became an increasingly attractive destination for valleys folk.

There were other retail centres on the rail system. Pontypridd was an attractive destination for the Rhondda people, Caerphilly served much of the Rhymney Valley, Merthyr attracted people from nearby, and even Bargoed was a destination for shoppers from the upper Rhymney Valley. The fares reduction of 1983 was a double-edged sword for these towns. The dramatic reduction in off-peak fares to Cardiff meant that people who previously felt unable to afford the journey beyond Pontypridd or Caerphilly could now travel to Cardiff for the same price or not much more. On the other hand, the fares to these local destinations - especially Pontypridd - were also reduced and brought in new customers who rarely travelled before the reduction. Those towns changed as retail destinations - Pontypridd and Bargoed declined generally and many of Caerphilly's shops and cafes were turned into offices for estate agencies, insurance companies, building societies and other services - but the railways had less impact on their fortunes than the growing appeal of Cardiff, the increase in car ownership and the mushrooming of out-of-town superstores (which accounted for five per cent of UK sales in 1980 and 37 per cent in 1992).

There was, and still is, a close connection between the local railways and retail. Many teenagers got their first taste of independence when they were allowed to travel to Cardiff to visit the shops with their friends, and their natural mode of transport was the railway. Frequent services which ran to a pattern that was easily remembered, cheap off-peak fares and rapid penetration to the centre of Cardiff made the trains attractive to adults as well.

Some of the store managers in Cardiff told John Davies they witnessed a significant drop in business on the odd days of rail strikes in the 1980s.

"I was pleased to hear that, not because of the strikes and reduced custom but because it confirmed that rail had a significant share of the market for shoppers," says John. "It wasn't enough to persuade the Chamber of Commerce in Cardiff to help us. They said they'd love to help but improving the railways was BR's job."

It was not until the mid-1990s that shops and restaurants in Cardiff began running joint promotions which offered discounts to rail travellers, but it could be argued that the cheap fares and good reliability were enough to sell the services in the 1980s without the need for extra incentives of that sort.

If the special demands of the Saturday market merited changes to the timetable, the Sunday market - which barely resembled the weekday trade in any respect - called for even greater changes to the post-1953 pattern. Passengers using the local trains to connect into and out of main-line services at Cardiff Central were few and far between during the week. On Sundays, by contrast, passengers travelling to or from other destinations on BR accounted for most of the railways' custom on the valleys system.

One improvement to the Sunday services was to ensure that the main local services – on the Rhondda and Rhymney lines – connected with InterCity trains on the London route, something they had failed to do when running to the traditional three-hourly Sunday interval. On weekdays connections were not accorded the same priority for several reasons: there were so many lines to serve from two platforms that it would have been impossible to despatch trains to every valleys destination from Cardiff Central five minutes after the London train arrived; the local trains were frequent enough for transfer between long-distance and local services to be convenient in most cases; holding trains for guaranteed connections would have played havoc with a local system on which the train diagrams were closely tailored to the journey time permitted by the infrastructure; and since there was little demand for connections there was little point in gambling the attractiveness of the service to its core market simply to suit a small number of long-distance travellers.

Connections were a different matter on Sundays, however, and John found a novel solution to the problem of Caerphilly tunnel being closed for maintenance on winter Sundays.

"We put on buses which ran from Caerphilly to Newport, via Machen, instead of going to Cardiff. That way people could catch the same InterCity train from Newport as they would have if the Rhymney-line train was running through to Cardiff," says John. "Again people thought that was a crazy idea, but we wanted to look at it from the passengers' point of view. Our main market on Sundays was not to Cardiff but to desinations beyond Cardiff. Why take them to Cardiff, so they would have to catch the train

Right: This typical Valley Lines information board at Aberdare in 1989 bears the Valley Lines branding in the top right corner and headline fares on posters. Although this was a reversion to a practice introduced to the valleys in 1953, it was a radical departure from BR's policy of providing detailed information on such hoardings rather than marketing its most attractive products. The eye-catching £2.40 here is the cheap day return fare to Cardiff. The effect is undermined by the strip at the bottom which informs passengers that they will have to pay peak fares on rugby-match Saturdays (described in chapter 4).
Stephen Miles

Below: The poster used to advertise a special fun day at Barry Island, when the funfair was open only to rail passengers.

to London an hour later, when they could catch the earlier train at Newport?"

Passengers for Cardiff could take a train from Newport and arrive not much later than they would have had the bus run through to Cardiff.

Cutting out the dog-leg through Cardiff for eastbound passengers by offering a bus between Caerphilly and Newport is one place where John feels there is scope for innovation in the future.

"We were precluded by law from running buses at any time other than in emergency, but there's a lesson in what we did for the future. If there's a market, you should cater for it. Rail supporters say a bus is the thin end of a wedge, but if you're using a bus to create a new, seamless part of the rail service - whether it's at a certain time of day or along a corridor where there's no railway line - then why not?"

Cardiff Queen Street has been closed on Sundays every winter for many years, and it would have been difficult to justify the staffing costs of opening it on winter Sundays in the 1980s. On summer Sundays, however, the station was a hive of activity because of the Barry Island trade. Again, this was a market which John learnt about by using his eyes and ears rather than by relying on the findings of some survey or other.

"I spent a lovely fine morning on Cardiff Central station. It was an education. There were a lot of young people catching the bus from the big estates in Cardiff and taking the train from there to Barry Island. I saw people coming to the station and seeing that there was no train for another hour or 90 minutes. They got the bus instead. I could see all this business passing through our hands. There were lots of people around and they didn't have the patience to wait."

Further investigation revealed that hordes of young people were catching the buses from Rumney and Llanrumney, estates on the eastern edge of Cardiff, and alighting near Queen Street station, where they caught - or attempted to catch - the train to Barry Island.

"In the summer we had always had a significant Barry Island market, but we had to do a lot of heart-searching as to whether we were serving that market properly. The market was changing, and was no longer dominated by families travelling together for a day by the sea. We decided to make sure there was a good service from the heads of all the valleys we served at a good commercial time. But the key, as I found out by observing at Central and Queen Street, was Cardiff itself. There was a huge demand with the young people going to the clubs. It wasn't the funfair which attracted them, it was the other things that happened at Barry Island - some of them unmentionable in print!"

This changing market involved another influential factor. The young people from Cardiff, whose bus services ran to frequencies of every 10 minutes or greater, were not used to consulting timetables and organising their days out accordingly, as the

valleys folk and the less casual family groups had been doing since time immemorial. They rolled up at the station at all times throughout the morning. If there was no train imminent, they would take the bus.

After all this market information had been thrown into the melting pot at Brunel House, a radically different approach to the Barry Island Sunday market emerged. The result foreshadowed the change which would be instituted across Britain after the introduction of Sprinter trains. Instead of running a few long trains from the tops of the valleys through to the resort, shorter and more frequent trains were laid on. There was to be a train to Barry Island every half an hour, a shuttle from Cardiff Queen Street filling the gaps between the trains from the valleys. This arrangement also suited another passenger flow which John had

Sunday ★ April 28th '85
SPECIAL 'FUN DAY' ★ EXCURSION ★
BARRY ISLAND
Pleasure Park

FOR ONLY £3.50 PER HEAD ADULTS & CHILDREN AGE 5 AND OVER (Ask for a FREE ticket for under 5's)
BOOK IN ADVANCE
'JUST ONE PRICE TO PAY FOR A GREAT VALUE DAY'
"INCLUSIVE OF AS MANY RIDES AS YOU WISH" (Excluding all coin operated rides)

─── TIMETABLE ───

RHONDDA Tickets from your Local Station
TREHERBERT 10.35 LLWYNYPIA 10.47 PORTH 10.57   NO ADDITIONAL DISCOUNT FOR RAIL CARD HOLDERS
TREORCHY 10.39 TONYPANDY 10.50 TREHAFOD 11.01
YSTRAD 10.42 DINAS 10.53
ARRIVE BARRY ISLAND 11.45 RETURN 17.55
MERTHYR Tickets for your Local Station
MERTHYR 10.00 TROEDYRHIW 10.09 QUAKERS YARD 10.23
PENTREBACH 10.05 MERTHYR VALE 10.14 ABERCYNON 10.28
ARRIVE BARRY ISLAND 11.14 RETURN 17.00
ABERDARE TICKETS FROM HUGH EVANS TRAVEL, 36 CANNON ST.
ABERDARE. Tel: 876185
or
MOUNTAIN ASH TRAVEL, OXFORD ST. MOUNTAIN ASH. Tel: 472272
ABERDARE 10.00 MOUNTAIN ASH 10.25
ARRIVE BARRY ISLAND 11.33 RETURN 16.35
PONTYPRIDD TICKETS FROM YOUR LOCAL STATION
PONTYPRIDD 10.15 10.51 TREFOREST 10.19 10.55 TAFFS WELL 10.28
ARRIVE BARRY ISLAND 11.03 11.33 RETURN 16.35 17.35

discovered - for travel to the Bessemer Road Sunday market near Grangetown station. The number of people who used the train to reach Bessemer Road was significant enough to convince John that winter Sunday morning services should be retained on the Barry line when they were removed from the rest of the system.

The close relationship between the rail services and the prosperity of Barry Island was evident in early spring 1985 when BR arranged an exclusive day at the funfair for rail passengers on two weekends shortly before the season started. Special trains were run from the heads of the valleys, including Aberdare, to Barry Island and the passengers had the run of the fair.

"It wasn't a runaway success but it was useful. It was using marginal capacity on our part and on the part of the funfair owners, who were getting their rides ready for the summer."

The People's Railway

The rail system in the valleys in the 1980s is accurately described as 'The People's Railway' for two reasons: firstly, the people themselves had a direct bearing on the way the service was operated and developed; and secondly, the people had such a strong affinity with the railway that the trains were used to an extent unrivalled elsewhere in Britain. The second reason is backed up by the information which came out of one of the relatively few surveys conducted on the valleys system in the mid-1980s.

John Davies was sceptical of the data which the railway was collecting on auto-pilot when he arrived in Cardiff.

"In the early 1980s the staff used to provide returns on Saturdays for the number of passengers on the trains," he says. "They didn't have a clue how to count passengers. They would sometimes say there were 500 people on a train and knew damn well there were only 290 seats. The conductors used this phrase 'Full and standing'. That drove me mad. It was used everywhere. 'Full and standing'. Did that mean 10 people standing or 100 people standing? As a basis for train planning it was a useless statistic.

"I wanted the staff to describe trains as half full, threequarters, one and a quarter, and so on, but I couldn't get that. We got rid of the returns - they weren't worth the paper they were written on.

"Instead we went to the stations ourselves. Alan Beardsworth could size up a situation in no time at all. He used to count the empty seats on the train. A three-car DMU had 290 seats. If there were 20 empty seats there were 270 passengers. When there was standing, it was 290 plus the number standing. It might have been 10 or 20 people out, but it was better than 'Full and standing'."

Before the introduction of Sprinters in 1987 Provincial headquarters required the Cardiff management to conduct formal passenger surveys. Professionals were drafted in from outside to do the counting.

"They were briefed somewhere else, and when we got the results we could spot errors straight away. We knew certain trains were four-car trains, but they had only counted two cars. They couldn't walk through from one DMU to the other, and hadn't been told they would have to count the passengers on both. It showed that you can get people to do these marvellous presentations of data but the data can be useless."

John had already gathered the information he needed to run the railway in 1986, and it was the results of those surveys that verified the success of the developments.

"We had difficulty getting people to work on Saturdays to do surveys for us, so we asked the Glamorgan Rail Users' Federation to do a big survey at Pontypridd on a Saturday. We gave the members a free ticket to the place of their choice anywhere on the BR network by way of payment. We were very pleased with the work they did.

"We discovered just how many people travelled in the Rhondda. I remember distinctly that the number of journeys equated to 10% of the population of the Rhondda Fawr valley. On the basis that most journeys were returns, 5% of the local population were travelling that day. That doesn't sound a lot perhaps, but, when you consider the number of other things people could be doing on a Saturday and the number of people who could be travelling by car, that was a really astonishing figure. It wasn't 5%

of the transport market, it was 5% of the entire population. It included all the people who were immobile, infirm and who never went anywhere – and there are a lot of people like that in the valleys – so we thought it was tremendous."

"I made a lot of enquiries around the country to see if there was a comparable figure anywhere else. I couldn't find anything anywhere near that. I talked to people who said it was amazing that that proportion of people were travelling on the trains. I was able to claim, with some justification, that the Rhondda had the highest per capita usage of the train in the country. There may have been some London commuter services, but they would have been a specialised commuter market rather than Mr and Mrs Joe Public travelling, which is what we saw in the Rhondda. The Rhondda line is a people's railway, as most of the lines in the valleys were. It wasn't serving a niche market - everybody used the train."

Such success was not borne simply from the sensationalism of the 1983 fares change or the improved frequencies on most lines. As much as anything, the 1986 figures were testament to the effectiveness of the way the services were marketed.

Marketing the valleys services was a relatively straightforward exercise to John, who had risen through the ranks from being a marketing executive for rail freight in South Wales and then passenger marketing manager in Norwich. Because the valleys services were developed according to perceived demands in the marketplace, the marketing exercise was a matter of informing people that the trains were now meeting their needs. This was far simpler than trying to sell people a product they didn't need or which was fundamentally unsuitable, as had been the case to some extent in the Norwich division.

Another factor which contributed to the efficency of the marketing campaign was the local management's feel for the market. They knew that money was a prime consideration in the deprived valley towns, and therefore focused their posters and advertisements on the cheapest fare to Cardiff. Other details, such as train frequencies, journey times and other fares were displayed in smaller typfaces.

Leaflets and Vouchers

A central pillar of the early marketing strategy was a leaflet drop to thousands of houses in the catchment area. A different leaflet was printed for each locality, and an intimate knowledge of the market paid dividends when it came to deciding which information would be displayed most prominently to each target market.

"We segmented the whole valley network into about 15 areas," says John. "We could do a bespoke message for each one. It would sometimes be a basic message. If there was space on the commuter trains, on the Coryton line for example, the main message would be the ease and cheapness of commuting by train. In smaller print we would say that if you travelled after 09.30 it would be cheaper. In areas where commuting was perhaps causing overcrowding, say on the Barry line, we would major on the opportunity of cheap fares after 09.30 with a strong subsidiary message that you could also use the train for commuting. The weaknesses, in the areas where we had capacity to sell, and the strong selling points would be combined where possible."

The Coryton line provides an example of market knowledge being put to good use. Many people living near that line didn't realise the train service existed, let alone know how often it ran or to where. Consequently the message needed was completely different from one that would sell the service in somewhere like Tonypandy, where everyone knew about the train and had inherited the habit of using it.

"The area of Cardiff which the Coryton line serves is like a transit camp, with people moving in and out. It could be quite an advantage for them to use the trains when they move to the area, but they don't know about the trains because they are new to the area. If you don't circulate the homes they'll never find out. You can't see the railway in that part of Cardiff - it's either in cutting or hidden in trees and the ground is so flat that unless you live in a street which faces the railway you won't see the trains or the stations. Even if you pass over a railway bridge in your car every day you don't realise it's a passenger-carrying railway line. There are plenty of bridges in South Wales that pass over freight-only lines or trackbeds where the rails were lifted long ago.

"The trains are highly visible in the valleys - they're always in the public eye. But in Cardiff you've got to get the message across, and tell these people what the train can do for them. You're not selling the train, you're selling its benefits. That's why we focused our campaign on the benefits to the local people of using the trains. The kind of message we conveyed was, 'Do you know you can get to Cardiff for £1, the train runs every 30 minutes and it takes only 10 minutes to get there?' They would respond, 'Is that so? We'll give it a try.'"

After the leaflet drop had gone through its product lifecycle it was given a rest, but unfortunately it was never tried again.

"Sometime afterwards I suggested reintroducing leaflet drops, but I was told, 'That won't happen now. We do things differently.' That was a shame, because there is a case for recycling good ideas from time to time after having given them a rest. A lot of the cutting edge of advertising in the valleys was lost in the later years," says John.

"We felt leaflet drops were preferable to press advertising because, even though press advertising reaches more people, it is perishable after a day unless you got the message into people's heads. If you did a leaflet drop and people knew the package included railway timetables and information, there was a much higher retention rate. Going through the leafleting agencies, you could reckon on 70 or 80% being delivered. The rest would be dumped somewhere, or else some unfortunate person would have 100 leaflets and the next houses none ar all. We knew that went on but generally it was a most effective way.

"The research Central Advertising Services did on feedback found that most people appreciated the leaflet drops. Even people who didn't use the trains themselves kept the timetables so that they would have information for their families and relatives, particularly children. The retention rate was high, therefore the penetration was good, and that was one of the reasons why the traffic grew so much."

Another effective marketing tool was the discount voucher, which entitled households to 50p or £1 off train fares. This initiative was aimed particularly at the Rhymney Valley, where John was still determined to find more custom to support frequent train services.

"The return on the number of vouchers as a proportion of the number that went out was at least twice as high as we were told supermarket promotions would achieve. The expert who looked at this said we'd done really well. Discounts had never been offered on the trains in the valleys before, and they offered big savings on fares of about £2. They helped bring non-rail-users onto the trains.

"Discount vouchers were frowned upon by the hierarchy because they always saw the problems, not the benefits. The problems were the opportunities for fraud. We knew there were some railway staff who collected vouchers from their friends – people who they knew wouldn't be travelling by rail – so they could substitute the vouchers for cash in their takings. We knew it was going on but we had no hard evidence.

"We did have proof, however, that most of the vouchers were handed in by passengers because the number of people travelling increased. That was the proof. You could try various things to stamp out abuse but that could take so much time and energy that you'd miss the point of the promotion. I think it was a shame that they stopped voucher offers completely a year or two later. They'd been happening elsewhere in the country too. I think it was a result of the innate caution of people whose prime purpose in life was not to get a good bottom line but to run the railway in a rigid, autocratic way."

The Valley Lines Identity

Getting the local press on one's side is a help to any marketing campaign and the valleys system was fortunate enough to get some sympathetic media coverage in the mid 1980s. Few organisations in British history have had such a bad press throughout their entire existence as British Rail, and to some extent BR

Continuous marketing effort is needed for the Coryton branch because it runs in a cutting behind the houses and is therefore away from the public view. Here a Pacer pulls away Birchgrove station in December 1991, before Canton had got round to fitting local destination blinds to its latest trains. *Stephen Miles*

deserved the poor publicity because of its ineptitude in public relations and because it was generally too monolithic and entrenched to carry out the kind of improvements which the press – and indeed the public – would notice and praise. Geoff Rich, who edited the South Wales Echo for many years, once told John that his paper would never be lenient on BR because he felt it was not providing the service that the people of the valleys deserved. Such an allegation could not be levelled at BR when it reduced the local rail fares wholesale in October 1983 and the favourable headlines that ensued were the first signs of a thaw.

The decision to give the valleys services their own branding was motivated primarily by a marketing need, but the branding generated yards of good press copy and gave reporters and headline-writers a useful handle to identify the whole system in two words: Valley Lines.

From the outset, 'Valley Lines' was the obvious branding for the system. People who took an interest in rail had known them as the 'valleys lines' for decades, and the locals had used similar terms. When the idea of a branding was first mooted, Valley Lines was the suggestion of people inside and outside BR.

"The people higher up in BR, in Swindon and Paddington, thought Valley Lines was far too trite. We needed something cleverer. So we ran a competition in the Western Mail for a name. We had an august body of councillors and somebody from the Western Mail to judge the entries. There were hundreds of suggestions for names, and we decided unanimously that Dragon Lines would be best. We'd have a Welsh dragon as part of the logo," says John.

"When we contacted Central Advertising Services they threw up their arms and said, 'Horror of horrors! This is a terrible name. It conjures up images of big Welsh women harrassing their menfolk!' They advised us to take a number of names and research them among groups of people. After we'd discussed the names with several groups there was a clear consensus that the name should be Valley Lines. It was so obvious!"

So having gone to the expense and trouble of a public competition, the winner of which had long since been presented with a cheque, the Dragon Lines were going to be the Valley Lines after all.

"We were embarrassed, but the PR advice was that it was all a story. People would poke fun at us but we got in the news. They were laughing with us rather than at us."

The Valley Lines branding was far more powerful than it would have seemed to outsiders. Dragon Lines was the sort of name the Welsh would expect to have been imposed from outside, by people whose stock of Welsh images was limited to male-voice choirs, leeks, rugby matches, colliers, castles and red dragons. The name would have been accepted, used spasmodically and given a quiet burial in the early 1990s. Valley Lines was different. It had pedigree, and it described the location of the railway. Valley Lines wouldn't be found anywhere else in the world. Indeed, there was concern in BR that the name had too strong an identity which would alienate people who lived to the south of Cardiff. Tests on the Barry and Penarth lines established that the residents associated their local trains with services that went to the valleys and the name did not upset them in the least.

Most important of all was that the name imparted a sense of possession in the communities it served, many of which were somewhat parochial in their outlook. Valley Lines belonged to the valleys; they constituted the people's railway.

The branding hit the nail on the head and survived a concerted assassination attempt by Regional Railways in the early 1990s.

"I fought tooth and nail against that," says John. "They wanted to expunge it because they didn't want too many images. I said this was a local railway and the local people identified with the Valley Lines name. I told them, 'If you try to impose the name Regional Railways nobody will know what the hell you're talking about.' They did some research shortly after and found exactly that. They didn't take any notice of that research and tried to bury the identity. It's been revived now but in very poor form."

It may have been revived by the rail operators, but it never needed reviving in the collective conscious of South Walians. Throughout its official exile the name Valley Lines was used consistently by local people and the press; the latter frequently wrote 'regional railways' or 'the regional railway' because Regional Railways had failed to enter the vernacular.

Having settled on the Valley Lines name, the management in 1985 then had to mould it into a recognisable logo, with a slogan attached. As ever, the management were impatient and used their autonomy to move the project forward at breakneck speed.

"We set a date to launch this logo in February 1985. We wanted a celebrity to launch it for us. We tried to get Ruth Madoc, who was in Hi De Hi at that time. She was busy in pantomime at the time we wanted her and was very expensive. Instead we hired Noreen Bray, who was very good as the newsreader on BBC Wales. So that was sorted out. Now we had to get the logo made."

The groans from CAS are almost audible now. John Davies was on the phone from Cardiff; he wanted a choice of three logos for application to trains, stations and literature - and he wanted them by the end of the week.

"CAS said that as part of the bargain we should choose our final logo equally quickly, to give them time to get the details finished by the launch date. The person I was responsible to at that time was Bill Kent, Western Region deputy general manager, who was based in Cardiff. He was on leave when the three logos came from CAS, so I took them round the office in Brunel House and asked the staff which one they preferred, then did the same in the area manager's office. There was a general consensus for the one we adopted, which was a V shape with a red dragon and BR logo. We added the slogan to make it look complete and balanced, and told CAS to get on with finalising the design work.

"A few days later Bill Kent came back from leave, so we thought we'd better ask him and hope he liked the one we'd chosen. He didn't. We said, 'Well, we're sorry you don't like that one. We've already chosen it because of the time limits.' He got really upset. 'Why the hell did you ask me then, if you've already decided?' he shouted. He very nearly stopped us having that logo because he got so upset at being asked after we'd made the decision, which in hindsight was understandable."

Sometime afterwards, shortly before the formation of Regional Railways, John protected his logo from its first assasination attempt by making a presentation to Provincial Sector headquarters. They agreed that the identity was similar in concept to that applied to trains and stations in metropolitan areas of England and Scotland where Passenger Transport Executives had a say in rail services.

"They didn't think the Valley Lines logo was suitable for pole signs at the stations and I agreed to have the logo revamped by a design agency. I told them to avoid a big V on the pole signs in case people thought we were sticking two fingers up at them! The design agency came up with a super new version, but Regional Railways subsumed it before we had a chance to apply it. The consultants had planned a total branding campaign which I wish could be used now."

The adopted slogan for the original branding read 'Frequent and friendly'. John and his colleagues thought this was audacious, but true.

"Generally speaking the staff were more friendly on the Valley Lines than elsewhere. People told us that in the reasearch we'd carried out. They liked the conductors because they'd have a chat and a laugh. They lived in the same area as the passengers and they knew the people. So we thought we'd use that in our slogan."

When Sprinters were introduced, the slogan became 'Fast, frequent and friendly'. Graffiti writers would sometimes add a comment on the railway's revenue protection, making the slogan 'Fast, frequent and friendly – and free'!

As the launch date drew closer it was Ian Walmsley at Canton depot who came up trumps with his beloved DMUs. He wanted to prepare a DMU to demonstrate the branding to the press on launch day but there was insufficient time to get transfers made. He used orange tape to form a V on the yellow front end, with horizontal lines continuing to the edge of the yellow paint from the tips of the V. A signwriter painted a red dragon on the ends and the words Valley Train below the cab's side window and *Trên y Cwm*, the Welsh translation, at the other end.

"That was controversial, and some of those higher up didn't approve of this kind of thing. Ian showed it to us a few days before the launch. I was highly impressed with his work."

Not long after this branding was established on the trains a wag at Canton depot painted a sheep, in the style of South Wales Echo cartoonist Gren, on one of the DMUs.

"He drew this sheep and called the train the Baa-goed Express. It only made one outing in that condition. There was an explosion in headquarters, and it was reported in the press that they were upset at the negative aspects. I was away on holiday at the time, and when I came back I was annoyed that our PR people hadn't turned this episode to our advantage. I thought the sheep was hilarious. We couldn't have kept it on the train because the sheep had Gren's copyright on it, but as just a one-off we could have made something of it. There were people higher up who had this staid attitude. They didn't like us poking fun at ourselves and couldn't understand the valleys humour."

To fit in with the new image, the Valley Lines map was redesigned with London Underground-style colour coding for each line. Something similar had accompanied the 1953 recasting but had long since disappeared.

"Neil Sprinks, our public relations officer at the time, was worried that we had nothing new to show at the launch, only a new name and a new map. If that didn't strike the public imagination we could fall flat on our faces. He had the idea of getting the prototype Class 150 Sprinter to Cardiff for the launch.

"We had it over the weekend of the launch when it made two trips on the Coryton branch on Saturday evening and a special trip to Merthyr on Sunday. On the Monday morning we decided to take it to Aber and back on a scheduled service. We had all sorts of problems because it slipped badly on the rails at Lisvane and as a result it was late coming back down to Cardiff. The conductors weren't used to using a public address system on the train because they didn't have one in the old DMUs. The conductor on the Sprinter made a right hash of trying to explain the delay. I saw that conductor recently on an InterCity train, where he was the senior conductor. I asked him if he remembered getting tongue-tied on the first Sprinter to run in the valleys and we had a laugh about it."

That conductor had to break ranks, along with three colleagues, to operate the Sprinter. They were sent to Derby to train for the launch against the unions' wishes.

"The unions said there were procedures for training people to drive new trains and that everyone had to go through prescribed hours of training. There were two drivers and two conductors

A cheerful painter at Canton depot pauses in his work of applying the Valley Lines branding to a train for the first time. For the launch of the identity the dragon had to be hand painted, but transfers were used for subsequent units. *Ian Walmsley*

who had the guts to stick two fingers up at the unions and say they wanted to go and do it. They went on a fast learning curve, and one of those drivers is now a driver leader for the Valley Lines."

Fortunately there were no problems with the Sprinter on launch day; John had wisely decided to limit the demonstration run with the media on board to a simple trip from Queen Street to Bute Road and back. At last the media were genuinely impressed with British Rail, with the Sprinter, the branding, the logo, the map and the way the launch was handled.

Nobody in the Swindon hierarchy could have predicted what really captured the media's imagination that day – the Welsh words *Trên y Cwm* on the side of the train. Indeed, if the show had been organised by the hierarchy the other side of the Severn the Welsh translation of Valley Train would never have got a look in. To this day, it remains the only time ordinary service trains have carried a Welsh branding. Even though bilingual branding was well established on buses around Wales, including those of National Welsh in the valleys and Cardiff Bus, the corporate railway stripped away the bilingual element at the first opportunity. In 1985, though, the day belonged to the local managers, among them Ian Walmsley who used his initiative and a roll of tape to come up with a cheerful branding which the media just had to love at first sight.

The A470 Challenge

The residents of Pentrebach, near Merthyr, might disagree that the Valley Lines were the people's railway. When they lost many of their off-peak trains they were the victims in a plot which was hatched to save the Merthyr line from near extinction. Paradoxically, it was because the Valley Lines management had such a good understanding of what the people needed that the timetables were altered to cut out the Pentrebach stop for many trains.

The construction of the A470 dual carriageway north of Pontypridd was awesome to behold from the windows of a DMU rasping up the gradient on the opposite side of the valley. No

expense was being spared, and the mountainside which had once hosted the fateful spoil heap at Aberfan[1] was crawling with bulldozers and earthmovers. This was to be a fast, motorway-standard road which carried the promise of Merthyr's economic salvation.

Meanwhile, the railway infrastructure was getting no improvements and the ageing DMUs had to be content with a permanent way laid decades earlier and subsequently pounded by innumerable mineral trains. Not surprisingly, there was a widespread feeling that the new road would ring the death knell for the Merthyr line.

John Davies was not prepared to see the apple of the Taff Vale Railway's eye withering away under his control. Once again, he turned to the marketplace for inspiration.

"We took the road head on. We decided to cut the journey time to under 50 minutes to Cardiff Central and 45 minutes to Queen Street. We could market those times and interest more passengers. We couldn't run the trains at faster speeds, of course, so we had to cut out two stops. We kept Troed y Rhiw and Merthyr Vale because they were contributing the most passengers. Stops at Pentrebach and Quakers Yard were cut out. We introduced a service that was highly competitive with the new road and succeeded in holding our market share against the odds."

The managers saved the railway in the teeth of investment of millions of pounds in the best road ever built in the valleys. The critics had been proved wrong; the rail service didn't look pathetic alongside the lavish new road after all. Critically, at a time when the new road should have been used heavily for its novelty value, the railway managed to attract enough passengers to justify retention of the hourly service to Merthyr throughout the day. Had the hourly service been reduced then, it would not have reappeared by today.

The price John had to pay for playing his cards this way was a campaign of harrassment by the people of Pentrebach and Quakers Yard.

"Pentrebach were the correspondents, who kept writing to me at length about the problems they were having. There was a concerted campaign there which nearly drove us mad," he says.

"Quakers Yard were more streetwise. They organised a public meeting, which I rashly attended on my own, in the village hall at Edwardsville - the village beside the station. I went to the meeting by car because I would never have got home to Neath by train from Quakers Yard that night, even if there had been a train calling. I borrowed the chauffeur car of the deputy general manager, without the chauffeur. It was a Ford Granada 2.3. Thinking they might not appreciate seeing me arriving by car, I parked at the other end of the village and walked up to the village hall.

"But somebody had spotted me getting out of the car, and the first thing that happened as I walked into the village hall was that I got vilified in public for arriving in a plush car when I'd taken most of their trains away. There were 200 people at the meeting and they gave me hell. I wished I'd taken somebody else with me. Anyway, I issued a challenge: I'd put back at least some of their trains provided that they in turn promised they would use them more. If they didn't we would be back at square one."

The residents took up the challenge, and the Quakers Yard stop is a regular call today. The trains were decelerated as a result, but by then the marketing of faster services had been driven home.

"We found through research that, as long as the Merthyr trains took less than an hour to get to Cardiff, ran on time and were dependable, the people didn't mind. But by planning before the event we turned a potential disaster into an opportunity."

When another threat arose from the new A470, disciplined marketing and a piece of blatant opportunism reminiscent of a Thomas the Tank Engine story came to the rescue. National Welsh was introducing an express bus service on the Merthyr to Cardiff corridor and John was all for having a public race between rail and bus.

"The bus company got their messages mixed up in one of the worst advertising campaigns I've ever seen. We were pleased with

[1] *Aberfan was the scene of a disaster in 1968 when a heap of slurry engulfed a school and many children lost their lives.*

27

our material. We focused on the basic benefits of cheap, convenient travel and a friendly service. That was the value of using Central Advertising Services, who cut out the rubbish.

"When National Welsh introduced X4, an express bus service from Abergavenny to Cardiff via Merthyr, we advertised heavily against them. I failed to get the South Wales Echo to sponsor a contest to see which was faster in the morning peak from Merthyr to Cardiff, the X4 or the train. The very first day they operated, a rail inspector went on the train and I went on the bus. The bus got stuck in traffic at Taffs Well. Although it was scheduled to be faster than the train, it had lost quarter of an hour by the time it got to Cardiff.

"We made headline news in the Echo that night and, according to the managing director of National Welsh, we'd completely ruined his marketing campaign at a stroke. We were delighted with that."

There were other pranks too, pranks that could only be played by managers who were alive to the situation around them, who could plan the right response and who had the freedom to act quickly. One example concerned Penarth Road, a busy road out of Cardiff, when it was dug up by the gas board.

"We had an advertising campaign in Penarth, telling people the train ran every half an hour and avoided the roadworks. We earned the wrath of the highways people at South Glamorgan County Council but the public transport people in the same council thought it was marvellous. It was the sort of tactical action we took. We spotted weaknesses in the competitors' marketplace and tried to exploit them."

Correcting Mistakes

Most of the improvements described in this chapter were instituted during the bureaucratic lull that accompanied a step change in the Provincial Sector's influence. When it was established in 1982 the Provincial Sector was confined to a head office in London, and in 1984 it put in place its first outbased managers. There were six on the Western Region, four in Swindon and two in Cardiff. Initially there was to be just one - John Davies - in Cardiff, but he argued that there was too heavy a workload for one person and Alan Beardsworth was kept as his assistant.

The eventual aim of this reorganisation was to divide the rail network into sectors that concentrated on certain traffics and where one tier of management had control over trains, marketing, operations, timetable planning, civil engineering and everything else. This, essentially, is what John had been striving to achieve in Cardiff. He had largely succeeded, too, thanks to Frank Markham, the liberal divisional manager.

Indeed, the revolution which the Valley Lines underwent between 1983 and 1986 could be viewed in retrospect as vertical integration's finest hour. All the graphs which were meant to climb were climbing, among them passenger numbers, revenue, train miles, revenue per train mile, passengers per train mile. At the same time the graphs which were meant to fall were falling - train costs, staffing costs and maintenance costs. All this was achieved in a remarkably short time by managers who were taking full advantage of being let off the Western Region's leash before being recaptured by the dog wardens of Provincial Sector/Regional Railways and before those wardens had a chance to impound discount vouchers, leaflet drops and even the Valley Lines branding.

"I realised that I could do a lot more under the Provincial Sector in 1984 because the sector's organisation was so slim that they didn't have time to look over your shoulder at what you were doing. I could get away with things I couldn't have done before, because previously you couldn't take risks on the railway," says John.

A corollary of introducing improvements for the passengers at short notice was the ability and humility to spot and accept mistakes and to correct them quickly. An example of the new system at work was the recasting of evening peak services to make maximum use of resources and provide the maximum number of peaktime seats.

"In the evening peak period there were some long layovers - 40 minutes at Coryton and something similar at Penarth. So we worked in more peak services and put in additional trains from Cardiff to Radyr and Caerphilly. Instead of running a six-car train all the way up the valleys, as had been happening since DMUs were introduced in 1958, we would run a three-car train as far as Radyr, Llandaf or Caerphilly ahead of the train which was going to the end of the line, which would not stop at the intermediate stations served by the short working. The DMUs on the short workings were then able to run back to Cardiff quickly and form another peak-period service.

"We built up the number of seats and were able to take more passengers. It became a principle which Provincial Sector/Regional Railways adopted to great effect. We were doing it early on along with some other places, especially the Birmingham area on their former Great Western lines to Stourbridge and out of Moor Street. There were many places where these things didn't happen until much later - Provincial Midland and North East. In those days Network SouthEast wasn't doing this either, until Chris Green got down to what he termed 'sweating the assets'."

In 1985 Rhymney trains which had left Cardiff Central on the half hour for many years were shifted to depart on the hour as part of a recasting of services. The 16.00 departure ran through to Rhymney, followed by the 17.10. Passengers for stations as far as Aber were catered for by the 16.30 departure, while those travelling to Llanbradach and Ystrad Mynach could catch a train at 16.55. However, the 16.30 to Rhymney had departed at that time for years and the commuters had got to love their train, which all of a sudden was truncated to Aber so that it could rush back to Cardiff and form another departure before the evening peak was out.

"Our view was that because there had always been a 16.30 to Rhymney that didn't mean to say there would be one forever. And anyway we didn't have the resources to run one at that time. We were using that train twice in the same evening peak. We were really proud of ourselves. We would sell the change and people would buy it," says John.

"However, the Rhymney line passengers in the late afternoon weren't best pleased with the change. Although we were confident that people would change and get used to the new timetable, they didn't. Within a few weeks we had to drop this plan. We perceived a shift away from the railway. It wasn't a huge shift, but it was certainly noticeable."

The train diagrams were rejigged and new timetables issued which restored the much-loved 16.30 to Rhymney. This, in turn, upset the operations managers at Western Region headquarters, who would rather see long-term customers deserting the railway than witness the sanctity of the Great Britain train timetable being defiled.

"We told them we couldn't wait till the next timetable change because people were voting with their feet. Headquarters sent people down to see me and I treated them politely. I gave them a cup of coffee, we had a chat and then I'd say 'No. This is what we are going to do.' We could get away with changes like this because the vast majority of our passengers were local. Our trains were running so frequently on all routes that it didn't inconvenience people too much if they suddenly discovered the timetable was different from the one shown in the national timetable. We did inconvenience some people, naturally, but we protected the majority."

"The solution to the problem of the 16.30 to Rhymney was just as neat as the first recasting. We wondered why we hadn't thought of doing it in the first place. The problem was that we didn't start with the customer. The customer forced us to do what we should have done in the first place."

For a few happy years the Valley Lines were the people's railway all round. They had the people's branding, the people's marketing and the people's timetables. All the service enhancements were driven, albeit unwittingly, by the people, and the people's railway was run by managers who were even prepared to recast timetables and incur the wrath of their superiors to correct action which was not in the people's best interest.

CARDIFF AND ITS LOCAL LINES

Top: At Cardiff Central the Valley Lines come into contact with the main-line system but have their own exclusive platforms, numbers six and seven. Occasionally platform four has been used for Valley Lines departures, such as the 17.08 Cardiff Central to Barry on 26th May 1987. This Class 150/1 Sprinter is operating the first diagram scheduled for Sprinter operation on the Valley Lines, a trip to Barry Island while the unit is in between turns on the Brimingham to Cardiff route. The unit was diagrammed to return empty to Cardiff. *Stephen Miles*

Centre: Until September 1990 platform three at Cardiff Queen Street had a dead-end track accessible from the south only. In August 1990 a new connection at the north end of platform three was under construction and was nearly complete in this photogrph showing a Penarth-bound Sprinter arriving. The connection allowed down trains to overtake one another if one was delayed but a bottleneck still exists to the north of the station where only two tracks can be accommodated on the bridge over Newport Road. *Stephen Miles*

Below: The north end of Queen Street station is unrecognisable in this view taken nearly 30 years earlier than the previous picture. The 15.40 from Queen Street to Rhymney is departing from the station without coming into contact with the tracks out of the Taff side of the station. The station was later rebuilt with the Rhymney and Taff lines merging at this point and crossing Newport Road on a new two-track bridge. The lines diverging on the left were the Rhymney Railway's access to Cardiff Docks. *John Hodge*

Top: The junction at Radyr remained unchanged when the City Line was launched in 1987 but provision of a bay platform behind the fencing visible here would have improved the service's reliability. A Coryton to Taffs Well service negotiates the junction as it comes off the City Line in April 1988. *Stephen Miles*

Centre left: Although commuting to Cardiff increased as coal mining declined in the valleys, the railways had been carrying large numbers of workers into the city for decades. In March 1963, after the introduction of DMUs but before the demise of the hat, commuters leave Clarence Road station ready for a day's work. The destination blind is misleading; the train would have come from Barry Island or Cadoxton. The picture shows Clarence Road station, near Cardiff Docks, in the brief period between its rebuilding and its closure. *Western Mail and Echo Ltd*

Bottom left: The old order on the Coryton branch – a 45xx GWR tank loco sandwiched between auto-coaches fondly termed The Coryton Flyer by the South Wales Echo in June 1955. The line, built by the original Cardiff Railway Company, once continued almost to Pontypridd but was cut back by the GWR to Coryton. *Western Mail and Echo Ltd*

Below: The newer order on the Coryton line in 1987, shortly after South Glamorgan County Council funded a bright brick surface for the platform. The DMU is displaying two destinations, both of them incorrect, and is in its last few months as a three-car set. *Stephen Miles*

Right: Sprinter 150 242 prepares to break the ribbon at the opening ceremony for Ty Glas station in April 1987. The unit, allocated to Leeds, was borrowed ex-works for the ceremony as Cardiff had yet to receive the first of its Sprinters. South Glamorgan County Council, which funded Ty Glas station, evidently had in mind the City Line branding for the entire Coryton to Radyr arc but in the event the name stuck only with the Radyr to Cardiff section. The close spacings of stations on the Coryton line is apparent; the platform of Birchgrove station can be seen below the overbridge.   *Western Mail and Echo Ltd*

Below: Shortly before the total withdrawal of old DMUs, a Class 116 set works a Radyr to Coryton shuttle over the City Line in December 1991. Pacers were already in use, providing two of the three City Line diagrams that day. This view of Fairwater indicates the quality of the track on this quiet loop line, formerly used only by freight trains. Far busier services in the valleys run on single tracks which still rest on wooden sleepers.   *Stephen Miles*

Above: Two trains at platform six, Cardiff Central, in July 1991. The inflexibility of the layout here meant that if the Sprinter in this view had arrived late and missed its slot at the platform, it would become even later through waiting for the Class 101 DMU to depart and clear the next block section.   *Stephen Miles*

Left: Stephen Miles A Class 108 DMU, set C968, hints at two destinations - both incorrect - as it waits to depart from Cardiff Bute Road for Caerphilly in 1990. The branch stretches away on an ugly embankment which Cardiff Bay Development Corporation is anxious to demolish, to make way for a wide boulevard. The derelict steam locos on the right were moved to Bute Road from Woodham's scrapyard at Barry for restoration to working order.   *Stephen Miles*

YNYSWEN NEW STATION

THE QUICK CONVENIENT BEST WAY TO TRAVEL

CHEAP DAY RETURN
PONTYPRIDD £1.10
CARDIFF £2
AFTER 09.30

MONDAYS TO SATURDAYS
HOURLY SERVICE THROUGHOUT
THE DAY EACH WAY
FROM MID-MORNING
UNTIL EARLY EVENING

⇋ Valley Lines

DIESEL TRAINS

IMPROVED SERVICES

CARDIFF VALLEYS
PENARTH - BARRY - BRIDGEND

15th SEPTEMBER 1958 to 14th JUNE 1959
OR UNTIL FURTHER NOTICE

CHEAP FARES FACILITIES

COPY OF TRAIN SERVICE BOOKLET OBTAINABLE
FREE FROM STATIONS, OFFICES OR AGENCIES

WESTERN · BRITISH RAILWAYS · REGION

THE QUICK, CONVENIENT, CHEAP WAY TO CARDIFF.

£3 WEEKLY TICKET

YOUR
RUSH HOUR TRAINS
FROM
PENARTH
07 28, 07 55, 08 15, 08 35, 08 55
TWO MINUTES LATER AT DINGLE ROAD

⇋ Valley Lines
We're getting there

TRAIN TIMES
AMSERAU TRENAU

VALLEY LINES
Merthyr Tydfil
Aberdare/Aberdâr

2 June to 28 September 1996
2 Mehefin i 28 Medi 1996

Aberdare/Aberdâr	Merthyr Tydfil
Cwmbach	Pentre Bach
Fernhill	Troed-y-Rhiw
Mountain Ash/ Aberpennar	Merthyr Vale
Penrhiwceiber	Quakers Yard/ Mynwent-y-Crynwyr
Abercynon North Abercynon Gogledd	Abercynon South/ Abercynon De
	Pontypridd
	Trefforest
	Trefforest Estate/ Ystad Trefforest
	Taffs Well/ Ffynnon Taf
	Radyr
	Llandaf
	Cathays
	Cardiff Queen Street/ Heol-y-Frenhines
	Cardiff Central/ Caerdydd Canolog

For full service between
Pontypridd and Cardiff
please see separate
timetable.

Am gwasanaeth llaw
rhwng Pontypridd a
Chaerdydd gwelwch a
amserlen ar wahân

Valley Lines

YOUR FARE DEAL ON THE

RHYMNEY LINE

Timetables and Fares
Until 30 September 1984

Mid Glamorgan COUNTY COUNCIL

THROUGH TRAINS TO BARRY ISLAND

This is the age of the t...

PICK-UP A BARGAIN ON THE BARRY & PENARTH LINES

24 OCTOBER TO 29 OCTOBER
½ PRICE FOR ½ TERM

...ditionally, reductions up
...30% make travelling by
...in the bright way to go

...is the age of the train

CHAPTER 4

RUNNING HARD TO STAND STILL
How Efficiency Was Improved

Business sectors were added to British Rail's empire in 1982, each one dealing with a separate aspect of the railway business but gaining control over all the resources needed to run those services. InterCity sector took charge of high-quality express workings, mainly radiating from London, Network SouthEast was responsible for the dense suburban and inter-urban network radiating from London, and the residue of passenger services was left to the Provincial Sector. This change presented Provincial managers with an unprecedented opportunity to reverse the fortunes of many declining local services but the top brass at the British Railways Board tended to regard the new situation as an improved organisation for cost-cutting. It was by deviating from the wisdom preached from the pulpit of Euston House – by exploring opportunities for expansion in the same exercise as opportunities for cost-cutting – that John Davies was able to make the Valley Lines a conspicuous success in the early years of sectorisation.

In early 1984, shortly before Provincial was devolved into an organisation with outbased management, John Davies and the other designated Provincial managers were summoned to London for a meeting with the sector director at the time, John Welsby (now the chairman of British Rail). He showed them a wallchart on which was drawn a tall bar representing the sector's costs. A tiny bar alongside represented the income.

"He drew a dotted line showing the effect of a 10% cut in costs, and another to show the effect of a 10% increase in income," says John Davies. "There was still a massive gap between costs and income, but the cut in costs closed much more of the gap than the increase in income. He said, 'The message to all my Provincial managers is: Don't worry too much about increasing income, concentrate on getting the costs down. That's the only way you're going to make an impression.'"

John Welsby's message was simply an expression in words and bar charts of traditional BR management intuition. That intuition had been responsible, for example, for cutting out two of the afternoon trains on the Pontypridd to Merthyr line, a move which reduced costs a little but also damaged income because the withdrawals destroyed the strict interval service north and south of Pontypridd in the afternoons.

Naturally, John Davies didn't agree entirely with John Welsby.

"I understood the general thrust, but if you're going to carry on cutting costs like that without making an effort to improve income, how are you going to take the staff along with you without them striking and doing silly things? All the management textbooks will tell you that organisations which rely entirely on cost-cutting without anything to complement it are the ones that generally fall, because that process gathers its own momentum and you cost-cut yourself out of business.

"I couldn't get John Welsby to agree and he was much better at arguing than I was! I withdrew hurt when I put this to him. But, having withdrawn hurt, I then decided that if I couldn't persuade him directly, I would persuade him indirectly by doing it. That's the method I adopted - to build the business up at the same time as having a really hard look at costs. That's how we came to be an organisation focused on the bottom line rather than focused on costs.

"I know I was right because eventually I had the evidence to support it, but I think one reason why some of the Provincial services didn't perform as well is that they carried on with this idea. The railway was very good at reducing costs in many areas but it wasn't very good at generating business."

Had John Welsby appreciated how much extra business could be gained in the South Wales valleys alone, he might have preached a different sermon in 1983. At the time, however, there were no precedents, certainly not outside London or the InterCity network, and the idea of a railway increasing its revenue severalfold while reducing its costs at a time of rapid growth in car ownership would have seemed like pure fantasy. Sadly, the top brass never pinched themselves to check whether they were dreaming or not; when the Sprinter programme was underway several Provincial businesses witnessed spectacular growth in business but new rolling stock had to be doggedly authorised, in compliance with Department of Transport rules, on the premise that two new vehicles would replace three old ones. The railway's obsession with cutting costs and paying little regard to income put a firm lid on the amount of extra business that could be accommodated, a lid which remains firmly shut in the mid-1990s.

For its first few years, however, the Provincial Sector was equipped with a considerable amount – a surplus in fact – of elderly rolling stock. One of John Davies's first acts as Provincial manager in Cardiff was to consider ways of filling spare capacity as well as stripping some of it out. The West Wales lines, operated by a mixture of DMUs and loco-hauled stock, were in more desperate need of attention than the Valley Lines and were shockingly inefficient to a manager accustomed to the Eastern Region's tight control of DMUs.

"Some of the diagraming in West Wales was appalling. People ought to be hung, drawn and quartered for what they didn't do there! They simply carried on as they had done for years and years. We reduced the fleet in West Wales from 72 vehicles to 32 vehicles in two years. We were carrying more passengers in those 32 than we were in the 72, because the resources had been so badly used," says John.

He used West Wales as an example for several years when he was a guest speaker at train planning courses at Crewe, where he would tell his audience that giving unilateral attention to the cost of resources was not an ideal method of working. The nature of the market had to be taken into account.

"If you planned a timetable with a DMU that went from Swansea to Milford Haven in just under two hours, came back to Swansea after 10 minutes, then went to Milford Haven again after 10 minutes, you could run the whole service with x number of trains. But 40% of the business in West Wales was actually interlining with InterCity and other services out of Swansea. If the resource-based timetable had trains leaving 10 minutes before the trains from London arrived and people had to wait 50 minutes, you'd have a lovely timetable on paper but you'd carry hardly any passengers. You have to look at the market, look at the resources, then try to match the two.

"Our timetable in West Wales wasn't an ideal operator's timetable. It was a resource-efficient timetable, but we also met the market's needs."

When the Provincial reorganisation of 1984 was planned two services - Cardiff to Portsmouth and Cardiff to Crewe - were left unattached to profit centres. John Pearse, Provincial manager at Swindon, took charge of the Portsmouth service and John Davies took the Crewe service under his wing. Within a few years both routes expanded rapidly to become showcase cross-country services but in 1984 they were so inconspicuous as to slip through the net of reorganisation.

"This is the way things developed haphazardly," says John Davies. "It's inconceivable now that Cardiff to Crewe would be regarded as an also-ran. I wasn't able to give it the attention it needed, although I did realign the loco-hauled services to connect better at Crewe."

He also made a small change to the Sunday service on the route, a change which illuminates his method of looking at efficient use of resources and increasing revenue side by side.

"There were only two Sunday services and I had one of those hunches that there should be a better service on Sundays. There was a six-hour gap between trains - one ran at about 14.00, the next nearer 20.00. This was clearly wrong, but how could I prove it? I couldn't see how I could research the need for this extra train, so I took the other line. I contacted the manager of train diagrams and asked him how cheaply he could crew an extra train if the stock was rediagrammed. Because passenger and freight were together at that time, the diagram manager found out there were a number of freight drivers riding back on passenger trains south of Hereford. He said, 'If you put in a train at 16.00 or 17.00 we can actually crew this neutrally by simply absorbing unproductive driver time.' I didn't have to go to anybody and ask permission. I told them to time a diagram for an extra train in each direction and I would justify it."

"It may sound daft, but that's the way things were done. It was difficult if you didn't see a gap in the market but in this case it was unlikely to fail. All too often managers didn't look at the market – they looked only at the costs and therefore nothing happened."

Another development on the Cardiff to Crewe route while John was there was the opening of Cwmbran station, in 1986. This station served a large new town north of Newport and its part funding was the last act of the outgoing Cwmbran Development Corporation, which had originally regarded provision of a station as the lowest of its priorities. From its opening week the station was twice as busy as predicted, even though its train service left something to be desired initially. John arranged for an additional service of DMUs to be started between Cardiff and Hereford so that Cwmbran would be served by more than the six loco-hauled trains and one DMU which worked over the whole length of the line each day. The additional DMU services - which again did not call for any extra rolling stock - also proved attractive to the considerable flow of people using the train from Hereford and Abergavenny to connect with eastbound InterCity trains at Newport.

In 1983 the rolling stock was generally used more sensibly on the Valley Lines than on other routes under Cardiff's control. Indeed, John soon found that the thrust of cost-cutting would have to come from other areas. Nevertheless, there was more rolling stock in the valleys than was needed to cope with the business inherited in 1983.

"With the fares initiative we wanted to fill that excess capacity. If we didn't we would start cutting back on rolling stock. We did start filling it, and two years later we came up against the ceiling. We had 17 three-car diagrams and two single-car diagrams in 1983 – 53 diagrammed vehicles. By 1985 the single cars weren't enough. They were used to strengthen three-car sets to make four, but we needed five cars. We sent our two single cars to the West Country and got two two-car Class 117 DMUs in exchange. We increased our fleet by two vehicles and our running costs went up as a result, but at that time we were able to justify it. That wasn't easy, because nobody wanted to seek more rolling stock anywhere."

Rolling-stock productivity was notched up in some areas, notably by reducing long layovers and by replacing some six-car workings in the evening peak with two three-car workings, allowing one set to return to Cardiff to form another peak period service.

Before long some Valley Lines services were, paradoxically, in danger of bringing in too much income. Overcrowded trains needed strengthening with another DMU, but in most cases the cost of running that extra unit would have been more than the extra income it brought in.

"You can fill vacant seats but there comes a time when you have to revise your marketing campaign. The step change, where suddenly your resources cost more than the income they brought in, was always a danger area and it was a case of recognising when that was arriving. We had to have a skill and understanding to reduce costs without having a detrimental effect on the service."

The problem of too much custom hit the Valley Lines hard two years after the fares initiative when the trains became severely overcrowded on Saturdays before Christmas and on weekdays in the last weeks before Christmas. The brightly lit shops and streets of Cardiff shone like a beacon to thousands of present hunters; the valley trains were cheap and frequent, stopped close to the shops and avoided the traffic congestion on the roads.

"There was a strong view from Provincial headquarters that we must price up the peaks. We hadn't got any more rolling stock so we should go for selective pricing. We decided to charge peak fares on Saturdays before Christmas and on Saturdays when rugby internationals were being played in Cardiff. It turned out to be one of the biggest mistakes I made," says John.

"We justified the change on the grounds that a peak fare was for peak conditions and peak conditions existed on these particular days. I pretended, naively, that I could eventually persuade the public. They didn't agree with us, because they'd never been used to paying these fares. The staff didn't like it because they got a lot of abuse from people. I had tremendous correspondence, I had people screaming down the phone at me. I tried to justify it in logical terms but logic didn't sink in. I was told time and time again that we were deliberately abusing our monopoly position."

The new practice was particularly hard on the passengers from South Glamorgan – from the Coryton, Penarth and Barry lines. Peak fares were about 25% higher than off-peak fares from the Mid Glamorgan valleys, but from the commuterland of South Glamorgan peak fares were 50 or 60% higher. This differential was justified for normal peak periods, but for pre-Christmas and rugby Saturdays the effect was a punitive fares increase of up to 60% for South Glamorgan passengers. To remedy the situation conductors were instructed to discount the normal peak fare on those Saturdays so that a more realistic price applied in South Glamorgan. However, computerised Aptis and Portis ticket machines were in use by then and the machines could not cope with this variation in the fares structure.

"The upshot was that it took so long to issue tickets that some people got away without paying their fares altogether," says John. "In 1987, the third year we applied these fares, I wrote out a new fares chart for a special peak return ticket for 'peak off-peak' travel. I advertised this in the newspapers and it was shown in the fares manual, but when the time came the conductors couldn't issue the fares shown in their books. I discovered that the fares hadn't been downloaded into the ticket machines. They couldn't over-ride their machines because there were checks to stop it happening and it would have been tantamount to fraud. I got onto headquarters and they told me the workload of inputting these fares into the computer system was too great. They'd forgotten to tell me when I submitted the fares chart several months earlier."

A third attempt at making the system more palatable to Christmas shoppers and passengers on rugby days - many of whom were not travelling to or from the match - was later tried. It involved applying peak fares to journeys from Cardiff between 16.30 and 18.00. Passengers travelling at that time with cheap day returns were surcharged. Again that caused resentment and the concept of peak Saturdays and peak pre-Christmas weekdays was dropped, only to be reintroduced in 1995.

"It was the right idea in terms of maximising income but the wrong idea in the long term because it worked against us. I learnt a hard lesson there. The theory is fine, but if you alienate your customers you are the loser eventually. Over time people found other means to travel, and I think we did lose business through that. I'm prepared to admit it."

This fiasco had stemmed from the simple fact that there were not enough trains to meet the huge demand for travel on certain winter Saturdays. Quite early in the saga, when it first became apparent that the commercial reasoning would not satisfy the disgruntled public, John asked the sector director, Sidney Newey for permission to follow a different tack.

One of the reasons put forward by BR to justify higher fares on busy Saturdays – rugby and Christmas shopping days – was that the cost of hiring extra rolling stock had to be covered. Such rolling stock was plentiful because most other urban systems in Britain were quieter on Saturdays than weekdays. This DMU, seen leaving Pontypridd with a train to Aberdare on 11th March 1989, was borrowed for the day from Tyseley, Birmingham. Ironically,the two end cars were originally allocated to work in the valleys but moved to the Midlands in the 1970s because there was insufficient traffic in South Wales to justify their retention there. *Stephen Miles*

"I asked him if he would look more favourably on increasing the allocation of rolling stock if I could make x hundred thousand pounds out of this fares increase. He said it was just not possible in the system for that to happen. I knew it wasn't possible, but I was hoping I could have bucked the system. The system couldn't allow it to happen because it was all skewed around the income you were already getting, not around the income you could get if you had more rolling stock.

"But I kept up the public pretence that I was making my case for more resources by earning more to pay for them. Prior to Sprinters, we were bringing in supplementary trains from Birmingham on weekends which we had to pay for. On rugby international days we had to bring in even more stock from outside. All this went down very poorly with the public and I got a bad press."

The moral of the story was that no matter how vast an increase in passengers the Valley Lines could potentially attract, they would only ever be allowed the same resources as they had needed in the doldrums of early 1983. (This is still a problem in 1996. The Pontypridd to Cardiff line is being resignalled to allow trains to run at five-minute intervals, but the rolling stock available is unlikely to be able to provide a more frequent service than the four trains per hour established in 1988.) As John Welsby had said, cutting costs was everything to the Provincial Sector and increasing income was largely an irrelevance. This attitude was about to prevail in the sector's programme of replacing rolling stock; the peak Saturdays fiasco had taught John, as he had suspected already, that it was futile to hope rolling stock could secure the future prosperity of the Valley Lines. Instead he would have to seek economies in other areas to keep the Valley Lines fighting fit.

Sunday Cutbacks

Demand clearly existed for frequent weekday and Saturday services in the valleys but an increasing commuter and shopper business could have no effect on the Sunday loadings. Summer Sundays had a useful trade to the funfair and beach at Barry Island. Winter Sundays, however, were losing money hand over fist and there were no potential sources of travel to be tapped, certainly while Sunday shopping remained outlawed. Even when

John Davies's formula – of not cutting capacity wherever there was scope to increase the loadings – was applied, the knives inevitably had to be sharpened.

"The Sunday timetable was totally resource-based. There were three DMUs and six sets of traincrews who did the whole system. The timetable ran at roughly three-hourly intervals in each valley and didn't necessarily connect with main-line trains, even though most of the business was into and out of main-line trains. It was a service which was of no use for local travelling and not much use for main-line connections because it was resource-based," says John.

"There was a train at 04.30 out of Treherbert on Sunday mornings which was used only by railwaymen who worked at Cardiff Central on the 06.00 to 14.00 shift. Porth signalbox was open at 04.00. We said there was no point continuing with these trains. We had shown that we were prepared to expand where necessary but we now had to show that where services were useless we would cut them out. We proposed the total cessation of Sunday morning services in winter."

Despite the runaway success of the Valley Lines reforms in other respects, the staff reacted angrily. They called a strike in the valleys on Sundays.

"The staff were incredibliy stupid on this point. Instead of hitting us where it hurt - on the weekday services - they hit us where it didn't hurt. If we weren't going to run on Sunday mornings they would go on strike and stop us running on Sunday afternoons as well. The staff cut off their noses to spite their faces. They diminished their earnings. It didn't have any effect on the revenue because there was so little travel on Sundays. A lot of the staff realised this, I think, but the trade union leaders said it was a matter of principle. A trade unionist will fight to the death on principle even if it destroys him!

"We were told that people went to church on Sunday mornings and needed the trains. The valleys were godly in the 1930s and 1940s but they certainly weren't in the 1980s. That didn't stop them wheeling out people who were suddenly travelling to church on the trains!

"We went through this nonsense for six or seven weeks. Although it didn't cause us a problem I did worry about it - you do worry if you have a dispute. David Warne, operations manager, was fully behind our proposals and said if we had one more week of this nonsense we would cut out Sunday services altogether in winter.

"We were about to propose just that when they escalated the dispute and stopped the main line for a day, InterCity trains and the lot. The head office management caved in, and cobbled up an agreement. The trade unions wanted the previous service restored on Sundays, we wanted no morning service. The head office came up with an agreement that we would try the unions' plan for three months and then our plan for three months. We went through it. It was utter farce compounded by farce."

Sunday morning services in winter were withdrawn in 1985 and the afternoon timetables remodelled so that the principal valleys services were anchored to main-line connections at Cardiff Central.

John was to cross swords frequently with the unions as he reshaped the Valley Lines, which were saturated by tradition, but never again would the staff jump at the option of a local strike. For his part, John had to play his cards carefully to avoid precipitating any strikes that would affect a wider area of the network than the Valley Lines alone.

Staff Productivity

Swimming against the tide always takes considerable energy. John Davies clearly had plenty of it, but strength and stamina were equally essential on the part of the staff if the Valley Lines were to be revamped for the future. They got a taste of how much harder they would have to work when they had to sell tickets to the masses who took up the half-price fares offer in October 1983. Their commitment was even more important on the Valley Lines than in most other parts of British Rail because it was the staff themselves who would have to bear the brunt of efficiency drives once the spare capacity on the trains had been addressed.

"In 1984, when we had the first devolved Provincial organisation, we were able to look at the business with a clean sheet, and look at costs from the ground up. We asked ourselves, if we were starting the business now, what resources would we need, what costs would we incur, what did we have in reality and how could we bring these closer together? The reality was much worse than the perfect situation in most cases, but we could move fairly rapidly towards the ideal situation," says John.

"In the valleys the train costs tended to be high. The average fare was low and the distances short, so we couldn't get the income per train to compare with longer routes. We said, 'No matter how efficient we are, we'll always be in this straitjacket of operating an urban service with frequent stops and low average fares. We had to look to other areas to be super-efficient, so that when we came to bid for resources we would be able to say we couldn't match train costs for obvious reasons but we could match anywhere else with the best possible traincrew strategy."

"We tried to flush out as many nonsenses as we could. We couldn't do a lot of things because they were covered by national agreements, which were sacrosanct. When we tried to mess around with those we had threats of industrial action. We would have taken on the staff, as with Sunday services, on a local basis, but what used to kill it was that they threatened to bring the rest of the system out. Privatisation and franchising might have a therapeutic effect because it will be less easy for the staff to bring the whole railway out on strike."

One national practice which John successfully challenged was staffing all three-car trains with two conductors in areas where there were stations without ticket barriers. It was obvious that a single conductor could collect all the fares from a three-car train on a relatively quiet service. After a lot of tough negotiation it was agreed that trains would be staffed according to the number of passengers they carried, not according to the length of the train. The assistant conductors had to be justified by the amount of money they collected on each specific service.

"To this day assistant conductors are still justified on some lines by train length rather than loadings. The management in those places didn't work hard enough to get the productivity. We had to work hard at it because there were so many other factors working against us. At the same time we had to be cute and clever to get some of these agreements done locally without completely negating national agreements, otherwise it would rebound on us."

Other improvements in staff productivity could be gained simply by tidying up edges which had become frayed over time. For instance, conductors and drivers were synchronised to work in pairs. Previously they would separate when the drivers went for their half-hour breaks. Synchronisation created a better camaraderie among the staff and, more importantly, simplified the job of the supervisor whenever a train was waiting for crew who were on a delayed in-coming train. Now the supervisor would need to search for one pair of spare crew rather than having to look in one place for a driver and somewhere else for a conductor. If one was missing, under the old system, the waiting train could be delayed or cancelled.

The conductor alone could easily issue all the tickets required on quiet services like this one. John Davies was determined that assistant ticket examiners would be justified by train loadings rather than train lengths.
Western Mail and Echo Ltd

"As it happened, by synchronising drivers and conductors we actually saved some conductors' turns. When we sold the synchronising to the trade unions they agreed. Then I made the fatal error of saying at the meeting that, as it happened, we would save some turns too. They immediately forgot there would be improved services and said the management were only doing it to save turns."

The logic was obvious, however, and the synchronisation was instituted.

Another inheritance John rectified was the limited route knowledge of the drivers. Drivers based at Rhymney had route knowledge covering only the Rhymney, Coryton and Penarth lines, while Treherbert drivers could work everything bar the Coryton and Rhymney lines. This practice probably stretched back to the days when the Rhymney line belonged to the Rhymney Railway and the lines on the Taff side belonged to the Taff Vale Railway. By the 1980s the practice caused problems when trains were running late; the supervisor had to find not only a driver for a waiting train but a driver who was familiar with the train's route, a process which undermined reliability further.

Curiously, John wanted to develop in the valleys a feature he had disparaged when it was applied in other areas.

"After flexible rostering was introduced, drivers in many depots could equalise their earnings. Drivers who always had short-distance work would be worse off so they had a combination of long and short-distance turns, but the costs of doing that were considerable. I knew this would push up the costs in the valleys in the short term."

The Valley Lines formed a compact system and equalising earnings was not an issue. The amendment proposed by John would also make the drivers' jobs more interesting, and the staff were happy with the change. The opposition was more likely to come from higher up, as the cost of training drivers to work the alien routes would be considerable.

"Chris Green, then the general manager of ScotRail, was always telling us that we should jump at the chance to use any spare money in the budget. We did just that. Alan Beardsworth, my assistant, was clever at ferreting through the budgets of various departments - such as operations, signalling, civil engineers - to find small surpluses. Each department would bid for more than they needed, and Alan found the money that was going spare in each department and brought it all together. It was all legitimate - there was no fiddling going on. I was delighted. It wasn't a good way to manage things, perhaps, but it was expedient. It was streetwise, and we got things done because we were possibly cleverer than other people. Because there was bad control of costs you took your chances when you could. We saw the opportunity to train all these drivers now, and for evermore they would have total route knowledge.

"There were drivers from Treherbert who said, 'Good God, I didn't know Rhymney was so beautiful!' The valleys are very parochial. Merthyr and Rhymney are only four miles apart as the crow flies but some of the Rhymney drivers had never been to Merthyr in their lives! That may be an exaggeration, but it was the sort of situation we had."

The introduction of part-time staff was given a more hostile reception by the National Union of Railwaymen, which had instructed its local branches not to co-operate on the subject. Many of the staffed stations on the system didn't justify a full shift and rather than de-staff them altogether John decided to staff them for the mornings only using part-time workers.

"We had one of those big meetings with all the staff representatives. We put our case and they put theirs, which was resolutely in opposition to the idea. The area manager, John Jones, was taking the meeting and he said, 'OK. The management has decided that we will introduce part-time working and it will start from Monday in a month's time. Thank you very much. We've minuted the meeting.' They didn't think we'd put it in. They were expecting us to defer the meeting and bring it up again. They were so surprised when it happened that they couldn't react. We had no strike and not even the threat of industrial action.

"The Valley Lines were the first part of British Rail to get part-time staff and we never got the credit for it. That's a pity, because we stuck our necks out to get it."

Station staffing was the subject of another contested change. In the early 1980s BR's policy was to remove ticket barriers at stations and increase ticket inspections on the trains.

"It was designed not as a cost-cutting measure but as a more effective way of collecting revenue. They took away the physical barriers to travelling and got more people onto the trains, where the passengers had time to ask questions and could be reassured."

The principle, however, was intended for long-distance services. It was felt that conductors on local services wouldn't have the time to inspect each passenger's ticket if they also had to attend to the train at frequent stops. John, however, had seen the open stations policy working successfully in East Anglia and wanted to implement it on the Valley Lines. The threat of a strike was all too obvious so he invited Ken Winter, a Mid Glamorgan county councillor who was also the NUR's sectional council representative for conductors, to join a working party on the subject. (The NUR's sectional councillors were strategic staff representatives at regional level.)

"I had the utmost respect for Ken. He was a level-headed man, a hard negotiator, and somebody you didn't mess around with. But he had the common sense to know when he was on a winner or a loser. He said, 'The union disagrees with open stations and I disagree with it, but if you're going to go ahead with it I would rather you did it with our advice. We won't sign anything that says we agree, but we will try to persuade you to do it in a certain way.'

"The working party, which had two management and two trade union representatives, met a number of times and we gathered a lot of evidence. We conducted train counts and decided which trains to put assistant conductors on.

"I was convinced that this was going to work, but I was the only one who was. John Jones, the area manager, wasn't entirely convinced but said he would stand by me and I was pleased to have his support. I worked on the basis that if a railway is trying to attract people the last thing to do is put a barrier in front of them. Although some regular travellers would think this was a licence to travel for nothing, we just had to make sure that we had the right people in the right place to make sure the fares were collected, and there would be penalties for indiscipline if they didn't collect the fares. We weren't having 'It can't be done'. We said, 'You will do it.' In the cases where it genuinely was impossible, we would see if an assistant should be provided. I wanted those barriers to come out and never go back. I didn't want to yield to the traditional view that customers are always guilty until they are proved innocent.

"A lot of railway staff had the view that everyone was on the make, trying to avoid their fares. Really there was a hard core who would find a way of travelling without paying no matter what you did, and then there was the soft core who were opportunists who would get away with it if they had the chance. The cost of getting the hard core into the fold might be more than the income we'd get from them. I never said that, but that's what I felt. There was a threshold.

"Changing to open stations actually saved us a few staff, so again we were criticised – it was all a cost-saving thing. In fact it had just happened like that. As I'd had the union representatives with me from the start I could at least say that this had been done not with their connivance but with their recognition that there was some over-provision of staff."

Revenue collectors in East Anglia were known as 'greyhounds' – travelling a few stations out in the morning peak to assist the conductors on trains coming in from further afield, then travelling out on the cushions again to meet another incoming train. When the open stations system was introduced on the Valley Lines in 1986, 'greyhounds' were sent out to Taffs Well or Radyr and Llanishen or Caerphilly to cover several trips in each peak period. The Rhondda line, which was exceptionally busy and had many stations over a short distance, was equipped with an assistant revenue collector on every train. Ticket collectors were removed from the barriers at Caerphilly, Pontypridd, Barry, Cardiff Queen Street and Cardiff Central.

"The open stations system was an immediate success - best of all in the Rhondda valley. People said removing the ticket collectors from Pontypridd was a charter for everybody to come to Pontypridd without a ticket. But by putting somebody on every train in the Rhondda we ensured not only that everybody going to Pontypridd had a ticket but that the people who had previously been travelling free also paid their fares. Before we made the change, fraudulent travel was rife in the Rhondda. People travelled, say, from Tonypandy to Porth. There were no ticket barriers and the conductors couldn't work their way through the train quickly enough to collect the fares in between the frequent stops. When they had two conductors on the train the second conductor could collect fares throughout the journey."

The returns proved that the income in the Rhondda had shot up, and John invited any members of staff who doubted the efficacy of open stations to view the data in his office.

"I told them that all the figures came from them in the first place. Nobody ever came. They felt intimidated about going to the manager's office, and also they rather suspected that I might be right and they didn't want to know," says John.

"There were periods when the revenue losses got quite high because the trains were overcrowded and it was impossible for the conductors to get through, or we lost control of the staff - they weren't doing their jobs properly. The vast majority were doing their jobs, though, and the on-train takings went up and up and up. When I ceased being responsible for the Valley Lines in 1991, 55% of the take was from on board the trains. In 1983 it would have been 20% at the most."

In the early 1990s, Regional Railways decided to revert to ticket barriers in the peaks at Cardiff Queen Street and Central. People turned to John, who by that time was no longer responsible for the Valley Lines, and said the open stations system had failed.

"I said, 'No, it hasn't failed. It's Regional Railways that have lost control of doing it properly in the customers' interests. It's an admission of management defeat to put the barriers back there.' I used the instance of the 1960s, when most retail outlets went to the open shop concept which was much criticised at the time. But has any shop ever gone back to the old system, where you had a counter and you had to ask for things you wanted? The railway is unique in its inability to implement successfully new systems that reflect the changing customer requirement. I had this view in 1986 when we did it, and I have not shifted from it since. If anything, the more people protested (including the Glamorgan Rail Users' Federation who joined in the chorus) the more I strengthened my resolve."

For the open stations system to succeed it was vital that the conductors were motivated. Obviously an incentive scheme was needed, but BR's national incentive scheme was self-defeating. It used a complicated points system that combined tickets sold and revenue taken. When the conductors reached a certain threshold the commission money halved, thereby failing to give them any incentive to exceed that threshold.

"It was one of those things that was probably designed by a committee at the British Railways Board and given national application, probably sometime in the 1960s. We told them we didn't want that system and we had the reply, 'This is the system. We're working on a revised system but it will take some time.' We despaired, because we had to get our incentives right.

"We had to implement our open stations scheme with the national incentives applying, but a year or two later I sat down with area manager Roger MacDonald, now the managing director of Thames Trains, and we created a local incentive scheme. We decided on a system that was easy to understand, log and collate. The conductors would pocket 2.5% of the first income they took on the train, until the fares they'd collected reached a threshold of £100 per shift. Above that threshold, 5% would go into their pockets. The idea was to make them work very hard for that first £100 because they knew they were going to do better after that."

Assistant ticket examiners were not entitled to incentives under the national scheme, as their job consisted of examining and issuing tickets and nothing else. In the new Valley Lines scheme they got 2.5% across the board, with no incentive above £100 of takings. There were cries of 'foul' because the conductors had better incentives, but John thought the system was fair. Another row blew up over the part-time staff who were switched from the ticket barriers to the trains.

"When we introduced this incentive scheme in 1988 we had part-time staff who were taking home the equivalent of a full day's pay when they added their bonuses. There was a hell of a row about them having a full day's money, but we said, 'If they're taking that money home they've earned it. Those people have worked their backsides off to get this. We're getting the fares in and that's what matters'," says John.

That disagreement in itself illustrated how the local incentive scheme was working wonders on revenue collection. John recalls another illustration.

"I remember taking the 07.02 train from Aberdare one morning and the conductor – now a Channel Tunnel driver – was a very bright young man. In the 50 minutes it took that train to reach Cardiff he took more than £300, some of it through season tickets because it was a Monday morning. He kept the train on time, despite all the stops, and issued all those tickets without missing anybody. I asked him, 'Don't you think you should have an assistant between Aberdare and Abercynon because of all those frequent stops?' He said, 'What? And me get less commission? No fear.' That was the attitude of the younger people. The older ones found it a bit difficult. There were older people not used to this more efficient way of doing things and who possibly didn't have the energy to do it, yet some of them were very good at it."

Once again, an effective system was swept away by Regional Railways. In 1991, the local incentives were replaced by a 5% commission across the board, with no threshold.

"I thought it was crazy. If they worked for 2.5%, why give the money away? Regional Railways panicked because in most parts of the country the conductors just weren't doing their jobs.

"Our system sometimes lapsed, and we had periods of 5 or 6% of income missing, but I knew that on average the uncollected income was about 2.5%. The cost of getting some of that last 2.5% was more than the money we would get in. That was the way to do business, even if it looked as if we, as a responsible public organisation, ought to be chasing every penny. We never said that publicly and I sometimes played down the problems in the press because I was afraid I would be forced to abandon the open stations scheme by my superiors. Things like this needed time to get right."

A remarkable aspect of all these changes was that the efficiency of the Valley Lines was turned around so quickly, a speed that was no doubt assisted by the small scale of the system and the degree of autonomy the management was then permitted. The Valley Lines' quick start off the blocks was brought home to John early in 1987, when he sampled the recently opened line from Bathgate to Edinburgh.

"The three-car DMU on the line was full from Bathgate and Livingstone," he recalls. "I was very impressed by the number of passengers. I was less impressed by the fact that they had a conductor and three assistant conductors to issue tickets. On the Valley Lines we would have had a conductor and an assistant for the same type of journey and they would have taken the same amount of revenue. Somebody in ScotRail hadn't focused on the fact that it might be costing them more to collect that revenue than they were taking. A lot of parts of the country were having the same sort of problem."

Crucially, great strides forward had been taken in staff productivity on the Valley Lines by early 1987. The retrograde steps of later years had yet to be taken and John was able to point to an efficient, tightly controlled local operation when the battle lines were drawn for the allocation of new Sprinter trains.

Pressure to Cut Costs

When BR was split into sectors in the early 1980s railway managers knew little about where their true costs were incurred. For many years they had never needed to know; for a century or so most railway managers sat on fat profits and for decades afterwards they had a comfortable cushion of regular subsidy although after 1968 this was progressively squeezed. Step by step in the 1980s costs began to come into focus.

"Where costs were shared between services or sectors the allocation of costs was on a very arbitrary basis and we weren't in a very good position to know the correctness of our allocation," says John. "Above that there were huge areas of overheads which obviously affected the costs of the services. We knew little about them because no information was provided for the management."

"Most of the pressure to cut costs was at ground level. In all the passenger sectors, improvements in productivity were legion between 1983 and 1993 but overheads remained a major drain. Those areas that were controlling costs at a high level – research and development and major engineering, whether it be civil, signals or trains – were in many instances impermeable to change. The result was that you tended to get emaciated services – cuts going through to the bone to try to balance the books while people higher up were getting away with not having to work so hard to get their costs down."

An early part of John's drive to identify costs was compilation of league tables for the various Valley Lines services. The tables were crude initially, because the methods of collecting data were crude.

"Gradually we fine-tuned this to get an idea of which was the most profitable of our routes, or the one that was making the least loss - that's a better way of putting it. The best-performing service was Treherbert to Barry Island. The second was Merthyr to Barry Island, which surprised us because the number of passengers was much smaller than on the Treherbert line. However, the service on the Merthyr line was less frequent than on the Treherbert line by then and the loadings per train on the Merthyr line tended to be higher. The worst performing route, apart from the short Coryton and Penarth lines, was the Rhymney line."

The Rhymney line was a poor performer because it had a bigger difference between peak and off-peak loadings than the other lines. While the Treherbert line needed only one extra three-car DMU to cope with its peaks, the Rhymney line was allocated four three-car DMUs over and above its off-peak allocation. When all the factors were taken into account, the service that was superficially the best performer turned out to be the worst. To the traditional railway mind, or even to more up-to-date thinkers, the correct response to those findings would have been to start cutting services on the Rhymney line. This, however, is where the thinking of John Davies and John Welsby parted ways.

"This information started focusing how we built up our off-peak trade. We worked hard to push up the off-peak loadings on the Rhymney line by fares reductions – more so than on other lines. We wanted to reduce this imbalance between the peak and off-peak. I gradually got to the view that trains that stood around between the peaks were wasted. In terms of capital employed they were an appalling waste, but we had a high peak in some cases so we had to cater for that. All the additional custom we achieved off-peak was costing us next to nothing to provide but bringing us extra income. That's why the financial performance of the Valley Lines improved so dramatically."

So much for John Welsby's advice to improve financial performance by focusing on costs alone. The operating ratio – a traditional railway yardstick which compared income with direct costs, excluding overheads - for the Valley Lines soon vindicated the wisdom of treating income and costs as parts of the solution to the same problem. In 1983 the operating ratio for the Valley Lines was 150%, meaning that the trains were costing 50% more

to provide than the income they brought in. By 1990 that ratio had dropped to 98% - the Valley Lines were operating at a slight surplus of income over costs.

While this rapid programme of change had undoubtedly transformed the Valley Lines from an anchronism to the basis of a modern transport system which deserved investment and respect, the management and staff – like their counterparts in other parts of the Provincial Sector who achieved similar feats – never got the recognition they deserved. This was largely because the staff at sector headquarters were racing up a parallel learning curve just as quickly as the staff on the ground.

"We didn't know how headquarters costs were made up and we would think we were doing really well and suddenly we would get saddled with another dollop of costs that we didn't know about. Most train maintenance costs were a headquarters item for many years. They were closely guarded – the mechanical and electrical engineering department had its own fiefdom. There was a jamspread allocation of costs which hid the inefficient areas and failed to highlight the efficient ones. Gradually the costs came down to depot level and we had a depot jamspread, and then the depot was able to allocate costs to different service groups in that depot. It all took time to get out of a system that was big and unwieldy and where people's reputations were made on such things. Gradually people were beavering away at headquarters level to make sure that more costs were accountable to the people who ran the services. Headquarters people had no incentive to improve efficiency – the thing was so massive to them that it was impossible to identify where things were going wrong. It was a good thing that those costs were passed down to us, but it was dispiriting to us at the time."

Recognition and applause would have done more than boost morale. It would have had a concrete effect on the future of the Valley Lines and many other Provincial services. In 1986 the Rhondda valley line was carrying more passengers per capita of catchment than any other in Britain, and possibly in Europe. It also had one of the best train frequencies per capita in Europe, more than 97% of its revenue was collected and its resources were closely matched to demand. The Rhondda probably had one of the most efficient train services in Europe per capita. Had this been proclaimed at the time other railway managers could have looked to it for elements of best practice, just as the Cardiff management might have found elements of best practice elsewhere had due credit been given. Had it been proclaimed long and loud the case for rail investment in the Rhondda could have been stronger, too.

In three years John Davies had proved that it was possible to increase income significantly enough to offset operating costs. Had this been acknowledged the Provincial Sector might have come to realise that extra trains and extra investment could be justified if there was considerable extra income to be gained. At that time the government, after all, was primarily interested in the bottom line – reducing BR's subsidy rather than its borrowing limit – and might have been convinced that some extra investment to meet the latent demand in certain areas would be justified within a few years by growing income and a fall in the subsidy required.

In the event the Provincial Sector had set its mind against any increases in costs and, therefore, against increasing the orders for new trains. (The sector's number of Class 158 units was even to be significantly reduced). No efficiency drive under the sun could have increased the allocation of Sprinters to the Valley Lines, and in the 1990s the Provincial Sector's pigeons came home to the valleys to roost.

THE RHONDDA LINE

Top left: The mountains which mark the full stop at the head of the Rhondda valley loom over Treherbert station in this 1984 picture. The tracks once continued to Blaenrhondda, at the top of the valley, but Treherbert was the terminus for the trains from Cardiff in 1896 and, since no railway managers made a conscious decision to extend those services to Blaenrhondda, it remains the terminus in 1996.

Centre left: Wagons, sidings and the double track Rhondda line are all visible in this February 1977 view of Treorchy station showing a Class 116 DMU in blue livery. Five years later the double track visible in the distance was singled, placing unfortunate constraints on the subsequent development of services.

Below: The highlight of the TVR 150 celebrations was the return of steam workings to the Valley Lines on a few weekends in October 1991. A number of local people have turned out to watch 2–6–4T No. 80080 at Ystrad Rhondda. The station and loop are much newer than the train, having been built with remarkable speed in 1986.
Stephen Miles (3)

Top right: The sight of a Western class loco on a rake of 10 coaches passing Porth was not so unusual in the 1970s as it might seem today. Until the late 1970s, long-distance Merrymaker excursion trains had been a feature of the railways in the valleys but the practice ceased because they required an inordinate amount of managerial effort. The Rhondda Fach line, often touted as a candidate for reopening, curves away to the right.

Centre right: The up platform at Trehafod was rebuilt so land formerly occupied by the three-track railway formation could be released for the new road beside the station. On 11th March 1989 a Sprinter departs with a Trehafod to Pontypridd shuttle service, part of an emergency service instituted after flooding affected the line between Porth and Trehafod.

Below left: Another unusual train in the loop at Ystrad Rhondda is Sprinter unit 150 138, imported from Birmingham to help shift the huge numbers of Christmas shoppers using the Valley Lines on a Saturday in December 1991. The driver is obtaining his token from the cabin beside the train.

Below right: Twelve years after the top photograph was taken the layout has been altered at Porth but the twin tracks have been retained to the south. This up train has just switched to the former down line as it begins its journey up the single-line route to Treherbert. The proximity of the railway to the Rhondda's dense housing is evident. *Stephen Miles (4)*

Top left: Three of the five trains which were stabled at Treherbert sidings on Sunday 12th February 1995. For decades, drivers based at Treherbert were not passed in route knowledge on the Rhymney line.

Top right: The number of passengers visible on the platform at Treorchy in this 1991 view supports the suggestion that the Rhondda line may have been Europe's best-used line per head of population at the time. The long-siding nature of the line is evident, as is the wonderful motorbike track thought-fully created by British Rail alongside the railway!

Left: The lines to Merthyr and Aberdare are visible on the right as a Sprinter on the Rhondda line passes Pontypridd Junction signal box. *Stephen Miles (3)*

A view which many people would have in their mind's eye as a typical Rhondda scene - but it is not what it seems. The pit-head winding gear has been retained only because the former Lewis Merthyr colliery at Trehafod now forms the Rhondda Heritage Park. One of Mid Glamorgan County Council's new roads sweeps up the valley beside the four-car train. *Stephen Miles*

CHAPTER 5

EIGHT WEEKS ON A KNIFE EDGE
The 1987 Timetable Change

The Valley Lines enjoyed a run of good luck over the first four years of their revival. From 1983 the steady improvement of train frequencies and productivity had produced all the right results. But in October 1987 the good fortune ran out abruptly. On the fifth of the month a new timetable was introduced to take full advantage of new trains, the Class 150/2 Sprinters, which had the novel feature of automatic couplings. Management did not realise until it was too late that the new timetable was too ambitious, especially as it coincided with the opening of the first new passenger service in South Wales since well before the Second World War.

Coupling and Uncoupling

When the new timetable swung into operation the automatic coupling and uncoupling which formed the nucleus of most of the innovations failed to work effectively, throwing the whole system into confusion. The fleet of trains was now of two incompatible types - old and new trains which were unable to couple up to bail one another out. Too many Class 116 DMUs had been abandoned immediately, leaving no spare capacity. Passengers had no idea when their train would turn up, many couldn't understand the Sprinters' powered doors and at least one got carried along with his coat trapped between the door-leaves. The complaints came flooding in, embarrassing advertisements for the new service on hoardings and local radio were hurriedly withdrawn, the local media wallowed in the chaos and Provincial headquarters was less than sympathetic, convinced that the gung-ho Valley Lines managers had had their come-uppance.

A new timetable was hurriedly devised to obviate all automatic coupling and uncoupling, but it would be nearly two months before it could be put into practice. For eight long weeks the future of the Valley Lines hung on a knife edge as the entire staff sweated blood and tears to keep the trains rolling and the management gambled everything on the hand that would be dealt in late November.

From the outside, the fiasco looked like a tale of over-ambition, incompetence and naivety on the part of John Davies and his assistants in Cardiff. In reality the mess had resulted from an unfortunate coincidence of numerous factors - many of them resulting from actions at a higher managerial level.

The 1987 timetable change was not as revolutionary as it might have seemed at first. In fact it was more evolutionary than revolutionary and took the promised assets of the Sprinters to achieve improvements which progressed naturally from the developments of the previous four years.

Bargoed station proved to be the biggest fly in the new timetable's ointment. Services on the Rhondda line had been improved to half-hourly in 1986, while Rhymney and Merthyr now had hourly services throughout the day. The Rhymney Valley was served half-hourly from Ystrad Mynach southwards. Half-hourly services from Bargoed, an important mid-valley town, had been an objective for Mid Glamorgan County Council and BR for some time. The difficulty – which even today has not been addressed satisfactorily – was that trains did not have time to run from Cardiff to Bargoed and return after a few minutes if a rigid half-hourly interval was to be maintained. The Sprinters' coupling abilities provided the solution, or so it seemed. Every hour a four-car set was to run up the Rhymney Valley and split at Bargoed. One unit proceeded to Rhymney and the other returned immediately to Cardiff. When the first train returned from Rhymney half an hour later it would pair up at Bargoed with a third unit

which had just arrived from Cardiff and the four-piece formation would run down the valley.

"We thought we'd got a wonderful solution, with loads of capacity and no down-time at Bargoed," says John Davies.

In the event, the Bargoed operation was a disaster. The Sprinters frequently refused to couple or uncouple there because the track was too uneven.

Coupling and uncoupling Sprinters in service was mainly restricted to Cardiff Central, Queen Street and Bargoed. Pontypridd was another location where dividing and combining trains suggested itself, but John steered clear of that because the platform track was curved at Pontypridd and British Rail's early problems with the Class 150s had often occurred on curved track.

"As it happens, it would have worked at Pontypridd because the track was in good condition!" says John.

Another of John's aspirations was to provide four trains per hour south of Caerphilly and Pontypridd, the latter to be achieved when the Aberdare line opened in 1988. Ideally the Barry line would also have had four trains per hour, but the intensive coal traffic sharing the line forced the managers to settle for three per hour to Barry and to Penarth (the latter destination being as much as anything a more convenient place to turn trains round than Cardiff Central). It was also important in summer to run trains through to the resort at Barry Island from the Rhymney, Merthyr and Treherbert lines.

The big drawback, however, was that the two main routes into Cardiff from the north would be operating on 15-minute intervals, while the two main routes to the south would be on 20-minute cycles. Matching the two up for through running – while also ensuring that Cathays was served by most trains to and from Barry and Penarth – was like knocking a square peg into a triangular hole and called for ingenuity in the timetable planning office. The facility to uncouple and couple Sprinters quickly in Cardiff Central and Queen Street promised to make the job easier.

Improvements within Cardiff were also ambitious. The City Line, which opened with the new timetable, and the Coryton branch both got half-hourly services - but not without tribulation.

The timetable also ushered in improvements which were not so problematic. Among those were better evening services which generally were a success, particularly on the Barry line. The upper ends of the Merthyr and Rhymney lines were among the only local railways in Britain to have as good a service on Sunday afternoons as on weekdays – a train every hour.

The Coryton line gained evening and Sunday services for the first time in its history. John was warned by his experienced assistant Alan Beardsworth that attempting to run Sunday services on what was essentially a commuter route would end in tears, but the service was motivated by the need to clock up high mileage on the Sprinters to justify having them in the first place.

"It was a novel idea, but a crazy one, to get better productivity for the new trains," says John. "We created a Sunday Coryton to Penarth shuttle which took 26 minutes from end to end. Some drivers were in danger of being carted into a mental institution because they were driving trains back and forth along the same piece of line, picking up hardly any passengers. It was dispiriting, and the only thing that kept them at it was the pay at time and three-quarters!"

Overall, then, the 1987 timetable was to bring an incremental improvement to most services. However, as it turned out the total number of increments added up to too much change in one helping.

One that got away on the dress rehearsal day for the new timetable in October 1987. Here the Rhymney portion has successfully parted at Bargoed station from the other unit, which will return to Cardiff, but all too often the Sprinters failed to couple and uncouple on the uneven track here.   *Stephen Miles*

The inability of the Sprinters to couple and uncouple in many situations was the new timetable's most vulnerable flank and probably its biggest single fault. The couplings needed to be within a millimetre or two of each other on the horizontal and vertical planes if the numerous electrical connections were to be made between the two. Unfortunately, some of the trackwork on the Valley Lines was in such bad shape that two couplings often found themselves out of alignment. Track joints caused a particular headache because of the difference in levels that could exist between two adjacent rails. The track in Cardiff Central and Queen Street was frequently pounded by double-headed coal trains. Much of the trackwork in the valleys had been in situ since before the decline of the coal industry and the withdrawal of steam engines, which transmitted a hefty lateral knocking motion through the wheels to the track. In a nutshell, the mess was a result of trying to run sophisticated trains from the electronic era on infrastructure that dated back to the steam era.

John Davies did foresee problems with the coupling process.

"I'd had reports from the Manchester area, where it had caused all sorts of delays," he says. "In the months leading to October 1987 I made representations to Provincial headquarters saying I was having second thoughts about so much coupling and uncoupling. They said, 'Don't be so stupid. Of course it will work.'

"I went up to Derby to see a coupling demonstration with Sprinters. It looked like simplicity itself. After that I thought maybe Manchester had got it wrong and I was wrong to doubt the reliability of the couplings."

This episode arguably demonstrates a fault at a higher level than Valley Lines management. The people responsible for testing and accepting the new Sprinters should have made available test results on coupling and uncoupling on different types of track. The causes of the problems at Manchester should have been investigated and other areas warned of the reasons for the coupling difficulties.

Ideally coupling of Sprinters should have been tried out well in advance at all the locations where they would be required to carry out the task on the Valley Lines. This exercise, had it been considered necessary, would have been difficult because the Valley Lines received their Sprinters much later than they should have done. Two units were made available earlier in the year for basic crew training, but the main allocation arrived less than three months before the big-bang change. This delay, caused partly by late delivery from train builder British Rail Engineering Limited and partly because Provincial diverted earlier vehicles to other areas, was to have a significant effect on the new timetable in October 1987.

Had the problems become apparent earlier, it might have been possible to reballast the tracks where uncoupling was to occur and ensure the trains had a level surface on which to perform.

The new trains were initially formed into three-car sets and used in place of Class 116 DMUs until the new timetable began, but this transitional period was far too short. If the staff were unfamiliar with the new trains, the passengers were even more confused.

"The passengers needed tuition as well as the staff. It would have been better if we'd had the Sprinters in service longer for passengers to get used to sliding doors."

Passengers who were used to the basic and brutal swinging doors on the Class 116s suddenly found themselves confronted by a train door with no handle. Panic could ensue, especially among passengers wanting to alight. There were also delays while the conductor broke off from checking and selling tickets to return to the rear cab and unlock the doors (operating rules prevented drivers from pressing the door-release buttons in their cabs). Worse still, passengers sometimes got caught in closing doors, and the local media devoured with relish the story of a passenger being carried along with part of his coat flapping outside the train.

Another unfortunate problem outside the control of Cardiff management was the shortfall in Sprinters allocated to Cardiff Canton, the upshot of which was an awkward mixture of old and new DMUs operating the new timetable. The rail strategy document produced by Mid and South Glamorgan county councils stated that 27 Sprinters (running 24 diagrams) would be needed to handle all the main Valley Lines services with the exception of a few peak-period turns. In the peak old DMUs could then have been deployed on the shorter, self-contained diagrams without having to mix with Sprinters. To cover the core services off peak, excluding the Coryton branch and City Line, 17 Sprinters were needed.

"If we went for another seven units for peak diagrams, we could cover the whole off-peak with the main allocation plus three of those extra seven. That left four with only peak-period work. To justify two of those we approached the Midlands area and established the idea of a joint Cardiff to Birmingham service, using two of our 150/2s off peak and one 150/1 from the Midlands area. That left two units needing deployment. One was to do a day's work in West Wales and the other to run the boat train to Fishguard and back to Cardiff between the peaks," says John.

"There was also an imbalance between the morning and afternoon peaks, because the afternoon peak is more spread out. We decided to deploy the one Sprinter we had spare because of this on the 17.15 from Cardiff to Milford Haven. This was justified because it maintained and improved the West Wales crews' traction knowledge of Sprinters. It was claimed, however, that the 17.15 was the train I caught home to Neath every day and that I was not happy with the prospect of making the journey in an old three-car DMU! In practice I hardly ever used that train, especially in late 1987."

It was clear in John's mind that 27 Sprinters could be justified but there was trouble ahead.

"Apparently the instructions as to how the bids for Sprinters were to be submitted were not clear, and we didn't submit our bid properly. Provincial headquarters said it was badly submitted and that they couldn't see any justification for 27. Their real reason was that they never had 27 to allocate because, unknown to me at the time, they were allocating 20 Sprinters to TransPennine, to cover until the Class 156s and 158s appeared."

Once he heard of the TransPennine allocation (for services between Liverpool/Manchester and Leeds/York) John gave up the fight for 27 Sprinters. Every Sprinter had to be justified in hard economic terms and the trains were strictly allocated to the areas which showed they could generate the best income per train.

John does not believe he threw in the towel too early.

"In hindsight, we would never have won and I had a hell of a job explaining it at the time. The TransPennine thing killed it. You can't blame them; they had very high costs running loco-hauled trains on TransPennine and it was a necessary stop-gap solution. But once you pit a cross-country service against a suburban network like the Valleys, the suburban network has had it. There's no way any suburban network can generate the income per unit to compete for resources with a cross-country service. The distances involved in suburban services are so much lower and the income proportionally lower."

The prospects of competing with other areas due to receive Class 150s were not good either. The units in the Edinburgh area would be used on much longer workings – as far afield as Dundee. The East Midlands and Manchester, with its Manchester to Blackpool long-distance workings, were obviously going to show better income-per-unit results than the Valley Lines. It turned out that, because income per unit was the be-all and end-all to the Provincial Sector, too many units were allocated to the Manchester to Blackpool workings. John recalls travelling to Blackpool and noticing that the four-car Sprinter formations were running almost empty at times.

"Because their earnings were high they got a large allocation. They could have made a better case if they had a mixture of two-car and four-car diagrams. They got away with it, but they had to change eventually because the whole hierarchy could see what was going on.

"By then it was too late. Had I known in early 1987 I could have made a stronger stand for the Valley Lines allocation but I wasn't in possession of all the facts."

Not surprisingly, relations between Cardiff and Swindon reached their lowest ebb in 1987. Relations were hardly rosy at the best of times; after all, the Valley Lines had been built up using the Las Vegas rules rather than the Swindon rules.

"The railway has never been good at taking decisions based on risk. They have to be based on certainties," says John. "You never progress unless you take a decision based on risk, but you have to win more than you lose. On the Valley Lines we didn't have time to go through the standard risk assessment because in that time the traffic would have passed us by. They asked, 'On what basis did you make these decisions?' I replied, 'It was a hunch. I know the Valleys well.' You can commission all sorts of surveys, but nothing beats getting out into the market and knowing what it's doing."

Much of the reasoning behind the strategy for higher frequencies was based on what John saw with his own eyes. At Queen Street there was overcrowding on the cramped island platform which could be eased if people had less time to wait for their trains. Frequencies of four trains per hour would spread the load more evenly on trains in the lower Valleys, eradicating the problem of some trains being packed to standing while following ones ran almost empty.

In the summer before the 1987 change, Provincial director John Edmonds (now the chief executive of Railtrack) visited the area on one of his quarterly reviews. He reviewed one part of the Provincial empire every three months, and this time it was the turn of the Valley Lines to be scrutinised.

"We explained to him all the contingencies we had for this new timetable. I said it would be the best timetable the valleys had ever seen. I heard a long time afterwards that he was very impressed by my statements, but he didn't know the sand on which they were built! He had a lot of good points but he was very ruthless. I didn't really believe he was the kind of person I could argue with about resources. I couldn't make a case on paper against the Sprinters being used elsewhere, so I had to be very upbeat."

Until 1987 nothing significant had gone wrong with expansion on the Valley Lines, so the upper management was content to give cautious support. Come the trouble of autumn 1987 and the same people withdrew their support.

"I had been very trenchant when I said what I must have for the Valley Lines. I made a lot of enemies at Swindon because they didn't have my faith in the growth prospects of the Valleys, but they did support me once I'd convinced them. When things started to go wrong they weren't supportive. They said, 'You made this bed. Now you sleep on it.' It wasn't a happy experience."

Having undermined the Valley Lines' allocation of new trains quite late in the day, the higher management then made clear they were not prepared to allow the Valley Lines to retain more old DMUs after the new timetable's problems became apparent. Cancellations and the frequent failure to combine two Sprinters meant that trains were overcrowded, to the point where passengers were left behind. This was a serious matter for passengers wanting to travel, say, from Cardiff to stations on the Merthyr line. They faced an hour's wait until their next train, and there was no guarantee that that would appear on time or that it would run at all.

Staff, media and public viewed the overcrowding as the outcome of changing from three-car to two-car trains. The Sprinters were built as two-car trains partly because the government insisted that new stock should replace old on a two-for-three basis. John had also insisted on cutting the three-car Class 116s to two-car sets by removing the centre trailer. This gave them less weight to drag up the steeply-graded valleys.

"Going to two-car trains was extremely controversial," says John. "In the first week there was a feeling of 'I told you so' because people had been warning of overcrowding. They kept the centre trailers at Canton for a long time – they were convinced I would want to put them back into service.

"I had nearly every other railman telling me it was crazy to remove the centre trailers, and in fact there wasn't much difference in the timings of three-car trains and two-car trains, but I wasn't going to have any problems. It was important that they had a good power-to-weight ratio because they would have to operate diagrams designed for Sprinters, with their superior acceleration. A three-car train substituting for a Sprinter on the Rhondda line could put the whole service out for hours because there was very little slack in the timetables."

As far as Swindon was concerned, there was no question of the Valley Lines getting any more trains. How John got his way illustrates how the Valley Lines revolution generally was achieved.

"On the third day of the new timetable I heard there was a train from Treherbert which was so overcrowded that passengers couldn't get on at Radyr and Llandaf. On the Thursday I went to Llandaf to see for myself, and a BBC television crew arrived at the same time and they saw it for themselves. Then they turned round and said, 'Now Mr Davies, what are you going to do about it?' I said that we'd already arranged for two old DMUs not to be sent to the knacker's yard but to be kept in service."

"Really I had arranged no such thing. As soon as the interview was over I ran down to Canton and asked them whether they had got rid of the old DMUs. They hadn't. Swindon were adamant that I wasn't going to keep them, so I told them what I'd said on television. 'On your head be it,' they replied. I asked them to explain on television why these trains were not going to be used after all. I had been put on the spot so I was going to put them on the spot. We got the trains!"

Those two extra trains, deployed on shorter workings like the Caerphilly shuttle, relieved the pressure and more Sprinters were run as four-car sets.

Nightmares at Queen Street

Because so many aspects of the Valley Lines were being changed at once, John decided to run a dress rehearsal on the day before the timetable was introduced. That in itself caused problems, especially because the rostering was such that the normal weekday traincrews could not be used on the dress rehearsal Sunday. Passengers were invited along and paid a flat fare of 50p.

45

The City Line opened on the same day, and it was at one of the opening ceremonies with South Glamorgan County Council dignitaries that John began to suspect that the new timetable was going belly up.

"I couldn't go anywhere or do anything about it because I was trapped in the ceremonies," he says. "When they finished I dashed back to Cardiff Central. That was the worst moment of all for me, the moment when I realised just how badly things were going."

Had he known what was in store John might have despaired even more. At the time he thought there were teething troubles which would be sorted out in a couple of weeks but as the first week wore on it became apparent that even a couple of months would not correct the situation. The Sprinters' refusal to couple and uncouple on the poor track at Bargoed caused cancellations on the Rhymney line and shortages of stock in Cardiff when too many four-car units were tied up on the Rhymney line.

The other weak point was the mile of double track through Cardiff Central and Queen Street. This was the hub of the Valley Lines system yet it had very little spare capacity and almost no flexibility in terms of reversible working. The busiest stations on the system by a long chalk both consisted of one platform face for each direction – probably insufficient infrastructure to run such an intensive service. Because every service had to use this double-track section, failures on it could – and did – throw the whole timetable into disarray.

John recalls, "A few days into the new timetable the supervisor at Cardiff Central panel box said, 'For God's sake Mr Davies, come and see what we have to put up with every day.' I went along. Every hour they were having minor heart attacks as trains from Barry and Penarth came in to Cardiff Central and had to combine. They prayed it would work, because otherwise they would have to reverse a train out from the platform before the next service could enter the station."

There were also nightmares at Queen Street, especially in the evening peak when a four-car train from Bargoed was meant to split to form trains to Barry and to Bute Road. The latter unit returned to Queen Street to form the evening long-distance commuter service to Milford Haven. The idea of running the latter through from Cardiff Queen Street (rather than starting it at Central) was to provide a convenient service for the many office and shop workers in the vicinity of Queen Street station. On most days the train wouldn't uncouple, so Bute Road was left with a half-hour gap in services at the height of the evening peak.

Naturally, the passengers were infuriated by all the disruption and, quite apart from the problems associated with the Sprinters, some unforeseeable gripes arose. The Coryton service had previously departed from the branch terminus on the hour or half hour, but the new service departed at xx.10 and xx.40. Many commuters were upset at having their routines disturbed in this way - to the extent that they deserted the rail service for good. They didn't return when, in 1989, the departures were restored to on-the-hour and half-hour.

The City Line formed a psychological obstacle, especially for people on the Merthyr line whose services were mostly running via Fairwater instead of Cathays. Ever since the days of the Taff Vale Railway, Merthyr folk had been used to their trains departing eastwards from Cardiff Central, but all of a sudden they were reversed to depart westwards via the City Line. Passengers were so incredulous that they refused to believe the announcements for Merthyr trains departing from platform seven instead of six at Cardiff Central.

"When they went to Central or Queen Street they often missed their train because it went a different way to what they were used to," says John. "It took a long time for us to realise they needed the reassurance that it wasn't going towards Barry but was in fact their train."

Sending Merthyr trains round the City Line also upset Merthyr line passengers who wanted to alight at Cathays, as they now had to change trains. Llandaf also missed out, as its service was cut from three per hour to two per hour. What densely populated Llandaf needed was a change in the opposite direction, and the suburb responded well to the 15-minute frequency that was introduced later.

To cap it all, the new service even discouraged passengers trying out the City Line for the first time. Because the trains were coming from Merthyr they were often overcrowded, especially in the morning peak and on Saturdays. Conductors were unable to proceed through the crowded aisles to sell tickets to people who had boarded at unstaffed City Line stations before the train arrived in Cardiff Central.

Reliability left a lot to be desired, too. The trains were diagrammed to run from Merthyr to Coryton via the City Line, back to Taffs Well via the City Line, to Coryton again, and then back to Merthyr. Incorporating the City Line in an existing service made sense in operational terms because it meant that to provide a half-hourly service on the City Line only one extra train would be needed. In practice, the consecutive turnaround times were very tight – five minutes at Merthyr, five at Coryton, 13 at Taffs Well, and five again at Coryton – and gave little room for delayed trains to get back on schedule. This in turn could affect other trains waiting to enter the single-track sections covered by these diagrams.

Valley Lines management kept the arrangement and gave it time to settle down, but the problems were so intractible that after two years the City and Coryton lines were allocated three dedicated units, operating a Coryton to Radyr shuttle.

Complaints Flood In

It was clear, as the media stressed every day, that the timetable had to be changed. The problems and solutions were also fairly obvious, but the difficulty lay in the mechanics of train planning and traincrew diagramming.

Before the change, David Gillett, area operations manager, had urged John to persevere and not to come back at the first sign of trouble to say he wanted to change the timetable.

"By the end of the second week he came to me and said, 'John, you've got to change this timetable'. On both counts he was right. The first time he was saying that I had to have patience and it would work, and the second time he was saying that everyone's patience was exhausted.

"It took a long time to make the change. The train crews were rostered on eight-week cycles so it wasn't till the end of November that we could put the new things in place. There was also a lot of work because somebody had to redesign all the diagrams and rosters. But how do you tell this to the public? We knew that if we got rid of the coupling and uncoupling most of our problems would be solved, but the public couldn't understand. They thought we should go back to fewer and longer trains. I had hell on earth trying to convince the media that it would be all right after eight weeks and it couldn't be done before. We just had to live through those eight weeks."

Naturally the complaints came flooding in, and John spent a couple of hours after work each evening to answer them (missing his beloved 17.15 train home every night!).

"I tried to write out answers to every complaint. It took an awful lot of time. I didn't find out till some time afterwards that there had been lots of complaints over the phone but my assistant Ken Williams had answered literally hundreds of them. He didn't tell me about them because he knew I was under pressure and was doing everything I could to put things right."

The pressure of the eight weeks was getting to everybody. John, normally a relaxed, soft-spoken man, even threw one of his superiors out of his office in Brunel House.

"I said, 'Don't come back until you've got some answers!'. He'd come to see me and said 'No, no, no, no' to everything. My voice echoed down the corridor, and other people opened the doors to see what was happening!" says John.

One illustration of the way the staff felt stands out in John's memory.

"There was a colourful character who worked at Treherbert - Harry his name was. He was colourful in every sense of the word: he had a shock of red hair. One day I found him prodding a Sprinter coupling with a bar, trying to entice it to uncouple. He turned to me and said, 'We're not going anywhere. I refuse to do any more. Get this thing sorted out!' Then he sat down on the platform."

A fortnight into the fiasco came the news that Glanrhyd bridge, on the Central Wales line, had collapsed in floodwater under the weight of a train. Four passengers were killed. Glanrhyd was in John's area as Provincial manager for South Wales.

"In some ways it was a relief to focus my attention on something different entirely. I had to leave the mess in the Valleys to concentrate on an even bigger mess on the Central Wales. That was where in particular I noticed a lack of support from Provincial headquarters. I think the Glanrhyd disaster was seen by some people in the hierarchy as a heaven-sent opportunity to shut the Central Wales line."

"We had to rediagram the trains. We needed an extra unit to maintain the timetable on the northern section. For the first few weeks we even had one replacement bus from Llandrindod down to Swansea - it was all we could do. On the north end we had to cancel the midday train from Shrewsbury because we couldn't resource it. I asked headquarters for an extra train but they refused. So I went to Provincial Midlands and found a Class 150/1 Sprinter. That, incidentally, is the only time a Class 150/1 has been used on the Central Wales line."

Back on the Valley Lines, things were beginning to look up because the staff were putting so much effort into improving operations. The morning peak even resembled the timetable on some days, although things always degenerated by the evening peak.

"There was a lot of cynicism among the staff and, while the supervisors might have disagreed with what we were doing, they rallied round nevertheless."

At last the eight-week period came to an end and the revised timetable could be introduced. Staff and public alike were surprised at the content of the revised timetable because it preserved all the service frequencies yet ironed out the worst of the problems. Nearly all uncoupling by trains in service was written out.

The Bargoed conundrum was sidestepped by giving one unit a 35-minute layover in the siding on Bargoed viaduct. This maintained the half-hourly interval service from Bargoed southwards but obviated uncoupling, at the expense of having a train out of use for over half an hour. The solution was good enough to last until 1993, and the change made then was far from ideal because it created 42-minute/18-minute intervals between southbound services - a textbook example of over-emphasis on cutting costs with no regard for the inconvenience caused to passengers and the undermining of the timetable's attractiveness.

The Bargoed solution of November 1987 meant that four-car trains would not be running up the Rhymney Valley throughout the day, but John believes that was not a problem because potential traffic from the Rhymney Valley had been over-estimated in the first place.

John even thought he had found a way to put the idling at Bargoed to productive use.

"The train crews needed a physical needs break every few hours and I wanted to use that time at Bargoed for the break. But to do that we needed more facilities for the staff at Bargoed and a proper walking route from the siding to the station. Nobody in Provincial headquarters would underwrite the expenditure."

It was thinking like that proposed for Bargoed which by 1987 had already turned the Valley Lines into the network with the most productive staff on British Rail. Only Merseyrail came close in traincrew productivity. Until 1983 the staff had seen nothing but retrenchment on the Valley Lines, so it was not surprising that even in 1987 there were many who doubted the rationale behind the new timetable. The conspiracy theorists saw it as a way to overload the network till it collapsed under the strain so that lower frequencies and even line closures could be justified.

"Such a big change as this should have been communicated better to the staff," admits John. "The railways have never been good about telling people, including staff, about change. The mushroom technique of management is what they use and we were guilty on this point."

"Whether the staff would have believed us I don't know. They weren't very keen that we were expanding the frequency without any more staff. The 1987 timetable was the last turn of the screw of staff productivity. Some people thought it was a good thing, a lot of them would have preferred to sit in the mess drinking tea for longer. It was all pressure, all go - especially for conductors who had to sell tickets."

One of the measures for which John fought was to get operations controlled locally, rather than from Swindon. A year before the timetable change a control office was set up in a portable cabin on the Valley Lines' island platform at Cardiff Central. It was quickly dubbed 'The Wendy House' by the staff, a tag which stuck even when the control room was transferred to a more permanent site at the west end of the platform. The idea was that controllers in Cardiff would react much quicker to day-to-day problems with train-crew shifts.

"We put unusual demands on the controllers. The staff were sceptical. Some of the controllers came from other jobs and had difficulty coping with such a huge change."

In the event, the staff were pleasantly surprised at the revised timetable introduced in November 1987.

"They were amazed when they saw all the frequencies intact. We had found a lot of other flaws which we cleared up as well. That was greeted with relief by the staff, and once it started working the customers flocked to the trains."

Surprisingly, perhaps, the Valley Lines' custom had not suffered significantly during the eight weeks of turmoil.

"The usage and revenue stayed fairly stable. People were remarkably resilient. They didn't have time to make other arrangements, but if we hadn't managed to put things right the custom would have gone down. People's patience was wearing thin. Fortunately, we had a reputation for dealing with things quickly. This didn't endear us to our superiors. They frowned on changing timetables in mid-period, but we did it frequently to put things right.

"We knew we had most of the answers and our customers, by and large, believed us."

The Valley Lines had survived a near-death experience in intensive care, eight weeks when trains just could not run to time, eight weeks when John Davies and his managers in Cardiff made enemies of the travelling public and their superiors in Swindon - all because of factors entirely within BR's own control. Was it naive, with hindsight, for John to have expected the staff, the trains, the public and his superiors to have coped with such widescale and sudden change?

"It wasn't naive. I was unwise in trying to do so much at the same time as opening a new line. I should have foreseen the problems on coupling and uncoupling," says John.

"We weren't the only ones to make that mistake. Manchester and Lancashire had the same problems. When Provincial's Network NorthWest came in they were arguably in a bigger mess. They had a bigger area and much less reliable rolling stock - Pacers.

"When I first came to the Valley Lines in 1982/83 the operation was very slack. Timekeeping was sloppy and revenue collection abysmal. All the time between then and 1987 I'd been notching up, but the notching up was going faster than the staff could cope with. In the 1987 timetable I had tightened up resources just a notch too much.

"We had this two months of utter chaos which was not good for the business, but because we responded and listened to what the customers were saying we sorted out not only the big things, like uncoupling, but also a lot of other problems. As a result we had tremendous growth in 1988 and into the early part of 1989."

In mid-1989 things were to go awry on the Valley Lines again, because Sprinters were taken off to cover for Class 155 long-distance units which had been hastily withdrawn for attention to door problems. The Valley Lines had managed to recover from the upheaval of 1987 but the disruption of 1989 was to be a blow from which the system never fully recovered.

THE RHYMNEY LINE

Top left: In March 1986 a Class 116 DMU waits to begin its journey from Rhymney to Barry Island. A policy of the timetable planners in the 1980s was to ensure that trains from and to the heads of the valleys ran direct to and from Barry Island, to cater for the crowds of daytrippers who travelled from the valleys to Barry Island's beach and funfair.

Centre left: A coal train hauled by 37701 passes through Ystrad Mynach at the start of its journey from Penallta Colliery to Aberthaw power station. The junction of the short branch from Penallta was a short way beyond the station and down trains like this one, seen in November 1991, travelled on the up line until they reached the crossover half a mile to the south. The branch from Cwm Bargoed colliery, visible on the left, has been proposed for reopening to passengers from Treharris and Nelson and currently carries the sole remaining freight service in the valleys.

Below: The tree-covered bulk of Britain's largest spoil heap, Bargoed tip, dominates this 1989 scene at Bargoed station. Much of the tip has now been cleared and the long-awaited bypass road may soon occupy the site of the signal box and station, in which case a new platform might be provided at the site of Bargoed's former island platform, on the right of this picture, to form Bargoed North station.

Stephen Miles (3)

Above: This view of Cefn Onn, just south of Caerphilly tunnel, was recorded by a photographer from the Western Mail and South Wales Echo on 31st May 1952. His caption read, 'The scene at Cefn Onn railway station on Saturday as the 6.7pm train slowly pulled in to clear the home-going crowds after an enjoyable afternoon amongst the rhododendrons and azaleas, which are now in full bloom.' A little over 30 years later this station was proposed for closure, and there was only one passenger left to protest. Shortly after this picture was taken the changes associated with the 1953 timetable eradicated old coaches like the clerestory-roofed vehicle by the tunnel mouth, as the valley routes were largely operated by fixed five-coach formations. However, the ex-GWR 41xx locos continued to work the main trains on the Rhymney line for a few more years.
Western Mail and Echo Ltd

Centre right: Another station in the Rhymney valley with staggered platforms is Llanbradach, seen here in 1989. On the hillside on the right rise the ramparts of the former Llanbradach colliery. *Stephen Miles*

Bottom right: To the delight of railway enthusiasts and local councillors, a gleaming Class 47 loco draws away from Caerphilly station after being named Castell Caerffili/ Caerphilly Castle. Locos of this type were seldom seen in Caerphilly at the time, but more recently Class 47s belonging to Waterman Railways have been hauling a daily commuter service between Rhymney and Cardiff. The ugly enclosed footbridge seen in the background here was pulled down in 1989 when the station was refurbished. *Western Mail and Echo Ltd*

Above: A train driver catches up on the day's news at Ystrad Mynach before taking his Sprinter back to Cardiff in July 1995.
Rhodri Clark

Top left: The first Sprinter to arrive at Rhymney – prototype unit 150 001 – pauses at the terminus in July 1985 on a special Sunday morning working. *John Davies*

Top right: A Pacer passes a cul-de-sac of terraced houses in the South Wales valleys style near Brithdir. This section of line was slated for closure when John Davies took responsibility for the Valley Lines in 1982. *Rhodri Clark*

Centre left: A Pacer unit is reflected in the puddles as it is shunted into the stabling sidings at Rhymney on a Friday evening in 1996. *Rhodri Clark*

Centre right: A Rhymney-bound Class 143 accelerates from Brithdir station in September 1993. The housing style in the upper Rhymney Valley, characterised by the long row of houses visible on the hillside beyond the train, is not especially conducive to local rail travel. In the upper reaches of the Rhondda, by contrast, the housing is packed along the valley floor, close to the stations. *Rhodri Clark*

Left: Since 1995 a train belonging to Waterman Railways has been hired to provide a commuter service from Rhymney to Cardiff each weekday morning and return in the evening. In spring 1996 a black Class 47, No. 47705 GUY FAWKES, buffers up to its four Mk 2 coaches after running round at Rhymney. *Rhodri Clark*

Right: In 1990 old DMUs were still venturing as far north as Bargoed. The DMU visible in the distance is waiting in the siding on Bargoed viaduct while a Sprinter from Rhymney forms the next southbound service. After the departure of the next train to Rhymney, the DMU will leave Bargoed, precisely 30 minutes after the Sprinter. The unproductive layover on Bargoed viaduct was reduced in 1994, but at the expense of creating an uneven interval between trains. *Stephen Miles*

continued on page 54.

CHAPTER 6

GENIES FROM A BOTTLE
New Lines, New Stations

Despite BR's successes in reversing the fortunes of the Valley Lines, the renaissance would have run out of steam quickly were it not for the support of several outside bodies. Over 10 years the local authorities in the area made significant investments in upgrading old stations and opening new ones. Many of those new stations were on lines where the local authorities were funding new passenger services, the flagship being the service to Aberdare which commenced in 1988.

While these highly visible improvements occupied the limelight, the support of the county councils was having an equally important effect backstage. Their confidence and willingness to stump up healthy sums of capital assisted John Davies when he had to fight the Valley Lines' corner at a higher level in BR. Indeed, it was the enthusiasm of those councils that staved off the looming threat of a disastrous rolling-stock replacement programme for the Valley Lines.

The commitment of South and Mid Glamorgan county councils predated the beginning of the Valley Lines revival. By the time John Davies arrived in Cardiff in 1982 the two councils had already devised a strategy for developing the local rail services. The main fruit it had borne was Cathays station, which had already passed the point of no return in the planning process. The new station opened in 1983 and was an immediate success, partly because the timetables were reshaped a little to give Cathays a good service. The reopening happily coincided with the popular fares reduction on the Valley Lines.

Cathays station was the only one of a number of projects which had managed to escape from a morass of bureaucracy and negative thinking – much of it due to lack of vision on BR's part.

"From what I could see, the railways had taken the view that they weren't going to move unless there was some evidence of money from the local authorities and in the meantime they had to manage the system and keep costs down. Talk of expansion seemed premature," says John.

"The county councils were keen to get things going but their ideas were more politically motivated than business motivated. Somewhere in the middle of all that there was a scheme crying to be let out, like a genie in a bottle. Everybody was getting frustrated because they kept talking about it. The county councils were putting plans forward and BR was stonewalling."

The vicious circle was broken when John Davies, aided and abetted by divisional manager Frank Markham, stepped in. John called a special meeting of council and BR representatives and told them he had the go-ahead to proceed with the councils' rail development strategy.

"They fell off their seats with amazement," John recalls. "The politicians were initially extremely sceptical, and felt this was another false move by BR. I went to a forum in Pontypridd Technical College where Bill Williams, chairman of Mid Glamorgan's transport committee, was criticising Albert Barnes, the previous divisional manager. He was saying terribly negative things. At the end of this tirade I got to my feet and said I'd like to introduce myself as the passenger manager. I got a laughing ovation. They didn't take anybody from BR seriously and thought, 'Here's another one from BR who's come to tell us what we can't have.' I told them they wouldn't get anywhere by running down BR managers in public and it was time we started talking."

The rail development strategy was dusted down and each project categorised according to its chances of succeeding. BR was looking for schemes that would improve its bottom line while the county councils looked for schemes that would improve their political standing. These two standpoints overlapped in the area of improved service to residents in Mid and South Glamorgan.

In category A were placed schemes which both sides agreed should be progressed, where the benefits were obvious. The Aberdare line was one. Many park and ride car parks which were proposed in the rail strategy also came under category A and the councils were given a pretty free hand to refurbish stations. This work tended to concentrate on providing smart platform surfaces and access ramps, while less attention was given to platform shelters. Through a combination of poor design and persistent vandalism, most shelters remained unpleasant places to wait for trains.

Category B was for schemes which the council proposed and BR opposed, or vice versa. These included some park and ride schemes whose value didn't seem convincing to BR, several line reopenings and one line closure.

Under category C were filed reopening schemes, such as Maerdy to Porth, for which BR felt there was no hope.

The siting of new stations was the area which aroused the strongest passions and the area where commercial and political considerations were most at odds.

"One proposed station was Hopkinstown, between Trehafod and Pontypridd. Hopkinstown happened to be in the ward of councillor Bill Williams! It was pushed and pushed. I kept saying, 'Go away. We're not going to look at it.' Another one where we didn't want to slow down trains that were running at a decent speed was Gabalfa, between Llandaf and Cathays. That was the only place where the trains got to 75 m.p.h. and we weren't going to slow them down for Gabalfa because there wasn't much potential custom there," says John.

Roath, between Cardiff Queen Street and Heath, was another proposed station on a fast stretch of line. Roath was placed in category B, as it could be served by the Coryton trains without spoiling the competitively fast run of the Rhymney Valley trains. In the event the station was not built.

Others in category B included Glyncoch, between Pontypridd and Abercynon, and Pontygwindy, between Aber and Llanbradach. Both were studied in some detail but rejected. A critique of Pontygwindy by Mid Glamorgan showed that most of the custom would have even abstracted from Aber, dividing its revenue between two stations and adding little extra business.

The first station to be progressed under John Davies was Lisvane and Thornhill, serving a fashionable and growing suburb of north Cardiff. South Glamorgan County Council was willing to fund half the cost of the station provided BR funded the other half. The station had the added attraction for BR of replacing Cefn Onn halt which was situated at the mouth of Caerphilly tunnel and came into its own when the azaleas in Cefn Onn park were in full bloom. That happened for only a few weeks each year and by the early 1980s botany had seemingly lost its appeal to rail travellers. The new station would continue to serve the park, being close to its front gates, as well as the nearby housing. A closure proposal was posted for Cefn Onn.

"We were naughty. Once you publish a closure proposal the train service has to be kept in aspic until the station is closed. We managed to reduce the service to a token service a few days before we served the notice of closure so by sleight of hand we closed the station, to all intents and purposes. We had a Mrs Mop coming from the Rhymney Valley to Cefn Onn to clean for someone who lived in a large house in Lisvane. She succeeded in holding up the closure procedure for a long time."

Lisvane and Thornhill was built to accommodate three-car DMUs and had to be extended, along with Cathays, a few years later when the Health and Safety Executive decided that trains with powered doors could not stop at platforms which were shorter than the trains. As some four-car trains were essential on both the Rhymney and Taff lines, the platforms on both stations had to be extended.

At its opening in November 1985 Lisvane and Thornhill was deliberately so named to underline its proximity to Lisvane, to the east, and Thornhill, to the west. Unfortunately the planning authority did not secure an undertaking from the property developers at Thornhill to provide a footpath and road linking the houses with the station.

"There is now a link, but it's not very good," says John. "I don't think the railway has ever got the full benefit of the extra housing built at Thornhill, which means the station will never have achieved its throughput figures."

On top of that the considerable park and ride facilities at the station are rarely used because people are afraid to leave their cars parked in seclusion at the mercy of the local yobbery.

Shortly after Lisvane and Thornhill's opening, South Glamorgan began planning another double-platform station, this time at Eastbrook which opened in November 1986 on the Barry line.

"There was good potential for Eastbrook. It was quite a large community with low car ownership. A lot of one-parent families lived there. Initially the combined loads of Dinas Powys and Eastbrook stations increased, but in recent years they have fallen off a lot because of improved road competition and unreliable train services."

In April 1987 a fourth new station was opened in South Glamorgan. For Ty Glas, John made an exception to his rule of not attempting to cater for people who commute to factories. Trefforest Estate, which by then was served only by peak-period trains, proved how factory estates were normally too scattered to be practical for rail commuting. A factor in favour of Ty Glas was that it lay on the Coryton branch, where journey times are not as critical as on the main valley routes. The station, since it needed only a single platform, was also cheap – costing £78,000. It was funded by South Glamorgan as part of a package of improvements to stations on the Coryton line. Each station was given a new platform surface in brick paviour and a barrel-vaulted shelter in the smoked transparent plastic which was then in vogue. The council also insisted on applying to each station the Countyride branding, which denoted public transport funded by South Glamorgan County Council. BR objected to this, partly because some station pole signs would show the BR double arrow, the Valley Lines branding, the name of the station and the Countyride branding! South Glamorgan was paying the piper and was ultimately able to call the tune.

The City Line

The final big project to be funded by South Glamorgan, the City Line, illustrates how an investment could be motivated by two completely different factors in BR and the local authority respectively. Shortly after starting work on the Valley Lines John began to appreciate the strategic potential of the loop line between Radyr and Cardiff Canton which had only ever been used by freight and excursion trains. The loop would be handy as a diversionary route whenever the Queen Street to Radyr line was closed and if growth continued the loop would provide a useful alternative route into Cardiff from Pontypridd to take pressure off the double-track junction north of Queen Street station. (The loop line might yet come into its own should a future train operator decide to extend some express workings from Portsmouth or Manchester beyond Cardiff to the university town of Trefforest and the local hub of Pontypridd.)

"We were worried about the possibility of the loop line being closed if all the collieries served by the Taff lines closed. There was a distinct possiblity in the mid-1980s that this could happen, or that the remaining coal trains could be run to Aberthaw power station through Queen Street instead of over the loop line. We were trying to think of a way to justify retaining the line when

Entire lines were threatened with closure in 1982 but in the event the only station to be closed in the valleys was Cefn Onn halt, replaced in 1986 by the new Lisvane and Thornhill station. One of the last trains to call at Cefn Onn is seen here. Rail enthusiasts dash to take pictures while a couple of older men watch and reminisce.
Western Mail and Echo Ltd

South Glamorgan came to the rescue, asking us if we could run a passenger service that way," says John.

"South Glamorgan did their own survey, without using consultants, and came up with a moderate passenger-usage proposal which we then analysed in every possible way to make sure it covered its operating costs at least. The objective was to get something to keep the City Line infrastructure, because we felt it was a long-term future safety valve. The only way to secure it at that time was to get a passenger service on it that would be difficult to close down.

"Frankly, the case was very marginal in financial terms, except that the original plan was not to have any rolling stock allocated to the regular service. The total rolling stock required was no bigger than had the service not been there because we diverted trains from the Llandaf route, although we did theoretically allocate a single power car in case we needed peak-period strengthening."

The first scheduled passenger service actually ran in 1985, two years before the City Line came into being. A DMU allocated to main-line work was diagrammed to work up the valleys in the mornings. Rather than send it back empty stock, John decided to use it for a Merthyr to Bristol service which ran non-stop south of Trefforest and used the Radyr loop line to reach Cardiff Central facing Bristol, thereby obviating reversal.

Three new stations were built for the City Line. A fourth, which had existed for years to serve the nearby Cardiff City football ground at Ninian Park, was upgraded for daily use. One of the new stations, Waungron Park, was situated on an embankment and its cost was pushed up when residents complained that waiting passengers would be able to look through their bedroom windows. Part of the solution was to offset the up platform, at the expense of building it out over a road on outriggers from the steel bridge parapet. To appease the neighbours, solid wooden fencing was provided opposite the down platform. As a result of this extra work Waungron Park's opening was delayed until November 1987, a month after the City Line's inauguration.

Left: The pine tree and lattice footbridge still make an attractive setting at Hengoed station, seen here in 1991 as a Sprinter arrives on a southbound service. The former Pontypool to Neath line passed over the Rhymney line behind the photographer and a high-level station was provided for interchange.
John Davies

Left: In June 1980, infrequent six-car trains were the norm at Caerphilly. The second set in this train bears the short-lived DMU livery of white with a blue waistband. The spartan bus station, complete with vehicles of Rhymney Valley District Council, is visible in the background, separated from the adjacent railway station by a replica of Offa's Dyke. Sixteen years later, this location's potential for transport integration has yet to be realised. *Peter Clark*

Below: The Saturdays on which rugby international matches are played in Cardiff guarantee a splash of colour on the Rhymney line. At Llanishen in March 1995, this Sprinter in the livery of West Midlands PTE was used to ease overcrowding.
Rhodri Clark

Top left: Shortly after, a Cardiff to Bargoed working draws into Llanishen station behind a Class 47 loco in the livery of Rail Express Systems. Two sets of maroon coaches, hired from Steamtown railway museum, Carnforth, were in use that day. This was a somewhat self-defeating exercise as the trains attracted so many railway enthusiasts that rugby fans and shoppers had to be left behind at some stations!

Rhodri Clark

Top right: In February 1973 the Western Region's programme of total modernisation of track was in full swing at Cefn Onn. Within 10 years, however, financial pressures meant that the Valley Lines could justify only the minimum of maintenance and renewal. *Peter Clark*

Right: Reclamation of the site of Bargoed colliery was nearing completion in June 1996 as a Pacer passed the site earmarked for a new Bargoed Central station. The semaphore signal controls entry to the single platform at Bargoed station.

Rhodri Clark

As described in the previous chapter, things went badly wrong from the opening day. Many of the problems were down to tight turnaround times in the City Line diagram and to passengers refusing to believe that trains to Merthyr were suddenly leaving Cardiff in the opposite direction to that taken since 1841. The original idea had been to send the hourly Aberdare services, once they started, via the City Line as well, thereby giving both the City Line and Llandaf routes a half-hourly service. That, however, would have entailed even shorter turnaround times than in the Merthyr/City Line diagrams. By the time an hourly service began on the Aberdare line, ideas about the City Line had been hurriedly revised.

"Revenue had nosedived from its original projections, which weren't that wonderful anyway," says John. "That was largely because of unreliable service. People in the City Line's catchment area weren't used to rail travel and they said, 'If they're not going to run the trains when they say they are, we'll switch back to the buses or whatever we were using before.' By 1989 we'd got to the state where we had to do something about the City Line. We decided to ring-fence the service and run it as a Coryton to Radyr shuttle which would require three units to operate, two of which were allocated to the Coryton line and the third incrementally allocated to the City Line.

"We could only justify that City Line unit if South Glamorgan went back to their committee and secured capital to pay for the unit. Otherwise we would say under the terms of the Speller Act we could terminate the service whenever we wanted to. For good faith we gave South Glamorgan the option. I think, secretly, we wanted South Glamorgan to come back and say 'no'. They came back and said 'yes'. So we had to carry on the City Line service although by this time we realised it was a dead loss."

Even with the shuttle service, the City Line rarely achieved respectable loadings except when Cardiff City were playing at home. One of the problems, John believes, is that the local people had no tradition of using railways. Danescourt and Fairwater stations were in cuttings, so some of the nearby residents were probably unaware of the service. Waungron Park was highly visible but straddled a bus stop from where a bus could be caught into town every few minutes. The bus took about the same time to reach the city centre – or less for passengers heading for Queen Street - and obviated the wait for the half-hourly train.

Against this sort of competition and over such a short route, reliability was vital but often deficient. Trains frequently ran late from Radyr, despite a healthy turnaround time there. This was because they shared the up platform at Radyr with the frequent Taff main line services, which took priority even when they were running late. The problem would have been avoided had a bay platform been provided at Radyr for the City Line. Although the necessary platform and tracks were in place, this was ruled out because of the costs of signalling the bay. The bay option is now open, however, since the Radyr area is being resignalled.

Another factor was that the shuttle timetable effectively caused the City Line to be operated as a single line, although the only section of single line is the short curve past Canton depot. Trains were booked to pass just west of Ninian Park station but up trains were often a minute or two late leaving Cardiff Central. They therefore held up incoming workings within spitting distance of Ninian Park station. When the up trains had negotiated the single line there was often another wait if a train from Barry or Penarth was late. The minimal infrastructure at Cardiff Central meant that the City Line trains could not run into the station and be overtaken there by delayed services. All of this added up to a frustrating stop-start run which was often slower than the journey into town by bicycle!

The single-line section past Canton depot was restricted to 20 m.p.h. because of gauge clearance.

"The sidings either side of the track were too close. Now the sidings are disused and the speed restriction could probably go from 20 m.p.h. to 40 m.p.h. overnight if the operators thought about it," says John.

Some small comfort was derived in 1989 when the City Line's operating costs were reduced a little by the introduction of Class 108 two-carDMUs in which only one vehicle was powered. Staff feared that those units would be under-powered for the steep climbs encountered on the Valley Lines, and there was a risk that, although they were intended for the City Line shuttle, they could escape to roam the wider system.

John says, "I remember panicking once, when the controller said, 'John, we've just had to send one of those units out to Merthyr'. In the event it lost a bit of time but it did get back. One evening I saw a train waiting at a green signal at Queen Street and I asked the driver what the problem was. He said, 'I've got two engines out on this train and I'm telling the signalbox I'm taking it into Canton.' When I told him there were no engines in the rear vehicle he got out and had a look. He came back and said, 'Oh no, there aren't, are there?' "

By coincidence, one of the members of the BR Western Region investment panel – which John had to persuade before the City Line went ahead – had previously lived in Danescourt. He was sceptical about getting people from that area to use a train service.

"I was very trenchant in getting the City Line through," says John. "In the event, I won the battle but he won the war. On the other hand we've kept the strategic route. It's on Cardiff Panel so there's nothing to be gained in taking it off. The City Line service has been reduced to hourly so it's on a hiding to nothing. I could have made a bigger mistake somewhere else."

Mid Glamorgan Spends its Money

If South Glamorgan County Council was left with a sour taste in its mouth after some of its rail investments, Mid Glamorgan's sweet tooth was quickly satisfied. The difference in the degree of success is partly explained by geography. Mid Glamorgan was a much larger county, therefore its rail services were inter-urban rather than local and the potential revenue was higher. South Glamorgan was a fairly affluent county, whereas the valleys in Mid Glamorgan are some of the poorest parts of Britain. The Valley Lines thrived on poverty, especially where poverty precluded widespread car ownership. The City Line provided the corollary, serving an area of privately owned houses, outside each of which a car (or two) sat beside an immaculate lawn and flowerbed.

The story of Mid Glamorgan's first big investment epitomises the Valley Lines in that brief period between the stranglehold of corporate British Rail and the suffocating bureaucracy of sectorisation and, later, privatisation. It is impossible to foresee a time when the railway will ever again be as flexibile, alert and streamlined as it was in autumn 1985, when Mid Glamorgan County Council informed BR that it had £300,000 left over from its budget for road building.

"The plan to put a crossing loop in the Rhondda line was one of those roundabouts - it kept going round in circles. The county council was hankering after a loop at Llwynypia and had been told it would cost about £1m, because it would involve colour light signals controlled from Porth signal box. There was no way they could find this sort of money and certainly couldn't foresee a payback on it," says John.

"By the time they came to us to say they had some money unspent from their Transport Supplementary Grant for road building, we had already dropped hints that we could provide a loop between Llwynypia and Ton Pentre using the No Signalman Token (Remotely-controlled) system. It had been applied on the Central Wales line and we didn't see why it couldn't work in an urban area. They said we could have the money if we could approve this expenditure by 31st March 1986.

"We were quick to respond. Our engineers worked flat out on estimates - the civil engineers on the loop and the signal engineers on the NST(R) system. They came up with a cost of something like £200,000 for the loop and signalling, including sprung points and point indicators. We told the engineers that we had £300,000 to spend so they said, 'We thought you might like a station as well. We'll do it for £100,000.'

"I went back to the county council with this proposal and they were overjoyed. We approved the project before the start of the 1986/87 financial year and by October 1986 it was open. It wasn't a wonderful job – the shelters are bog-standard structures – but at least we got it. People were thrilled. It was well used from the start

"We could never do that today. The safety gurus come in and start wrecking everything. It all has to go through thousands of committees, everybody adds their costs to the project and it quickly becomes unaffordable. In those days we were able to short-circuit things. I'm not saying it was unsafe, but a lot of bureaucracy got swept aside and we said, 'We've got this money. Let's spend it.'"

The project was a big leap. The Central Wales and Rhondda lines may be in the same country but they are worlds apart. NST(R) was proven on long rural lines which had a handful of trains each day, but nobody knew how it would work for a half-hourly service in an area where vandalism seemed to be the second most popular hobby after pigeon fancying.

"The things they worried about didn't happen. At Ystrad Rhondda they were worried the sprung points would be vandalised, particularly by shoving stones between the point blades. We did have occasional problems with the token cabinets being broken into and the instruments tampered with. Once they discovered there was nothing to pinch in there those things stopped happening. You can't get kicks out of breaking into a cabinet which you can't take away or destroy. There were a number of occasions, though, when they put superglue in the locks and the drivers had to cross the footbridge to get a token from the cabinet on the other platform."

Vandalism was so widespread that the local press reported at the time how the station shelters at Ystrad Rhondda and the nearby Ynyswen station had to be repainted the day before their opening ceremonies to obliterate the graffiti which had already accumulated.

"Where one track had been lifted on the Rhondda line there was a strip of ballast. Motorbike scramblers used to race the trains along there," says John. "There's a fair bit of lawlessness, particularly trespass, which is customary in the Rhondda and the other valleys. I doubt it will be totally eradicated because it's gone on for such a long time. It goes along with the fact that people regard the railway as theirs anyway. It's part of the fabric of the area."

Arrangements had to be made to redistribute the tokens at Ystrad Rhondda at the end of each day since all the tokens for the upper section would end up on the down platform.

The station caused some confusion initially. It was to have been named Gelligaled Park, after a local feature, but it was named Ystrad Rhondda because it was closer to the village of that name than the old Ystrad Rhondda station. The latter station was renamed Ton Pentre, as the villages of Pentre and Ton Pentre were adjacent. The new station broke up a long stationless section of railway. Such sections aren't ideal in a valley like the Rhondda, where the ribbon development is continuous.

Usage of the new Ystrad Rhondda station was bolstered by the result of another remarkable feat of lateral thinking – the raillink bus from the Rhondda Fach valley. The success of the Treherbert

line (in the Rhondda Fawr valley) suggested that a rail service in the Rhondda Fach, which branches off at Porth, would attract sufficient custom. There was a strong political will to re-establish a passenger rail service up the valley on the track which served the colliery at Maerdy, but BR felt the business prospects were poor. John drove up the Rhondda Fach several times to assess the railway's chances. Each time he came away convinced that it would fail because the main towns were on the opposite side of the valley from the railway. (In the Rhondda Fawr, by contrast, the line runs through the middle of the ribbon development so most people are close to a station.)

Meanwhile, another project which Mid Glamorgan proposed for the Rhondda seemed to merit closer attention. The Rhondda Fawr trains terminated at Treherbert because of the accident of railway history explained in Chapter 1 and Mid Glamorgan County Council wanted to see the service extended a mile to Blaenrhondda, at the very top of the valley. The track was intact part of the way, having been retained for freight use, but the station at the blocked entrance to the Blaenrhondda Tunnel would have to be rebuilt. What killed the scheme was not the potential custom or the physical aspects but the fact that trains could take no more than eight minutes of turnaround time at Treherbert, otherwise they would delay the next up train waiting to enter the single track section at Porth. Trains would need about four minutes each way to reach Blaenrhondda, leaving no time at all for the driver to change cabs or leeway to absorb delays. The option of abandoning the hourly interval pattern and running every 65 or 70 minutes didn't bear consideration.

The project was only practical if an extra unit was deployed. Before embarking on such an expensive solution BR and the council decided to test the market by laying on a feeder minibus, which would connect with every train at Treherbert. Rail tickets would be issued using Portis machines on the bus, and the only passengers carried would be people transferring to or from the train.

"We decided we would try the feeder bus and if the results were good we could revisit the rail reopening scheme some years later. I don't think we ever thought we'd revisit it, but it was a good test-bed for a rail feeder bus. The fact that it's still there 10 years on suggests that it hasn't been a bad idea. It was also able to serve Blaencwm and Ty Newydd, which the trains wouldn't have done," says John.

"There used to be more people on the rail-link bus from Blaenrhondda than on the frequent National Welsh buses. The through rail tickets were a great draw, as buses took longer to get down the valley to Pontypridd or Cardiff than the trains."

The concept of the feeder bus provided a compromise solution for the Rhondda Fach. The first option was to run this feeder from Maerdy to Porth station, or to a reopened station at Ynyshir on the southern stub of the Rhondda Fach line. Both locations would be difficult to access by bus. One proposal even involved the

21st April 1990 at Ystrad Rhondda. Where once trains had rolled past on a single track there was a crossing loop, new station and four-way interchange. Each hour passengers transfer between trains to and from Treherbert and Cardiff and the feeder bus to and from Maerdy, seen on the left. The river bridge clearly shows the formation of the unusual triple track laid to carry coal trains in the lower Rhondda.

Stephen Miles

SPRINTERS IN THE VALLEYS

Top left: The transition period at Ystrad Rhondda, as a three-car Sprinter meets a three-car Class 116 unit in September 1987. A fortnight later, all trains were reduced to two-car formations as train frequencies were increased.   *Rhodri Clark*

Centre left: The Sprinters quickly settled into reliable service on the Valley Lines. This unit is leaving Trefforest station in early 1988. The shelters are free of graffiti, which had previously plagued this location. Because of the presence of a cosmopolitan student population at the nearby Polytechnic of Wales, this was the only Valley Lines station where the graffiti was in Urdu, Arabic and many other tongues.
John Davies

Below: A Sprinter leaves the gateway to the Taff valley south of Taffs Well beneath the towers of Castell Coch, former residence of the Marquis of Bute, the industrialist who developed Cardiff to become the world's biggest coal exporting port. The white building is of similar vintage to the castle, having been constructed by the Taff Vale Railway as a crossing keeper's cottage.   *John Davies*

A little further down the valley, a Sprinter sweeps around the reverse curves above the picturesque Radyr weir on the river Taff.

Rhodri Clark

The Taff Vale Railway's quadruple-track main line is still in place, although the freight lines are out of use, as a Sprinter accelerates from Radyr heading for Pontypridd. This picture contrasts with the scene on page 63 some 30 years previously.

Rhodri Clark

On a rugby international Saturday, a four-car Sprinter formation heads up the Rhondda valley near Dinas. This part of the valley was too narrow for the normal ribbon development and the railway hugs the riverbank at this point.   *John Davies*

Mid-Glamorgan County Council paid for a Sprinter train to operate the new Aberdare service in 1988. Here one of the class is seen crossing the river Cynon near Penrhiwceiber, close to the spot favoured by the notorious coal train hijackers. Beyond the train is the derelict siding which creates a kink in the tracks, over which trains are restricted to 20 m.p.h. No funding was forthcoming to eliminate this impediment to improving train frequency within the clockface timetable.   *Rhodri Clark*

converting the railway route to a busway, with the buses joining the conventional road network through the National Welsh bus depot at Porth.

"That itself would have scuppered the idea. Even if National Welsh were running the feeder bus they wouldn't agree to do that," says John.

"We couldn't run the bus to Porth so Mid Glamorgan suggested going over Penrhys mountain and connecting with trains at the new station in Ystrad Rhondda. I thought it created a dog-leg, but it was better than no service at all. To our amazement we found there were as many people changing off the bus to go up the Rhondda Fawr as there were to go downward to Cardiff. An even greater surprise came when we found some people using the bus from Ferndale (where it originally terminated before being extended to Maerdy) were buying tickets to Blaenrhondda. They were getting on a rail-link bus, changing to a train, then changing to another rail-link bus – all on one ticket.

"We were learning about the market. There's a lot of local travel in the Rhondda and the train was a good way to travel. People travelling from one valley to the other, to visit relatives or go to a club up the valley, had a difficult journey and this bus made it easier for a lot of them. It boosted the use of the bus because it had more than one function. It's never run more than hourly and that perhaps is a pity, but you'd need two buses to run every half an hour."

Both feeder buses were put out to tender by Mid Glamorgan and subsequently subsidised by the council. The additional fare for the bus journey was kept low and BR gained the full revenue for the rail part of each journey. It is possible that the feeder buses could run commercially if a little more of the revenue were apportioned to the bus operator.

The least spectacular development in the Rhondda was provision of a new station at Ynyswen. It opened on the same day as Ystrad Rhondda but its funding came from the county council's 1986/87 budget and was justified as part of the rail development strategy.

"We were sceptical about Ynyswen. It's suspected that it was built because it was in the constituency of one of the councillors who was also a railwayman, although he will deny it!" says John.

Ynyswen is memorable for John chiefly because of the devious way he got it past the BR Western Region investment panel and the sheer good fortune which stopped him being caught. Although the county councils were prepared to fund the new stations proposed for the Valley Lines, each proposal had to be scrutinised by the investment panel for its members to determine whether BR's side of the deal would be sensible in business terms. There were costs involved in stopping trains at more stations, mainly the slightly negative effect slower services would have on revenue. At that time the railway was also providing design work and other background services for nothing, and the investment panels needed to know whether that work was justified.

"I was put on my mark a number of times at investment panel meetings," says John. "The chairman was Brian Scott, then deputy general manager of the Western Region and now managing director of Great Western Trains. Although Ynyswen's revenue projections weren't great, I thought it was worthwhile because it would only affect journey times for Treherbert passengers. Brian Scott was dead against Ynyswen. He said, 'This is not on. I don't want to see it referred to again.'

"I waited till a couple of meetings later when Brian Scott was on leave and someone else was in the chair. I put up another case for Ynyswen and got it through. Mid Glamorgan were delighted, and said the contracts had to be let quickly because it was associated with the Ystrad Rhondda package. Ynyswen station was being built before Brian Scott could spot it in the minutes!

"A year or two later, when he was general manager of the Western Region, Brian came on a tour of the Valley Lines and asked me to accompany him. We had a number of "set to"s on that tour."

In the intervening period, Gareth Jenkins, then Provincial's South Wales manager, had come up with proposals to alleviate the bottleneck at Pontypridd station. Pontypridd had only ever had one island platform but that platform, with its giant canopy, once hosted no fewer than seven platform faces. Two were through platforms, and there were four bay platforms for branch lines to the north and another bay let into the southern end of the island platform for the service to Caerphilly and Machen. By the 1980s only one platform still had tracks and this constriction presented a problem by the time eight trains an hour were calling at Pontypridd.

"In 1991 I compared the timetable for Pontypridd with the 1934 timetable. There were more trains in 1991 with one platform. To people who said the railways were in terminal decline, I said that nearly 60 years later we had more trains at Pontypridd and handled them in one-seventh of the platform faces."

Even so, the situation was far from ideal and Gareth had calculated that restoring the through down line would involve huge track and signalling costs which would take at least 25 years to pay back. The alternative was to build a new side platform adjacent to one of the through freight lines. This scheme had the bonus that Mid Glamorgan County Council would pay for it because it would release the trackbed of the former down line for a new road. This scheme eventually went ahead in 1991, involving construction of a new footbridge, moving a steel bridge parapet a few feet to the side and provision of a new pedestrian access route from the west side of the station.

When Brian Scott came for his grand tour of the Valley Lines the Pontypridd solution was in its infancy. When his train arrived at Pontypridd he asked John what plans he had to solve the capacity problem.

"He didn't think our solution was the best way to solve the problem. I think he commented, 'So the solution, in the station on the Western Region that's got more platform than anywhere else, is to put yet another platform in!'

"Later in that journey we got to Treherbert. It was midday on a Friday. I remember it well," says John. "We left Treorchy and my heart was in my mouth. We were sitting in the front seats of a DMU and I thought we were about to arrive at Ynyswen where the platform would be empty, and he would say, 'What the hell did we build this for?'

"My lucky fairy was there that day. The Polikoff clothing factory, which was close to the station, had just closed early for the day and there were 20 women standing on the platform to go to Treherbert. If I had rent-a-crowd I couldn't have done better! I said, 'Brian, look at this station. It's doing really well.'

"I think he'd forgotten about it, really. It was a little thing to him. We used to have all sorts of rows in the investment panel. I used to sit through long arguments with other people some of whom had dubious investment projects, particularly people from the technical departments. They had their pet signalling schemes which were found to be lacking when they went under the firm analysis."

This insight shows how crucial the outside funding was to the success of the Valley Lines. John had to fall back on his own cunning to gain approval for a two-car, single-platform halt at the top end of a valley even though BR was not paying for the station. Had the council funding not been forthcoming it is unlikely that a single new station - let alone three new rail services - would have been opened on the Valley Lines system.

The Threat of Pacers

Although the rail development strategy of the two county councils was purely about improving stations and providing new stations and services, its influence on the well-being of the core service ran much deeper than is generally known.

"Without the county councils' support we would probably have ended up with Pacers instead of Sprinters on the Valley Lines," says John. "I had a letter from John Edmonds, then managing director of Provincial, shortly before the final bids for Sprinters. He said he was pleased with the way things had gone in the valleys and this would contribute to our being early recipients of Sprinters. But I heard afterwards that there was tremendous opposition to the Sprinters coming to the Cardiff valleys because we couldn't get high earnings per vehicle. The hostility from headquarters towards what were considered to be unimportant bits of the railway was incredible. In economic terms there were better cases for Sprinters elsewhere in Britain, and it was the county councils' rail development strategy that swung it, even though the allocation of Sprinters for the Valley Lines was reduced.

"Can you imagine running the Valley Lines with Pacers alone? I was terrified of that. I'd seen how badly they performed in the Manchester area."

Pacers were a terrifying prospect because they were so poorly conceived and poorly engineered. The idea was to create a four-wheel railbus vehicle by mounting bus bodies on a minimal railway chassis and powering it with mechanics which were unproven in railway use. When the first batch, Class 141, was delivered to Yorkshire in 1983 the Pacer seemed a desperate solution to a chronic lack of investment capital. In the event the savings made by building the Pacers cheaply were eaten up in endless modification costs and revenue lost due to unreliability. The later Class 142 Pacers were allocated to branch lines in Cornwall and Devon but were quickly moved elsewhere because they couldn't cope with the curving and steeply-graded tracks.

Manchester was saddled with a huge quantity of Pacers, many of which met their Waterloos on the stiff climb to Oldham Werneth. Had they been allocated to Cardiff they would instead have fallen like flies on the 1 in 39 climb out of Abercynon on the Merthyr line or the bank from Cogan to Dingle Road. Greater Manchester was fortunate enough to have a patient Passenger Transport Executive and a concentration of railway resources. The Valley Lines, by contrast, had no statutory body to promote public transport and were only allowed the minimum number of trains and staff required to run their daily diagrams. Had the Valley Lines been entrusted to the Class 142 Pacers, unreliability would have hit the system hard. Passenger numbers could have declined to the point where closure of sections like Bargoed to Rhymney was back on the cards.

Pacers did eventually arrive at Cardiff Canton in 1991, but by that time much had been learned about the temperamental fourwheel railbus. The Pacers allocated to Cardiff were, in any case, of the slightly better Class 143 design. Nevertheless, reliability of Pacers arguably became the Achilles Heel of the Valley Lines.

For the time being, however, the confidence which the county councils placed in the Valley Lines and their commitment to further developments helped John to justify Sprinters. There was also a question of honour, since BR's contribution as a partner in the rail development strategy was to provide new Sprinter trains. Nothing is more certain to destroy a working partnership than one of the parties going back on its words.

The Aberdare and Maesteg Lines

The new loop and station at Ystrad Rhondda, as well as the new side platform at Pontypridd, were crumbs that fell from the banqueting table of road construction in the valleys. The reopening of the Aberdare and Maesteg lines also owed something to a road scheme – a project which was deferred ad infinitum.

One of Mid Glamorgan County Council's priorities when John Davies first examined the rail development strategy was to close the Bargoed to Rhymney line and provide a new station in Bargoed. The current Bargoed station is at the top end of the town while Gilfach Fargoed halt, apart from being less than one coach long, is a little remote at the other end of town. Mid Glamorgan's aim was to replace both with a single Bargoed Central station, an island platform located below Hanbury Square. A dedicated feeder bus from Rhymney would connect with trains at Bargoed Central. Later, when the threat of line closure was lifted, the plans were modified for a station with one through road and one bay platform. It was also decided at this stage to retain a station at the present Bargoed station site, this to be called Bargoed North.

Funding for the alterations would come from the budget for the proposed Bargoed bypass road, since the road would occupy the site of the present station building, platform and signal box. However, that road project itself was conditional on an even bigger infrastructure project, the eradication of one of Britain's largest spoil heaps. This huge project, which finally got underway in the mid-1990s, was bound up in all manner of planning niceties. In the mid-1980s Mid Glamorgan realised that the land reclamation, and by association Bargoed Central station, was at least five years away and decided to bring forward its plans to reopen the Aberdare line - plans which were way back in the original programme of rail development. Had those plans not been accelerated the Maesteg reopening which followed could have been so late as to fall outside the dissolution of Mid Glamorgan County Council in 1996, and it is questionable whether the two unitary authorites covering the Maesteg line would have implemented the scheme.

In the mid-1980s the Aberdare line was a great talking point not only among councillors, officers and rail managers but also among the general public, because in 1984 BR began running shoppers' trains from Aberdare to Cardiff. Those services made use of the platforms which had survived at Aberdare and Mountain Ash in a condition that was just about usable at that time. (Platforms in that condition would send today's Health and Safety Executive into apoplexy.) The platforms had been retained for spasmodic use by Merrymaker excursion trains so John Davies and his colleagues decided to test the Cynon Valley market by running occasional specials on Saturdays, using DMUs brought in from the West Midlands or London Paddington.

"There were a lot of sceptics saying people would use the trains initially, because of their novelty value, but questioning whether they would in future," says John. "The first time we ran shoppers' specials, on a Saturday in December, we had six-car trains. They were sold out. There were three trains in each direction. Two weeks later we had nine-car trains, and people were thrilled. Again people were saying the trains wouldn't make regular business. During the miners' strike, when the freight drivers at Aberdare had nothing to do, I went to their cabin and tried to pick their brains about the local market. They were fairly evenly divided between those who thought there would be regular passenger trains and those who thought there would not. I'd like to have another chat with them now to see which ones changed their minds, and when!"

The number of specials was increased, and by 1986 a two-hourly service was being run every Saturday for two or three months.

"Suddenly the Department of Transport blew the whistle on us. They said, 'You're only allowed leave to run a certain number of trains a year over a freight line. Above that number the operation is deemed unsafe.' They didn't use those words, but this was Mr Jobsworth speaking from the DoT. We'd started running on Sundays in the summer as well, to take people to Barry Island. They gave us an inch and we took a mile, but it was all for commercial reasons. We were doing well - it was proving that it wasn't a flash in the pan. We had trains waiting outside the single platform at Pontypridd because we'd fit these Aberdare trains in without a proper path."

When the time came, the Aberdare reopening passed swiftly through the investment panel, even though it involved purchasing a Sprinter to operate the service. Mid Glamorgan also paid for six new stations, rehabilitation of the track for regular passenger use and about £1M for resignalling the line. The last-named element involved installation of the Western Region's first Solid State Interlocking system, at Abercynon signal box. At Abercynon a new station was constructed on the Aberdare line in a scaled-down version of the Pontypridd paradox. The existing platform for the Merthyr trains was a huge expanse of tarmac but it proved to be cheaper to construct a new platform than to install a new junction for the Aberdare line at the north end of the old platform.

The contribution of £2M from outside BR, half of it from Mid Glamorgan County Council and half from the European Regional Development Fund, was a large amount in railway terms, although a pittance compared with road budgets. John instructed the Aberdare line commissioning panel, which was to take the scheme through its implementation, that everything would have to be kept within that budget. He had to put his foot down when the signal engineers came back with a much higher estimate for the work to be done.

WORKING IN PARTNERSHIP

Right: The uninviting Barry Docks station in 1993 is part of a dormant panorama which is currently being transformed in a huge redevelopment programme by the Welsh Development Agency and other bodies. On the right are railway relics from Barry's coal export trade.
Rhodri Clark

Top Left: The City Line was not the most productive investment in the Valley Lines by an outside body but the project did at least secure the future of the loop line from Radyr to Cardiff Central, a useful alternative route into the city from Pontypridd. In March 1992 Waungron Park's evening service was being provided by Merthyr-line Sprinters booked to run via the City Line rather than Llandaf.
Rhodri Clark

Centre left: In August 1963 a six-car DMU in the original light green livery arrives at Radyr on a Treherbert to Barry Island working while a 5101 Class tank loco. pauses on the freight lines. This scene was subsequently transformed by provision of park and ride facilities on the site of the sidings on the left of the picture. The area is now undergoing further changes with the replacement of semaphore signalling in a project funded by Mid Glamorgan County Council.
John Davies

Bottom left: Empty Cawoods coal containers bound for Tower Colliery leave the City Line at Radyr in 1988 under an array of signals which are shortly to be replaced. Mid and South Glamorgan councils spent substantial sums converting old railway land into station car parks, of which the one at Radyr is the best used. Even on this April evening many of the parking spaces were still occupied.
Rhodri Clark

Below: The Welsh Development Agency and other public bodies have invested huge sums in clearing the remains of the coal industry and providing new sites for industry in the valleys. A four-car Sprinter is seen passing one such site at Treorchy, Rhondda.
John Davies

"There was a feeling that the county council were paying for the work so they could get away with overcharging. I wasn't having any of it," says John.

The decision to provide two-car platforms was criticised, but that was all the budget allowed. Four-car platforms could be created later, if traffic justified them.

"Those words seem hollow now, because today there are still two-car platforms and still problems of overcrowding, particularly on Saturdays. It's worse now because the Health and Safety Executive will not allow four-car trains to run, pulling up at the stations. In the first year or two we did run some four-car trains but later we were stopped. Extending the platforms would need local authority money. My feeling is the money would be far better spent on improving the infrastructure to permit a half-hourly service to run when required."

Plans of this nature were considered by Mid Glamorgan in the early 1990s. An £8M package was drawn up to include resignalling the Radyr to Pontypridd line, raising line speeds on the Aberdare branch and providing stations for extension of services beyond Aberdare to Trecynon and Hirwaun. The idea was to run an hourly service from Hirwaun which stopped only at principal stations in the Cynon Valley. On the alternate half-hour an all-stations service would run from Aberdare. In the event financial restrictions allowed only the Taff resignalling element to go forward.

For a brief time shortly after the reopening, part of the line did in fact have a half-hourly service for short periods on Saturdays. An interim train ran as far as Mountain Ash while the normal train was proceeding to Aberdare and back. This was quickly stopped when it was realised that the Mountain Ash turnback was raising a potential hazard. The signalman at Abercynon could have allowed a freight to proceed to Penrhiwceiber behind the interim passenger train, and the passenger train's driver could begin his return journey unaware that the home signal at Penrhiwceiber would be red.

The new Aberdare service was launched in October 1988 using old DMUs. Signalling work was incomplete so a two-hourly service was operated. The absence of freight on Saturdays allowed an hourly passenger service on Saturdays.

"Patronage on the Aberdare line has always been better than the forecasts. Passenger miles are higher, and passenger journeys about the same as the forecasts. The journeys forecast included a lot more local journeys than ever materialised and a lot fewer long-distance journeys than we did get. The Aberdare line was competing with buses every five minutes for local journeys. It was much more successful for travel through to Pontypridd and Cardiff, particularly off-peak. The peak was disappointing. That did at least prevent the problem of finding more rolling stock to cope with the rush, so we took a relaxed view. Cynon Valley Borough Council felt it wasn't good value to have a service that wasn't very well used by people going to work. We pointed out that the number of leisure travellers far exceeded the expectations and evened out the flow, making a nice 'profitable' service. It was something most commuter lines would give their eye teeth to get. We were very pleased," says John.

"The Aberdare line came in two years after the Bathgate line, which I thought was a similar line although it had a long, fast run into Edinburgh. Also road congestion was far more serious than in Cardiff, so they had a head start there. We never did as well as Bathgate on the Aberdare line. On the other hand, our bottom line was far better than Bathgate's because they had extra ticket examiners on the trains. Staff productivity wasn't good in Scotland."

If vandalism was a problem in the Rhondda it was awesome in the Cynon Valley, where ladders weren't fixed to the signals in an attempt to reduce the incidence of lights being smashed. The technical services staff had to take a ladder in their van and carry it to each signal when they needed to reach the lights.

More formidable was the practice of ambushing coal trains. In a carefully organised operation, rocks and sleepers would be laid across the track to force coal trains to stop, at which point people waiting in the bushes would rush out, open the hopper doors on the wagons and help themselves to the coal which came gushing out. The train would not be able to proceed until the coal had been swept clear of the rails beneath the wagons. This was happening so frequently since the dark days of the miners' strike that drivers had nicknamed the rail route through Penrhiwceiber 'the Kyber Pass'. Naturally, the county council, BR and the British Transport Police were concerned that this practice could affect the new passenger service, either by causing mass cancellations or, worse, by a passenger train hitting one of the barricades while travelling at a fair speed.

"After the passenger service started the hijackings virtually stopped, because there were people around the railway all the time. There were drivers going up and down. The hijackers couldn't spend hours making their preparations in Penrhiwceiber," says John.

"The policing by passengers was as much of a deterrent as anything. What we discovered in the Cynon Valley once we restored passenger services was that people collectively said 'We've lost them once, we're not going to lose them again'. People would go down the train if the conductor was reluctant to collect their fares. They would find him out and pay because they didn't want there to be any excuse for closing the line again. There was a collective will for it to succeed."

One aspect of the service that contributed immeasurably to its success – especially in view of the propensity towards longer-distance journeys – was that all services ran through to Cardiff. In pre-Beeching days they had often terminated at Abercynon, and changing trains was tiresome on such a short journey as Mountain Ash to Pontypridd. This ground rule of running every train to and from Cardiff has never been broken.

The same principle was established at the outset for Mid Glamorgan's other line-reopening project. The Maesteg reopening was conceived in 1988 as a scheme to provide local rail services between Cardiff and Bridgend. Mid Glamorgan considered new stations at Pontyclun, Llanharan and Pencoed, as well as Brackla and Coychurch where new housing had mushroomed since the last time local services had stopped on the South Wales main line. South Glamorgan was interested in providing stations at Ely and St Fagans, the latter to serve the popular Museum of Welsh Life.

"Much to the disgust of South Glamorgan we turned down Ely. There was no chance of us stopping trains which were running at 70m.p.h. through there, especially in view of traffic on the City Line, which is close by. St Fagans would be OK if somebody would pay for the station."

The Mid Glamorgan stations all seemed feasible, but the infrastructure was such that local trains from Cardiff could not be terminated at Bridgend. The option of continuing the trains to Tondu was then discussed. An hourly service could not be maintained by one unit however, so to achieve adequate productivity each train would provide a half-hourly service between Tondu and Bridgend, continuing to Cardiff every hour and running into the bay platform at Bridgend in between. Mid Glamorgan was keen to establish a series of feeder buses from Maesteg, Blaengarw and Nantymoel connecting with trains at Tondu, but no sensible timetable could be devised to provide good connections into and out of InterCity services at Bridgend.

"It was then suggested that we might like to run to Maesteg. Mid Glamorgan decided it was worth investigating. They were good at market research. They didn't go to consultants and were better than South Glamorgan. I said I'd accept their findings. Maesteg is quite a large town, with about 25,000 people. Car ownership was low and the age-profile fairly high, so the propensity to travel by train would be quite high if the right service was provided. The answer to Maesteg, as with Aberdare, was to run through to Cardiff. The failure of the original service was caused by its discontinuity."

Another attraction in Maesteg was the central location of the station site – right beside the Gateway superstore. 'Maesteg Gateway' was suggested as the station name, but John questioned what would happen if the supermarket changed hands! Since two units would be required to run the main line stopping service anyway, it was decided to continue through to Maesteg.

"The research showed that, although there wasn't a huge potential for Maesteg, it would make a viable project when added to the main line stations. We'd learnt a lot from the Aberdare scheme, so we could have a more bullish assessment of commercial effects."

Ironically, it was the Maesteg branch which made the service a conspicuous success. The two stations which were built on the main line were initially somewhat disappointing but counterbalanced by a healthy trade from Maesteg to Bridgend and Cardiff.

Once again the budget for the project was tight, and problems were exacerbated by the blocking tactics of other BR sectors (described in Chapter 7). Costs were pushed up by a number of factors, including new Health and Safety Executive requirements, so a number of features had to be deferred. The footbridge at Pontyclun was not provided for the opening day and two stations on the branch - Ewenny Road and Wildmill - were built once the service was running. Wildmill suffered another delay when the HSE inspector found the platform shelter had been erected one inch closer to the edge of the platform than the distance specified in the regulations. The whole lot had to be dismantled and re-erected, delaying the opening. In the meantime, potential passengers used road transport which, statistically, was more dangerous.

"The inspector decided he was going to teach them a lesson," says John. "He had to make a point. He was a most inflexible person. They did ridiculous things there - a complete waste of public money."

The bay platform at Bridgend was rehabilitated and used in the early days for the first service of the day from Maesteg, which terminated at Bridgend and connected into a Cardiff-bound InterCity 125. Latterly the bay has been disused as all trains run through to Cardiff.

Mid Glamorgan's original plan for the Maesteg and main line stations was to give them a service that ran through to Cardiff Queen Street, for easy access to shops and workplaces. This happened to a limited extent, with some Maesteg to Coryton workings in the early timetables. However, the formation of shadow franchises in 1994 put an end to through running because the Maesteg line was placed under a different franchise from the Valley Lines system. The Maesteg line went through a period of unreliability, and consequently poor loadings, soon after the start of the shadow franchises but in 1995 there was a concerted attempt by local managers to improve reliability. This was coupled with a temporary fares reduction and special marketing.

"There wasn't the verve and the will in Swindon to operate this local service," says John. "It's fortunate that the local management intitiative has pulled the ridership back."

During the 1980s and early 1990s the Valley Lines' kitty for largesse was, not surprisingly, empty. However, John took the opportunity to thank the councils for their support when the 150th anniversary of the opening throughout of the Taff Vale Railway arose in 1991. Celebrations on a grand scale were planned, starting with an open day at Cathays works, where rolling stock from the 19th century to the present would be on display, and culminating in the return of steam-hauled trains on the Valley Lines after an absence of 25 years. Sporting, gardening and cultural events were sponsored and the steam runs took place on three weekends in October, to the delight of the local authorities. Rhondda Borough Council even hired the steam train for an afternoon to kick off its Industry Week celebrations in style.

Another person who was delighted with the steam runs was Dai Woodham, whose scrapyard in Barry had been home to many of Britain's preserved steam locomotives. Indeed, the BR Standard 2-6-4T used for the steam runs, No. 80080, had once languished in his scrapyard and he was thrilled to ride in its cab from Cardiff to Barry.

"We made a loss on the TVR 150 celebrations. They coincided with the formation of Regional Railways so there was insufficient management time available to organise the celebrations effectively," says John. "But the celebrations were good for morale on the railway and it was nice to be able to thank the councils and the local people for all their support."

Cardiff Bay Redevelopment

The county councils were not the only public bodies outside BR which were in a position to support the development of the Valley Lines. One such body was the Cardiff Bay Development Corporation, a quango charged with redeveloping the old docklands of Cardiff. A central plank of its redevelopment strategy was to create a wide boulevard to link the city centre near Cardiff Central station with Butetown, in the Cardiff Bay development zone. Unfortunately for CBDC, the Bute Road branch sat on an ugly stone-faced embankment along the full length of the proposed boulevard. "They said 'Get rid of it'. We said 'We can't just get rid of it. We have to go through closure procedures'," says John Davies.

By this time the Bute Road branch, once an important transport artery to the coal tipplers and the coal merchants' offices in Butetown, was a sleepy backwater. However, a rail service would be essential if CBDC's dream of creating workplaces for 30,000 people in the bay area was to be realised. CBDC saw light rail as the solution, as this would continue the railway presence but allow demolition of the ugly embankment.

"Light rail was a long way away - even further away in fact than we thought at the time. The whole Cardiff Bay redevelopment has been much slower than I expected."

"The director of engineering talked to me in the early stages and said CBDC had some money to spend on useful things. He said, 'Do you think it would be sensible spending some money on the branch as it is, just to keep it intact until we've got something to replace it?' He had worked for the London Docklands Development Corporation before coming to CBDC and knew that railways could be useful. I told him that we couldn't enhance the rail service to Bute Road because of the problems at Queen Street station."

Queen Street was, and still is, a bottleneck on the Valley Lines. There were only two through tracks. A siding accessed from the south served a side platform at Queen Street but was only spasmodically used. A shuttle between Queen Street and Bute Road could use the bay but would have to interrupt main line traffic on the busy double-track section south of Queen Street to access the Bute Road branch. BR agreed to provide a frequent service to Bute Road in return for CBDC's paying to provide additional trackwork and signalling in Queen Street station.

CBDC paid £600 000 for 200 yds of track (which made the Bute Road branch independent of the main running lines), three new sets of points and some amended signalling. Two of the connections were for the new stretch of track – the first to be laid on the Valley Lines system for many years – and the third turned the siding into a through platform road. "It helped not just the Bute Road branch but the whole Valley Lines service as well."

Trains from the Rhymney Valley to Bute Road could be sidelined immediately on arrival at Queen Street, and the new platform road could also be used for a late running train to overtake a punctual train which had already been let into Queen Street.

John pushed for a similar tweaking of the infrastructure at Cardiff Central, so that up trains could overtake one another when necessary. "We wanted to do lots of things around Cardiff Central. We particularly wanted to put facing-point locks in, so trains coming from Barry, Penarth or the City Line could run into either platform six or platform seven. It would have been possible for one train to overtake another if there was nothing coming in the other direction, and if a train failed we could get round it. We battled but the people above us stonewalled. Two-way signalling would be desirable but it's quite expensive to install."

The modest alterations at Queen Street weren't cheap either.

"A lot of the money went towards coping with new regulations on signalling which had followed the Clapham Junction crash. They were appalling. If we hadn't got some common sense into it, we'd have had the whole Valley Lines system shut down for two days so the signalling could be brought in and tested. In the end we reduced the service for a week so it could be hand-signalled without causing excessive delay."

The City Line was used to avoid using the junction at the north end of Queen Street too frequently, so the decision to keep the Radyr loop line came in useful.

"We got this upgrading scheme done quickly. We always took advantage of any money that was on offer to enhance the services. CBDC was originally committed to getting rid of the Bute Road branch as soon as possible, but it wasn't long before they had acted to secure its future for a longer period!"

This was just as well, as there has yet to be a serious submission for light rail in Cardiff. The concept of light rail poses big problems. A Y-shaped line running from Cardiff Bay and splitting to serve Central and Queen Street stations would be rather short. The operator would be faced with considerable overheads but the fares would be low. One of CBDC's objectives is to permit easy access to the promised employment bonanza in Cardiff Bay from the deprived valleys to the north. The existing rail service performs that function and CBDC has proposed a light rail system that would share tracks with heavy rail services so that services from the bay can continue to Caerphilly and Pontypridd. This would follow the technological concept piloted successfully in Karlsruhe, Germany.

There are problems in installing such a system in the UK. The differing buffing heights of trains and trams and the different end-loading standards mean that a system has to be provided to ensure that there can be no contact between the two. This could mean that all vehicles have to be fitted with ATP apparatus although simpler methods can be used under certain circumstances.

"They've talked about an initial projection of light rail from Cardiff Bay up to Pontypridd via Llandaf and the City Line," says John. "I believe that associated with that is the notion that there would be no heavy-rail trains between Pontypridd and Cardiff during the daytime, so people coming from Merthyr and the Rhondda and Cynon valleys would have to change at Pontypridd to light rail vehicles. That might improve the service between Pontypridd and Cardiff tremendously but it will undo the good work in developing the mass market for travel from north of Pontypridd. Once you make people change you've lost it all."

Manchester and Sheffield could justify light rail not only because they are big cities but because their heavy-rail stations are poorly sited for the city centres. Light rail was a way of getting rail services to penetrate the centres without the expense of constructing the exclusive rights of way which heavy rail would need. Karlsruhe itself was in the same situation. Plenty of other cities share the problem, including Bristol, Nottingham and Leicester – but not Cardiff. It would be practically impossible to improve the railway's current penetration of the office and shopping area of central Cardiff.

Poor penetration is a feature of some of the towns served by the Valley Lines, however. The big advantage that light rail could offer the valleys is the opportunity to extend the rails deeper into some valley communities, from Merthyr to Dowlais, from Aberdare to Hirwaun via the houses, and from Caerphilly to Senghenydd or even Machen.

Installing wires and making other preparations for light rail to run through lightly-populated areas to relatively distant towns is not likely to be feasible. More realistic would be converting the Coryton and Penarth branches to light-rail operation and building new routes to areas of Cardiff which have never been rail served – areas like the housing estates of Ely and St Mellons.

"Ely and St Mellons are heavy public transport areas but they're not sexy sorts of areas for light rail. I think that's the problem, and that's why building light-rail lines to those places didn't figure in the thinking after local councillors and many others went dashing off to Karlsruhe in 1991.

"At the time when everyone was euphoric about adopting the Karlsruhe system in Cardiff, I was urging caution. They tended to assume that the government in this country would become as elightened as the German government in terms of investing in public transport. I did some calculations then that showed the investment per passenger in Germany was five or six times more than in this country. The cost of converting the whole Valley Lines system to light-rail operation was £200M, and that would probably rise. If Manchester Metrolink can just run at a profit, after the capital cost has been written off in an area where 300,000 people live around a 20-mile line, how on earth can an 80-mile rail system with a 300,000 population be remotely successful? Once the politicians and others actually get to see the facts it could die."

The Welsh Development Agency became a highly influential body in the late 1980s and committed itself to an energetic programme of clearing away the dereliction and contamination left by the coal and metal industries in South Wales. One reclamation site was the area vacated by the pithead buildings of the colliery at Nantgarw. Closure of the colliery in the mid-1980s left the branch line from Taffs Well to Nantgarw redundant and by agreement the track was allocated to the Provincial sector. John was ready to investigate a passenger service along the branch if the site was to be used for housing or out-of-town shopping. In the event the WDA earmarked the site for industrial use and, as explained in previous chapters, John believed that scattered factories were not good generators of custom for local railways.

In line with its general aim of beautifying the valleys, the WDA funded cosmetic improvements to many Valley Lines stations. Fencing was replaced or smartened, platforms resurfaced with brick paviour, shelters improved and new or brighter lighting installed. Stations in the Rhondda and upper Rhymney valley were targeted. Treherbert was one of the most difficult projects, as its historic Taff Vale Railway station building had to be preserved but renovated as an operational ticket office. Trefforest's revamping was a major scheme that involved creating extra park and ride spaces.

Caerphilly was also tackled in a programme that saw the demolition of the 'Berlin Wall' separating the rail and bus stations. Rhymney Valley District Council and Mid Glamorgan contributed, as well as BR and the WDA, and there was a feeling that the old hipped-roof canopy ought to be demolished. Happily it was retained as an aesthetic and practical feature, although destaffing has by now led to the waiting room under the canopy being boarded up.

Another outside body which was well placed to assist the development of the Valley Lines was the Welsh Office, the government office dealing with most domestic affairs in Wales. The Department of Health, for example, has no direct involvement in health services in Wales, which are controlled by the Welsh Office instead. Similarly, the Welsh Office is responsible for transport investment in Wales. It maintains and builds trunk roads and gives grants for local authorities to build lesser roads. However, it has never given a grant for a rail investment.

When John Redwood, then Secretary of State for Wales, prepared his Roads in Wales 1994 document, he felt the Welsh Office's green credentials should be mentioned and wrote that many of the 29 stations opened in Wales since 1985 had been "supported by local authorities with resources provided by the Welsh Office". This is not quite true. Far from supporting the projects, the local authorities were the driving force behind them. The Welsh Office provided resources in the form of loans, which the councils had to pay back, rather than grant, although the government funded the repayments. One way of looking at this arrangement is that the Welsh Office had to grant the councils permission to spend their own money. This policy then left each rail scheme fighting for elbow room in council budgets which also had to take care of many sensitive local services.

Even a modest contribution in grant from the Welsh Office could have made a big difference to the City Line, by providing a bay platform at Radyr and ironing out capacity problems near Ninian Park, or to the Aberdare line, by providing four-car platforms. Even better would have been a commitment by the Welsh Office to provide some of the funds needed to upgrade the signalling and trackwork on the system, smoothing out the capacity problems at Central and Queen Street, for instance.

The Welsh Office is continuing this policy of not funding rail projects even after the Department of Transport has begun direct funding of new stations and infrastructure improvement in England.

"The Welsh Office has a transport policy division but says rail policy is a matter for the Department of Transport. The Department of Transport says Welsh policies are a matter for the Welsh Office, resulting in no strategic thinking at government level – not enough anyway," says John.

He found more sympathetic ears in the local authorities, where some individuals were willing to take a longer-term view of public transport development. The Maesteg line had scratched the surface of developing local rail services along the South Wales main line and planted in John's mind the idea of a local train corridor crossing South Wales from Swansea to Newport, with extensions at both ends to places like Llanelli in the west and Chepstow, Abergavenny and possibly Newbridge in the east. That seed began to germinate when, in 1994, the Swanline local service between Swansea and Bridgend was inaugurated. The service involved new stations at Llansamlet, Skewen and Briton Ferry, funded by West Glamorgan County Council with European Union assistance, and a fourth station at Pyle, funded by Mid Glamorgan County Council. However, that seed has started to wilt because of the simultaneous reorganisation of the railways and Welsh local authorites and the lack of strategic direction from a body covering the whole of South Wales.

"I put these ideas to the councils," says John. "I think I was getting some response from them that maybe they should be building these jigsaw pieces into a longer-term plan which would permit all sorts of journey opportunities without a change of train. It would improve people's employment prospects, and the scope for leisure travel too. Cardiff would be opened up to all sorts of small villages."

This plan could also take in the Vale of Glamorgan line between Barry and Bridgend, a double track route which is currently used by freight trains and diverted main-line passengers trains when engineering work is undertaken on the main line between Cardiff and Bridgend. Reopening the line had been an aim of South Glamorgan County Council since before John's arrival in Cardiff, and BR had placed it in its B category. The reopening was investigated in terms of a local passenger service extending from Barry to Llantwit Major, calling en route at a station near Cardiff International Airport. The problem was that the population of the villages that would be served was quite low and car ownership high. Revenue support would have been needed from the council. The amount being asked rose to unpalatable heights after the formation of Railtrack and shadow franchises, and one of the first acts of the new Vale of Glamorgan County Council in April 1996 was to put the scheme in abeyance because of the high subsidy requested.

More recently the concept of diverting some existing services to serve the Vale of Glamorgan has been floated. The line between Llantwit Major and Bridgend is rural and offers no prospects for traffic generation per se, but a service over that stretch could open many new journey opportunities between Barry and points west, including Bridgend, Maesteg, Swansea and West Wales.

"There are all sorts of scenarios, but minds were closed," says John. "I said the airport could be linked to the railway by a courtesy bus, but if passengers from Swansea and West Wales have to change trains at Bridgend or Cardiff as well, then the chances of getting enough business to the airport by rail are zilch. If you have a through train from Swansea, even every two hours, you might get some business to the airport then.

"The syndrome is, 'This is the resource we've got. We can't cope with this service, therefore there can't be a market for it.' "

The whole idea of a local rail service across South Wales did not go down well within BR.

"It wasn't in Regional Railways' grand plan of things and therefore it couldn't be a good idea. By this time I was no longer in the policy-making side of local services, I was simply representing the railways of Wales. It was considered that my views were no longer sensible because they were based on theoretical thinking rather than hands-on operation. I think I was starting to become far more wide-seeing. One of the problems of working out in a business organisation is that you don't get enough time for strategic thinking.

"You need time not just to think out these things but to take people with you – not just within the industry but your partners outside. You've also got narrow timeframes there, for political reasons, but there are also individuals there who are quite wide thinking. Darien Goodwin, public transport officer with Mid Glamorgan County Council, was a good case of somebody who was far-seeing. Mike Richardson in West Glamorgan and Rob Quick in South Glamorgan were the same. There were even some officers in Gwent County Council, which was outwardly uninterested in public transport, who were keen to develop wider strategies for public transport.

"These were all people who, I think, in time I could have taken with me because two things were becoming apparent. One was that the councils should start contributing to the basic infrastructure so they had a railway to run trains on in the future. The other was the need to think wider, think regionally. If you consider that the years 1983 to 1993 involved the rise and fall of the Valley Lines, the loss of an overview is part of the fall. The Balkanisation of the local authorities and the railways has set back strategic thinking in regional terms."

Perhaps the best remaining hope is the Standing Conference on Regional Policy in South Wales, which brings together local authorities and other organisations involved in the region. In the last two years John has outlined the idea of the South Wales local rail corridor to them, and it remains to be seen whether they can make it work once the dust has settled on the new unitary councils and the new rail companies.

For John Davies, one of the most satisfying aspects of developing the Valley Lines was to observe the way local people quickly began to covet their new rail services, especially the Aberdare line. The residents of the valleys which had been fortunate enough to retain their passenger services had always regarded the trains as something which belonged to them. Now their neighbours in other areas did the same as new stations were opened in their villages.

"*It's incredible that people write off railways as not being important. There are areas where they are central to the local economy," says John. "When the Maesteg line opened, the strange thing was that people were saying it was good because now they could go to Cardiff. Basically it meant that people who didn't have cars found it difficult to get to Cardiff before the railway was reopened. Now they didn't have that worry. It was strange how people have perceived that Maesteg is now connected to the outside world again."*

This factor is possibly under-estimated when feasibility studies are conducted into new local rail services. In 1991 consultants were commissioned by Gwent County Council to investigate the costs of restoring train services to Newbridge or Abertillery in the Western Valley of Gwent. The picture that emerged was not encouraging. When asked why there should be such a marked difference between this case and that of Aberdare and other routes in the Valley Lines portfolio, the consultants said one big difference was the general absence of young women commuting from the Western Valley to work in Newport or Cardiff.

Young female commuters have always been bread and butter to the Valley Lines. Since there is no genetic difference between the people of the rail-served valleys and those of the Western Valley, it is reasonable to conclude that the absence of rail services in the latter forces many of the local young women to choose between either staying at home and not attempting to get a well-paid job in Newport or Cardiff or leaving the Western Valley to live somewhere that does offer good commuting by public transport to Newport or Cardiff.

John feels the effect of railways can be observed even in the outward prosperity of various valley towns.

"*Merthyr, Aberdare and Pontypridd are moderately prosperous by valleys standards (although not by other standards). But you look at Tredegar, or Brynmawr. They're wrecked. They're awful places. It may be just coincidence, but when there's a rail service you have the choice. It makes a town a more desirable place to live in, to stay in, rather than emigrating out. If you're stuck in Brynmawr or Tredegar without a car, what do you do?"*

The area covered by the new county of Blaenau Gwent saw a far bigger depopulation (by 3.4%) between 1981 and 1994 than any other area of Wales. It may be merely coincidental, but Blaenau Gwent is the only county in Wales without a railway station.

THE ABERDARE LINE

Top left: Before Aberdare's daily passenger service was restored a number of trains like this one were run from the old platform at Aberdare to Cardiff on Saturdays. This picture, taken in November 1986, shows a diesel shunting loco and brake van lurking behind the old Aberdare High Level station. Health and Safety Executive rules forbid terminal stations from being built on graded track, so the track on which the DMU is standing in this view had to be relaid before the regular service was launched in 1988. *Stephen Miles*

Centre left: While the initial two-hourly service was operated on the Aberdare line, old DMUs like this battered Class 101 vehicle, were frequently used. This set, in use on 11th Feburary 1989, is a hybrid of Class 101 and 108 vehicles. The barrel-vaulted shelter was inadequate for the large numbers of people who used this station and it was soon replaced by a brick shelter and ticket office. *Stephen Miles*

Below left: Cwmbach halt, shortly after its construction, illustrates the spartan platform-shelter design used for the Aberdare line. Finding a good shelter was a perennial headache for BR. Brick huts didn't allow the inevitable urine smells to be washed away, barrel-vaulted shelters quickly became opaque when the perspex was scratched, and the sheet-metal construction shown here was no match for the vandals, besides looking ugly. *Stephen Miles*

Below right: An integral part of the Aberdare project was this feeder bus service which takes passengers to and from Hirwaun, with some journeys extended to Rhigos. Here the vehicle waits at Aberdare station in February 1992 for its next complement of rail passengers. Notice the confusing plethora of logos and the message 'I meet the train' across the bonnet. *Stephen Miles*

Top left: South of Cwmbach station a DMU traverses a section of track built between the closure of the old service and the start of the new one. It connected the line from Aberdare Low Level to Abercynon with the line from Aberdare High Level to Pontypool, allowing the track through the low level station to be removed and level crossings in Aberdare to be eliminated. *Stephen Miles*

Centre right: Vandalism in the Cynon Valley was such an acute problem that a roof of steel mesh had to be fitted to the footbridge beside Penrhiwceiber station. Happily, there were no miscreants present as this Aberdare-bound Sprinter left the station in May 1993.
Rhodri Clark

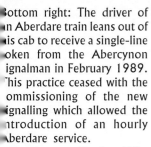

Bottom right: The driver of an Aberdare train leans out of his cab to receive a single-line token from the Abercynon signalman in February 1989. This practice ceased with the commissioning of the new signalling which allowed the introduction of an hourly Aberdare service.
Stephen Miles

CHAPTER 7

FRIENDS AND FOES
The Influence Of Other Rail Businesses

Superficially, the rapid reversal of the Valley Lines' fortunes in the 1980s might have seemed the result of innovation on a grand scale. Below the surface, however, the policies and practices that were new to South Wales were mostly adaptations of good practice on rail systems in other parts of Britain and even abroad.

Although the passenger system was compact, the Valley Lines didn't exist in a vacuum. Some tracks were shared with other BR business sectors, and by the 1990s their attitude towards the local passenger business was so obstructive that the Maesteg reopening nearly had to be abandoned. In the event, public money was wasted simply on assuaging the groundless fears raised by the other sectors.

Being part of a larger organisation brought many advantages but could also have its disadvantages. In the late 1980s the disadvantages became more prevalent, causing minor problems which gathered enough momentum to start destroying the business - a process which apparently has yet to be halted.

Maesteg – Opposition and Support

The project to restart passenger services to Maesteg was the only time in the history of the Valley Lines when the local management were swept along by support from the top. John Davies and his colleagues in Cardiff had had to fight tooth and nail for an allocation of Sprinter trains to operate the Valley Lines and most of the improvements made in the 1980s were a result of those managers taking full advantage of any independence they stumbled upon or of collaboration between local BR management and the county councils.

It would be fair to say, however, that the Maesteg service owes its existence to the support of Gordon Pettitt, who was then the managing director of Regional Railways. It was his backing that gave John the strength to knock down each of the many obstacles raised by two other BR sectors.

One of the early manifestations of the down-side of sectorisation in South Wales occured in the lower Rhymney valley. As each sector became more aware of its costs, so the age-old tradition of freight and passenger businesses helping each other out was killed off.

"People looking after their own fiefdoms too much could scupper the full effect of our plans to improve services," says John. "We wanted to go with Trainload Freight, which was running coal trains from Cwmbargoed down the Rhymney Valley line south of Ystrad Mynach, to create an extra signal at Llanbradach. That would have reduced the headway and allowed us to run a more frequent service to Ystrad Mynach. Trainload Freight said, 'We can't justify spending this money because your existing service can run with the existing signalling. If we paid for this it would be paying for you to run more passenger trains.' Our view was that we wanted to run more passenger trains without affecting the freight trains, but they weren't willing to spend any money for a coal business that might disappear in a few years."

The nub of the problem was the long block section between Ystrad Mynach and Caerphilly. Gaps of at least 25 minutes had to be left between passenger trains so that occasional freight trains could run up or down the line in between. A signal at Llanbradach would have allowed the passenger trains to follow the freights much more closely. Before sectorisation this relatively simple investment might have been viewed as a way of improving reliability and service in the Rhymney valley, but as a result of sectorisation the residents of Ystrad Mynach,

Llanbradach and the Aber area of Caerphilly were denied a more frequent service which may have been justified in business terms.

By the time the Maesteg scheme was on the drawing board, the attitudes of other sectors, in this case Trainload Freight and InterCity, had developed beyond apathy to outright opposition to improving the railway.

"I very nearly had to abandon the whole Maesteg project from intransigence within BR. The other sectors ganged up against us over the issue of line occupation between Cardiff and Bridgend. They said, 'You can't possibly run an hourly service. We want this path and that path.' I argued that I could remember the same line in the 1960s with far more freight trains, mechanical signalling and unfitted freights running at slow speeds, and now they were telling me that with fewer, jumbo freight trains an hourly passenger service couldn't be fitted in," says John.

"We had futile arguments about this. There was a general will that this project had to be killed at birth. It was not sensible to be running pootling little trains when you had high-speed trains and heavy freight trains on the line. That was the thinking behind it all, although they never admitted it."

The picture was bleak indeed when John also realised that there was simply no rolling stock available to run the new service. He felt he'd been beaten already by the time he made his submission to the Regional Railways investment panel (since the Maesteg scheme exceeded a certain price it had to go to headquarters level rather than the regional investment panel). The response duly arrived at Brunel House: Mr Pettitt was not impressed by the case for the Maesteg line.

"I had a call shortly afterwards to say that Gordon Pettitt would like to come down to have a look at Maesteg to see if there was anything in it. We went to Maesteg and he looked at the town and the site for the station. He said, 'This has got to be a good scheme for Regional Railways. Where are your blockages?' I told him that rolling stock was one blockage, and he found us the trains we needed by judicious fiddling around. A number of Pacers were coming from Heaton, Newcastle, to Canton and there were trade-offs at the Heaton end. Their allocation was over the top."

"The managing director, having taken a personal interest in the Maesteg scheme, then moved and shook at a high level and got us the promise of rolling stock. I then drove like a steamroller through the opposition from the freight companies and InterCity."

Those sectors still had plenty of other excuses up their sleeves. InterCity was concerned at the possibility of a Pacer failing on the Maesteg line, in which case the next train heading for Maesteg could be held in the down platform at Bridgend, delaying London to Swansea services. To placate InterCity, John promised that the Tremains loop, half a mile east of Bridgend, would be signalled for passenger use so that, in InterCity's doomsday scenario, the Maesteg-bound train could be recessed from the main line to await a clear run at the branch line. The changes, of course, added to the cost of the Maesteg scheme which was under so much pressure that two stations and a footbridge had to be deferred.

"I was told in April 1996 that the Tremains loop has never ever been used by a passenger train. That shows how InterCity were over-egging this thing. They were imagining problems that would not exist except on rare occasions," says John.

The next hurdle was how the Maesteg service would cause chaos whenever there was an electronics failure at Bridgend which happened occasionally - and the crossover between the up and down main lines couldn't be used. John's answer was that the train already on the branch would use the bay platform at

Bridgend to operate a shuttle, while the local train on the main line would be emptied at Bridgend and run down the mainline towards Port Talbot as far as the next operational crossover, where it would reverse to form the next local service to Cardiff.

Then the freight managers started predicting expansion of freight through Tondu. The rambling double junction at Tondu at that time was normally unused but Trainload Freight had its eye on several putative coal-mining schemes. One was the prospect of opencast mining at Maesteg, but John felt this was unlikely to happen because of local opposition to the plans.

"Then they talked about the Parc Slip opencast site which was to have caused the line between Margam and Tondu to be shut. At that time they said they wouldn't send coal out via Margam because they would have to haul it to Bridgend over Stormy bank and that would restrict the loads in each train. Instead they were going to reverse the coal trains at Tondu, and they would need paths on the single-track line between there and Bridgend. Tip recovery at Blaengarw was also imminent, and all these things together would make it impossible to path trains unless we had a loop at Bridgend. How much would that cost? 'Oh, a million pounds or so,' they said. We couldn't afford that! This was all on the possibility of traffic. We had endless arguments about it. In the end we had to write into the plans that if this happened we would go back to the county council and ask for another million pounds for a loop at Bridgend. This was shown up for the farce it was."

In the event the only freight trains to conflict with the Maesteg passenger trains were those carrying coal recovered from the colliery tips at Maesteg. A 90-minute gap in the morning was built into the original Maesteg line timetable to allow a freight train to run up the branch and be locked in at the top end, beyond Maesteg station.

"The coal recovered from Blaengarw went via Margam. It was for blending with other coal at Steel Supply in Jersey Marine, near Swansea. That's where we suspected it would go, but they insisted it would go to Cardiff for blending."

For a while, in 1995 and 1996, the coal travelled via Bridgend, when the direct line between Tondu and Margam was closed in advance of the Parc Slip opencasting. From Bridgend the coal trains went round the Vale of Glamorgan line and Ninian Park, Cardiff, to access the mainline and run through Bridgend in the other direction to get to Jersey Marine! There was nowhere to reverse at Bridgend or Llantrisant, and as the trains would have to reverse in Cardiff it was simpler to run round the Vale and avoid uncoupling the loco from the train.

Whatever the obstacles, the Maesteg scheme cleared them all. "Thankfully, with Gordon Pettitt behind me, I went to the next Regional Railways investment panel, sailed through and got the scheme approved." says John.

Help from the Engineers

John was also fortunate to have the wholehearted support of other disciplines within the railway in South Wales, most importantly the civil and mechanical engineers. The civil engineers demonstrated their flexibility and willingness to help when the Ystrad Rhondda loop scheme was implemented, but there were many other cases where similar flair was shown. Often those projects went unnoticed by the public because the county councils were not involved and they were simply internal BR achievements.

The councils' rail development strategy for the 1980s did not include any funding for improving the existing infrastructure. That is perhaps not surprising, since a new station is far more glamorous and vote-catching than a minute or two shaved off journey times. Mid Glamorgan did take up responsibility for investing in the infrastructure in its final year, paying almost the entire cost for resignalling the Radyr to Pontypridd line. The new unitary councils for Cardiff and Rhondda Cynon Taff have perpetuated this programme with funding for further improvements. Back in the 1980s, however, it was BR's job to make improvements like providing an extra signal at Ystrad Mynach and John was able to take advantage of a good working relationship with the engineers to progress many schemes that would get mired in bureaucracy nowadays.

"We were concerned about the lowish speeds between Radyr and Pontypridd, and expressed our concerns to the area business group. The group met four times a year to discuss operating and engineering issues in the context of business, and we would talk about solving the problems which we'd never set our minds to because we'd never looked at them in the business context before. The Taff main line was one of the first to benefit from that approach. The civil engineer came back to us and said he could save us millions of pounds. When we looked at it further it turned out to be a saving of about £10M over five years. It was quite simple. The civil engineer was saying we should approve a programme of gradual improvement on the line which could be fitted into our normal maintenance, like tamping and keeping the track circuits in good fettle. He proposed that at the same time they would make minor adjustments to the cant and other things to allow higher speeds. We could achieve, at a fraction of the cost, improvements that previously would have required complete relaying of the track. He asked us to prioritise. Our priorities were, first, Radyr to Pontypridd, second, Bargoed to Caerphilly, third, the Barry line, and fourth, the Merthyr line. Our lowest priorities were the Treherbert and Penarth lines, where there were too many stops to allow fast running anyway."

Another revelation at that time was that the sections of track that were no longer carrying freight would not need relaying for decades under the light axle-loadings of the Sprinters.

"When the Mid Glamorgan scheme to close the railway between Bargoed and Rhymney was abandoned, we took a hard look at the track. The civil engineers said that with a bit of regular maintenance work the rails would last for years and years. They said they were turning themselves into a maintenance company rather than a building company. The civil engineers always had great designs to rebuild the whole railway, whereas their real purpose in life was to keep it well maintained. They said it would keep going in its present state for 30-odd years but deterioration would set in if heavy locomotives started running on it regularly again.

On the main section of the Taff Vale line, speeds were raised from 45mph to 55mph, simply through improving the track while normal maintenance work was undertaken.

"We got it done at no cost. John Edmonds, at one of his quarterly reviews, said, 'What's this rubbish about you getting it done at no cost? Everything's got a cost – you're just hiding it.' I said the work was being done because it was in the civil engineers' budgets. We were doing it for good business reasons and I had to take the civil engineer's word for it that it was costing no more than normal maintenance."

An even more important change which the civil engineers' cooperation permitted was work to allow passenger and freight trains to use the viaduct between Cardiff Central and Queen Street simultaneously. Clearance problems meant that nothing else could move while a freight was negotiating this section, and the civil engineers initially estimated that the work would cost £1M.

"They did it for about £100,000 in the end. They moved some railings back and slewed the track slightly, and that enabled any trains to pass other trains on the viaduct, although it wasn't cleared for 23-metre passenger vehicles. We could never have run the intensity of service that we did without that improvement. Again the gut reaction was that it would be expensive, but you can often find cheaper ways of doing things. Ribblehead viaduct, on the Settle to Carlisle line, was another example. They thought they'd have to practically rebuild the viaduct, but in the event they singled the line over it and put in some waterproofing at a fraction of the cost."

The alterations to the viaduct in Cardiff, carrying the main artery of the Valley Lines, were needed to allow the many extra services planned in the 1987 timetable. At the same time the signalling at Taffs Well also had to be amended because half of the City Line services were to terminate there and cross from the up to the down line. The trains were routed into the stub of the recently closed branch line to Nantgarw colliery. This presented what appeared to be another expensive problem: while the City Line train was changing lines, the next down passenger train from

71

The double-track viaduct lifting the Valley Lines out of Cardiff Central and over the South Wales main line remains a bottleneck today, but deft engineering in the 1980s did at least lift the ban on passenger trains using this section when a coal train was coming the other way. Here the prototype Sprinter unit is descending towards Cardiff Central in July 1985, when it was used to shuttle enthusiasts between Cathays works and Canton depot as part of the 150th anniversary celebrations of the GWR.

John Davies

Pontypridd would have to be stopped as far back as Maesmawr, near Trefforest Estate, which was the nearest home signal with a safe over-running distance. Clearly it would be impossible to run five trains an hour from Taffs Well with such a restriction in the timetable, and the obvious solution was to create – at great expense – a new block post between Maesmawr and Taffs Well. However, the signalling engineers saw an alternative, and within weeks they had moved the Taffs Well outer home signal, along with its attendant distant signal, far enough away from the crossover to allow the next down train to come to a stop there with enough space for a safe over-run.

"They got the signals moved at low cost and very quickly, so that we could introduce the timetable as planned. You couldn't do that today - it would cost a fortune in design and take months and months."

Although it didn't last long, this lateral co-operation between different departments was one of the greatest benefits of sectorisation. The resignalling of the Rhymney line between Heath Junction and Aber was perhaps the most visible example of the collaborative system at work.

"The signal engineer in our business group was Phil Inskip. He was a smashing guy but he always had these doomwatch predictions. If it wasn't telegraph poles on the Pembroke Dock line about to fall with calamitous consequences, it was something else in another part of South or West Wales. In the valleys his prediction was that the lever frame in Aber Junction signal box was about to crash through the floor because the timbers were rotten and we'd have no signalling at Aber. We used to listen to him and laugh, then suddenly somebody realised that he was serious. We turned the problem into an opportunity, and decided to put in colour-light signalling. This is where a business ap-

proach made a difference. In the old system they would have taken the signal box away, kept the crossover at Aber and replaced the semaphore signalling with colour lights controlled from Heath. But in the new system we wouldn't have got that through the investment panel, because there were no compensating reductions in resources. The only way we could have made a case was to prove that the lever frame was going to collapse and the service wouldn't run."

Instead of that, however, John and his colleagues in Cardiff studied the option of moving the crossover to Caerphilly station, which was where the trains really needed to turn round. By terminating them at Caerphilly instead of Aber, 10 minutes could be saved on the out-and-back turn from Cardiff, which meant the local service to Caerphilly could be operated with one train less.

"When this was added to the investment submission, it all stacked up," says John. "The problem was that, instead of saving a unit, we decided to run more trains and increase our capacity. That got a very stormy reception at investment panel. The saving of a resource is something you can prove absolutely, but improving income is a straw in the wind. I recall the most appalling arguments and having to go back time and time again to show how this project would make money. The business case was made on running the trains straight into the down platform at Caerphilly and straight out again with a three-minute turnaround. It had the advantage of bringing 50% of the trains into the right side of Caerphilly station for people to get on and off, because the main entrance was on the down platform. In the end, that was a successful application of a business case."

Although the signal engineers contributed to these bargain basement solutions, the complicated hierarchy of the signal and telecommunications (S & T) side of the railway had its drawbacks.

The Caerphilly crossover was a deft business solution made possible by close contact between business managers and engineers. In October 1987 a Class 116 DMU sets off on the half-hourly Caerphilly to Cardiff shuttle as a Sprinter approaches the crossover with the next up service. In the distance, to the left of the tracks, are the buildings of the former Rhymney Railway workshops.

Peter Clar

The S & T engineers were different from the civil engineers in that the latter functioned through local engineers for all matters except major structures and bridges. On the signalling side in Cardiff there was an engineer responsible for maintenance functions and a small team for new projects. Matters were often referred to the regional engineer and others even to the BR Board's signal engineer.

"It came to a head when we decided to install a customer information system at Cardiff Queen Street. It was bought from a small company in Coventry which had not been approved officially by the hierarchy in the telecomms side. We went along to have a look at the system that was working in Coventry station. It looked good. We said that this company was the only one that did what we wanted in terms of what the customer saw. It was the only system that could show every station served with the next train, which was paged over as the train left. Somebody on the platform at Queen Street who was travelling to, say, Llanbradach could see at a glance if the train was going to Llanbradach and for good measure the display was in the line colour. Technically we weren't sure how good the system was, and the telecoms engineers hadn't approved it."

"After it had been installed it kept going wrong. We got the run around because the local telecoms people were saying one thing and the regional were saying another. In utter frustration I called a meeting with the company, the area manager and one representative of the signal and telecoms engineer. They said it was impossible for them to send one person, because certain people dealt with the contractual aspects, others dealt with the technical aspects and the local people dealt with the day-to-day operation of the system. The signal and telecoms department always sent at least two people to every meeting, which led me to suspect they were overstaffed. I said they had better send one person who was well-briefed, because I didn't want to crowd out the company with masses of railway personnel. As it was we'd be three to one."

"The real reason why things were going badly wrong was not just that the company wasn't delivering the specification but the telecoms department didn't know what it wanted and had difficulty sorting itself out. It was so hierarchical that one part couldn't tell the other what they were doing. There was fault on all sides. We should have evaluated its technical aspects more, but we saw what we wanted. The organisation couldn't deliver what we wanted because too many people got in the way with their own ideas of what should be done."

Another instance of poor communication arose when John ordered a bank of monitor screens for the entrance to Queen Street station. The idea was to angle the screens towards the doors so that people walking in could see when their train was due.

"When the scheme went in the engineers built the thing flush with the wall. The screens weren't facing the people as they came in so a lot of them missed the information. The brackets on the wall wouldn't bear the weight of the screens but, as so often on BR, things went ahead and nobody fed back any difficulties. They'd just carry on and produce the thing because they were the experts. We'd specified the screens but they didn't come back to us, the customer, to see if their proposed solution was what we wanted. We might have said there was no point having the screens if they were flat, or we'd see if we could find a different place to put them."

"It was symptomatic of the management on the railways that there were often too many levels. Policy decisions were taken at different levels, depending on the spend required, and there wasn't always proper co-ordination. In big projects it was generally good, because they went through a tough project appraisal. Some of the smaller things which didn't go through appraisal got lost in the immense size and complexity of the organisation. By the time you'd found somebody was going on in their own pet way it was too late. I'm sure the Cardiff valleys was not the only part of BR where this went on."

As for mechanical engineering, John and his team at Brunel House had a good relationship with Cardiff Canton and they were supported by sterling maintenance work to ensure there were sufficient superannuated DMUs available to run the advertised service. When Ian Walmsley began working at Canton DMU depot the Class 116 sets were achieving about 3,000 miles per casualty. Appalled by this figure and undaunted by the age of the units, he began a campaign of attending to maintenance details in all areas, especially the heaters, batteries and engine-coolant systems. A system was established to detect the most common faults and reduce the likelihood of them recurring. When the Class 116 sets were replaced they were achieving 25,000 miles per casualty - the best figure for old DMUs on BR at the time.

John says, "We had a good relationship with Canton through Ian Walmsley, who was left largely to his own devices managing the DMU fleet. For most of the time we had something around 85% availability, which was 10% better than was expected of trains of that age and condition. We had occasional bad patches, when the failures would come piling in together. That was down to Murphy's law as much as anything. The DMUs were prone to things going wrong that needed a lot of work. The wiring was difficult to get at and didn't get examined very often. If it perished all the electrics were knocked out, and key things were disabled."

The self-contained nature of the Valley Lines helped in this respect. Unless they were sent out on main-line turns, the Class 116s were never more than 25 miles from home and the same teams looked after the same trains every night, getting familiar with each unit's condition and idiosyncracies. Other units at Canton, such as the Class 119 cross-country units, were not as reliable, partly because they spent some nights at other depots.

"The DMU diagrammers in the early 1980s were proud of the fact that they had DMUs going all over the country on efficient diagrams," says John. "The problem was that they started going wrong miles from base without a prospect of returning to base for some time. Then nobody really took the responsibility to put things right."

"Today Central Trains has units that run from the Cambrian Coast line to Lincolnshire - right over the system. When I was responsible for the Cambrian lines in the early 1990s one of the problems we had was that the trains had a poor-quality look. You could never find out where to pin the blame - where the cleaning hadn't been done. In the 1980s the same thing was happening to Canton DMUs, until there was a concerted move by Provincial Western to get dedicated diagrams for the trains to spend each night at their home depot. That improved, overnight, the reliability, availability, miles per casualty and everything else."

Value for Money

Told of the achievements of the Valley Lines' renaissance in the 1980s, a typical rail manager in mainland Europe might respond, "So what?" In countries like Switzerland or the Netherlands, regions comparable to the South Wales valleys are served by trains three or four times the size of a Sprinter and just as frequently as on the valleys routes. If a regional authority in Germany, say, wants to increase the usage of public transport it invests and the results follow within a few years.

The response to our hypothetical rail manager would be to point out the context in which the Valley Lines revival occured. Seen against this background, developments in South Wales and many other parts of the Provincial system, are remarkable indeed. The most obvious difference between South Wales and an industrial region in Germany is the lack of sustained public investment in rail transport, and this makes the Caerphilly crossover scheme every bit as remarkable, proportionally, as the development of Germany's ICE high-speed rail service.

While countries like the Netherlands were pursuing strategies to reduce growth in road traffic, the many millions of pounds spent developing new roads and car parks in South Wales were bound to have an effect on the local railway.

Another difference is the absence of regional government in Britain, the absence of bodies which have the resources, the overview and the vision to lead a comprehensive local rail development strategy from the front. Instead, Britain is controlled from a centre which has little understanding of the everyday lives of people in the regions.

Even in the British context, the Provincial sector's achievements are noteworthy. Railway enthusiasts who were used to two-car Pacers or Sprinters as the norm for local and regional services would watch in open-mouthed amazement rakes of seven or eight Mk 2 coaches shuttling between Oxford and London Paddington throughout the day with a smattering of passengers on board. Network SouthEast and InterCity managers had their own pressures to cope with, but few could have sweated harder than John Davies and his colleagues to justify an allocation of adequate new trains for their services. The income streams in InterCity and Network SouthEast were high enough in the 1980s to cover basic investments fairly free-handedly while Provincial managers were having to fight for every penny of investment - even if the pennies, as in the case of Ynyswen station, were coming from local authorities rather than BR.

"I can't think of many parts of Europe where a combination of factors creates a good commuter service that's also very good value for the taxpayers. There are lots of very good commuter services in Germany, but there seems to be an awful lot of subsidy to German Railways," says John.

"For examples of appalling practice France takes some beating. Some years ago I was at Clermont Ferrand station in the morning. Clermont Ferrand is the only large city in the central area of France. It was encouraging to see the developments in commuter services there but I was also wondering how they could afford to run them. They ran almost entirely in the peak periods. Every unit seemed to do just one journey into the city and one journey back out in the evening. Sure, it provided an excellent service when it ran and the quality seemed quite good, but the earnings-to-cost ratio must be appalling."

"It appears that SNCF gets regional councils to pay for commuter services and then specifies what they can and can't have. The result is they pay far more than they need to. There's very poor resource productivity and I suppose the local authorities pay up because they don't know any better. I think they're being taken for a ride."

BR and the county councils in South Wales agreed in the early 1980s that the councils would not provide revenue support for rail services. The idea was that any new services started would be immune to future fluctuations in local government budgets if they were independent of council support. Only once was revenue support applied, when South Glamorgan wanted to prove that the Coryton line could sustain a frequent all-day service, and fortunately the experiment was successful enough for BR to take the service on without external support.

The drawback with the arrangement between the councils and BR, however, was that the Aberdare and Maesteg lines were unable to have late evening services. This was a bone of contention in the Cynon Valley because the Merthyr line, which generally wasn't as busy as the Aberdare line, had a late evening service simply because it had historically been supported by the Public Service Obligation grant. Mid Glamorgan County Council did consider providing revenue support for late evening services to Aberdare, but decided that the majority of people would be adequately served by the services running between 07.00 and 19.00. The upshot, if the thesis of Chapter 1 is correct, is that passengers in 1996 cannot return to Aberdare or Mountain Ash after an evening in Cardiff because in the late 1830s, when the Taff Vale Railway was planned, Merthyr was a more important town!

When John became Provincial's manager for Wales he inherited a revenue-support agreement on the Wrexham to Bidston line. "Two years afterwards I went to Clwyd County Council and said, 'You're getting very bad value for money here. I know you're going to come back to us one day and say you can't afford it any more, so I'm going to pre-empt that and say we can save money if we agree on some changes in the train service.' We then came to an arrangement," says John.

"It was quite possible for us to sit back and say we'd carry on running the trains because we got the money for the council regardless. Then, of course, somebody blows the whistle when they can't afford it any more and you've got a crisis on your hands. It isn't the local authority that gets the blame, it's BR - for taking the trains off. You have to consider those situations carefully."

It is conceivable that revenue support could return to the railways in South Wales. When the local operations are in private hands there will be a disparity between privately operated bus routes, which receive support for quieter services, and privately operated rail services, which receive no support from local authorities. The Office of Passenger Rail Franchising is underwriting only a two-hourly Swanline service. As John proved back in the early 1980s, two-hourly frequencies are nowhere near enough to attract passengers wherever they are making journeys of between three and 25 miles. The new local authorities will not want to see several million pounds worth of investment by their predecessors going to waste, so they could easily be held over the revenue-support barrel by profit-conscious rail franchise operators.

South Glamorgan County Council was prepared to enter into a revenue support agreement for the proposed Vale of Glamorgan service, for its early years at least. Since then, however, the scheme has been deferred because the revenue support demanded by the fragmented rail system of 1996 has increased.

The commuter rail systems John encountered in the United States also embodied poor productivity while being bailed out by revenue support, but those same systems carried some lessons that could be applied to the Valley Lines.

"The Americans are maligned for their passenger services. There are hardly any of them and it was no good looking at Amtrak for examples of good practice because they had a totally different way of doing things. But you hear less of America's commuter services, which are extremely good in some respects. I would never have learnt anything from them about low-cost operations. What they call the farebox recovery (and we call the operating ratio) was pretty low. The average city is lucky if it's getting 30 to 40% of its income towards operating costs from the passengers. When the Caltrans system for Los Angeles was being planned they were intending to start on a 10% fare-recovery ratio and get up to 40% when they were fully operational - mainly because they had to charge such low fares to get people out of their cars in a part of the country that's gone completely to cars."

In the late 1980s the Valley Lines were generating enough income from fares to cover all the costs attributed to the system. Although there were also some overheads from centralised functions which hadn't been attributed to the Valley Lines, the operation's bottom line was in a different league from that of Caltrans, or many other American systems. In recent times, however, the Valley Lines have lost a great deal of custom to the private car; perhaps the Californian system of low rail fares and heavy subsidies from local authorities is one which South Wales may have to adopt if it wants to prevent Cardiff becoming as polluted and congested as Los Angeles. (Such a time might not be as far off as many people imagine. On several occasions in the hot summer of 1995 Cardiff had the worst air quality of anywhere in the UK and had higher concentrations of some noxious gases than the maximum recommended by the World Health Organisation.)

Clean Trains

In Chicago, John witnessed a different approach to attracting car-oriented consumers and he felt aspects of Chicago's emphasis on quality could be applied to South Wales.

"When I was there in 1988 I looked hard at what they were doing on their suburban lines. They've had a lot of difficulties over the years, but in 1988 they had almost total reliability. Every booked train ran, even though they had frequent services in the peaks (although not very frequent off-peak). They had on-time arrival records of 97 or 98%, day in, day out. One of their hallmarks was providing rolling stock in excellent repair. There was not a spot on the trains – not even the cab ends of the push-pull trains. I remember looking at a train in Chicago Union station, on the old Milwaukee lines. I couldn't see dirt anywhere, even in the cracks between the corridor connections. I went through the train looking at the inside. It was super – just like a Swiss train. Then I thought, 'They pay attention to detail. Their pricing is reasonable (but then they're heavily subsidised), and their operation is first-class in terms of reliability and punctuality.' It seemed to me that this was the way we should be going in this country. It vindicated my view that the Valley Lines could be as good as anywhere if we paid enough attention to detail. Why shouldn't people in the valleys get as good a deal as anybody else? They're not second-class citizens."

"The American commuter railroads were second-class operations years ago – the only people who used them were the ones who didn't have cars. Now most of their business comes from park and ride."

Such lofty thoughts were all well and good at Chicago Union station, but soon John was back at Brunel House where he would need to produce evidence of a positive financial return before investing even in a new mop! Nevertheless, he donned his thinking cap and came up with some proposals for cleaner trains on the Valley Lines.

"It wasn't good enough in my mind to say we'd got difficulties and couldn't clean the trains. We would have to find cheaper ways of doing it. I did suggest that we should adopt a policy of the Greyhound Corporation of the USA. I travelled a number of times on Greyhound buses but I never saw a dirty one. They were shining, inside and out. In fact they had a slogan: 'The bus will always be clean'. Every member of staff was imbued with this. If a bus was dirty when it arrived somewhere the driver was entitled to debus the passengers, take the vehicle through the wash and give it an internal clean if necessary. The Greyhound Corporation's reputation was at stake."

"A few years ago I asked why a driver coming from West Wales to Swansea with a dirty train who had some time in his shift before going back out couldn't take it upon himself to take the train through the carriage washing machine at Swansea. I raised it at business meetings but there were too many agreements with drivers, tea breaks and everything else."

At that meeting John also expressed concern that trains operating the Heart of Wales line, between Swansea and Shrewsbury, were not being cleaned properly at the Shrewsbury end.

"The trains from Swansea weren't as important as the others because they were run by a different sub-sector. They would get cleaning resources if they were available," says John.

"That got even worse around that time, because for six months one train was booked to stay overnight at Crewe and was diagrammed to be fuelled there. If the depot in Crewe had time available they would fuel it. The result was that a number of times we had a train running out of fuel at Knighton in the morning. This wasn't a lack of attention to detail – it was people ignoring the basic things that were laid down to be done. Because it wasn't one of their sets it didn't worry people at the maintenance depot in Crewe that it ran out of fuel at Knighton. That was a problem for Provincial Western to solve."

Cleaning problems were not as easy to identify as lack of fuel. Trains didn't break down if they hadn't been cleaned, so tightening up on sloppy cleaning practices was more difficult.

"The area business group was concerned that Valley Lines trains were being sent out clean in the morning and by midday they were beginning to get full of rubbish and cigarette ends. Commuters going back in the evening would often sit in a sea of rubbish. This wasn't acceptable, and I first suggested that conductors, when their duties were lighter during the day, should be given a plastic bag and asked to pick up litter. There were lots of reasons why this shouldn't be done, including that they could only pick up rubbish. They wouldn't have the time or the facilities to clean around with a cloth, and certainly not to freshen up the toilets."

"So the area manager, Roger MacDonald, came up with the suggestion that we put in part-time cleaners. It was successful. It didn't cost us much. By having cleaners at each of the valley termini and a few at Cardiff we could cover the whole fleet with about eight people on turns of two-and-a-half or three hours. Recruitment was easy. Nearly all the cleaners were wives of drivers or other railwaymen who wanted the extra money. It had an immediate effect on customers. Nobody would say the trains were cleaner in the evening because if a train is dirty you notice, if it's clean you don't notice. If it's clean you have neutral views but at least you're satisfied. During the day these cleaners were going up and down the trains while they were in service and there was an awful lot of positive comment from passengers."

"I think it was one of the best things we ever did. It was unique in terms of commuter services. InterCity Cross Country had started introducing cleaners on their trains, although they didn't clean the toilets, because on long-distance journeys the rubbish accumulation was quite nasty. I tried to introduce it to the Wrexham to Bidston line after that but we couldn't afford to put a cleaner on such a small service. We persuaded some of the conductors to do it in the end."

Naturally, John had to argue the case for taking on extra staff. After all, Regional Railways' chief concern was to cut costs. Indirect methods of improving the bottom line were seen as largely irrelevant.

"We fought this case on the basis that if we didn't do something about the state of the trains for evening commuters they would drift away because it was something else they didn't like about the trains. A lot of business has since been lost for other reasons, but I think it was worth doing. If you analysed it thoroughly you probably saved on overnight cleaning because there was less to do."

The biggest reduction in overnight cleaning demands came from banning smoking on the Valley Lines – a step which John had been afraid to take because of the likely reaction! In the event it raised few hackles.

Although John had struggled to justify the plan for part-time cleaners, Provincial did make a change that revolutionised train cleaning. When the situation before that change is considered, it is a marvel that any paint showed through on the Valley Lines trains.

"The cleaning facilities in Canton were archaic. There was only one hot tap in the whole of the carriage shed," says John. "The first time we had a quarterly review with John Edmonds and his team we all stayed overnight at a Cardiff hotel. While we were sitting there at dinner, John Edmonds said, 'I've decided we're going down to Canton late this evening, when the night shifts have had a chance to start, and we'll do an audit.' At 23.00 we marched down to Canton. Considering the man he was – John Edmonds had a reputation as a hard man – he was actually very talkative with the staff and got on with them quite well. He was quite complimentary that, in view of the dreadful circumstances, they weren't doing too badly. Some of the things we looked at – not just Valley Lines DMUs but cross-country units and sets of Mk 1 coaches with locos – really were pathetic. I wonder that he didn't blow his top, but I think he had the sense to realise that blowing his top wouldn't change much."

The Cardiff management had attempted to bring in the Japanese quality-circle concept, which was aimed at empowering staff to improve their own working environment. However, the RMT union put a stop to such practices, saying that collaboration between staff and management should only happen via the union's long-lived consultation process.

"As a result, the improvements to train cleaning came along a lot later than they might have done. Cleaning, for example, had always been a sin bin for people who misbehaved. How could you possibly get a good job done when it was considered a thing to avoid at all costs?" says John.

"It was some years later that Provincial introduced a national policy that cleaning had to be treated as a profession. We saw a progressive improvement in cleaning – certainly it's difficult to criticise the Valley Lines today on internal cleaning. People who travel regularly will notice any deterioration in the cleaning and think the organisation doesn't care. They'll find other means to travel. I was delighted when I could support Provincial headquarters wholeheartedly in their moves to put train cleaning right."

PTEs and Sector Management

Many times in the 1980s and 1990s academics, politicians, rail campaigners, environmentalists and others argued the case for a Passenger Transport Authority and Executive to be formed to coordinate public transport in Wales or in South Wales. The arguments were persuasive, particularly as the English PTE areas and Strathclyde had seen far more investment in rail facilities than other urban areas outside London. John Davies, who had been keeping his eyes and ears open as he travelled around Britain, was not convinced.

"For years a PTE for South Wales was talked about. I was implacably opposed to it," he says. "I said we were managing all right without a PTE. If a PTE was going to improve bus services and help integration, rather than be an all-embracing controlling body, I might have held a different view. But I looked at the existing PTEs and considered how many of them were operating in what I thought was the public interest in its totality."

"West Yorkshire PTE was excellent in terms of developing new services, better frequencies and new stations, but I felt it had a daft policy on fares. There was one price for the whole West Yorkshire area, which was heavily discounted if you had a strip of tickets or season tickets. I remember going down the Calder Valley line and when we got to Todmorden – the first station in West Yorkshire – the train, which had been practically empty, filled up. You could go all the way from Todmorden to Leeds for the same price as Todmorden to the next station along the line. People were paying something like 55p single for a journey of an hour on the train. I thought this was stupid. I know it attracted a lot of people, but they would have paid more because there's a certain value in people's minds. As long as you don't exceed that value you'll get good use of the trains. The sad thing was that West Yorkshire could have had even more money for investment and expanded faster if they'd had a sensible fares system."

This philosophy might sound a little odd coming from the man who reduced the Valley Lines fares in 1983, but the West Yorkshire situation strengthened his guiding principle that what a local railway needed was not cheap fares but the right fares. Even amid the poverty of the Rhondda Valley it was possible for a train fare to be too low. As explained in Chapter 2, the fare from Porth to Pontypridd was quickly raised a little but this had a negligible effect on custom because the higher fare was still within people's value-for-money threshold.

Another feature of PTEs which John abhorred was that the system placed the railways under the thumbs of politicians. In South Wales he was fortunate to have a mature working relationship with the county councils, and BR could easily veto any scheme – like the proposed station for Hopkinstown – which had a strong political argument but a weak economic one. The last thing John wanted was for this productive relationship to be skewed by politics to the extent that had occurred in some PTEs, notably Merseyside.

"Merseyrail had a lot of good features. I was envious because they were highly productive in terms of units and crews, but that's where it ended. The PTE had a policy of creating employment and even the smallest stations were staffed all the time, although hardly any tickets were being issued at those stations. It had a spin-off because there was a lot of vandalism in the area, so it could have saved some money being paid out to repair damage, but it seemed to go to ridiculous lengths. I don't think it encouraged more people to travel than would have used the trains if the stations were unstaffed. They've lost an awful lot of custom in recent years, so that argument doesn't stand up. I think the decision was made on blind political grounds, so they paid out far more than they needed to. Again, your basic cost base is way up and you've got less money to invest. You could replicate that in most PTEs."

At the opposite end of the productivity scale for trains and crews was nearby Greater Manchester PTE. "The worst one, from an outsiders' point of view, was Greater Manchester. Generally they had poor services, weren't terribly innovative and often ran services for the sake of running them, with poor utilisation of resources for political reasons. All this was capped by some of the worst reliability problems on Provincial and Regional Railways. Between the PTE and the Pacers, the rail services in Greater Manchester were almost wrecked. The rail network north of Manchester had been in the doldrums for years and it beats me how it survived."

On a trip round the loop line through Oldham and Rochdale, John found that he knew the conductor on his train. He had been a part-time instructor on customer-care courses. "I said, 'It's nice to see that you do some real work as well! But why don't you issue tickets?' He said there was an agreement between the unions and the PTE that only assistant ticket examiners could issue tickets. Each train on the Oldham loop had one conductor and two ticket examiners. The conductor just did the opening and closing of the doors and rang the bell, and the ticket examiners sold the tickets. They had a train crew of four for trains that were generally less heavily loaded than the average Valley Lines train. They had double the traincrew for half the passengers. It did not make any sense."

Although John disagreed with the general functioning of the PTEs he felt their lively rail systems contained many positive lessons for the Valley Lines. One notable feature in the Strathclyde area and on the Tyne and Wear Metro was the use of automatic ticket machines at stations, but on balance it was felt that the Valley Lines were not suited to such machines.

"We never considered automatic barriers for the Valley Lines but we did consider automatic ticket machines. Our terminal development manager at Swindon visited Strathclyde and witnessed their system. He said, 'Don't bother with automatic ticket machines. If the vandals in South Wales are anything like the Strathclyde ones they'll destroy them'," says John. "Strathclyde and Tyne and Wear were far more concentrated systems in terms of population than the valleys and they could afford to put in automatic fare collection. Virtually all the stations had enough throughput of passengers to justify them, whereas the Valley Lines didn't have that."

One group of PTE-controlled services which John felt was similar to the Valley Lines was that operating out of Birmingham Moor Street and, latterly, Snow Hill to Stratford-upon-Avon and Leamington Spa.

"Those services impressed me very much. They ran for years and years like the Valley Lines with basically grotty DMUs which Tyseley depot seemed to manage to improve. There was quite a contrast with the Cross City line, which wasn't as well operated. I think they may have had staffing problems and possibly bad management there. They seemed to have a better way of doing things on the Stratford lines. The set of lines from Snow Hill was self-contained, like the Valley Lines, so that may have helped."

Again, there was a constructive lesson to be learned. When John was fighting for Sprinters for the Valley Lines he was up against the problem of low income per unit, mainly because the distances travelled in the valleys were shorter than on other urban networks. One way to bump up those figures could have been to integrate the valleys services with other workings from Cardiff, but John avoided this solution, with one or two exceptions, because it would have eroded the advantages the Valley Lines enjoyed as a self-contained system.

"Two things stymied the Valley Lines," says John. "One was that you'd be OK running out from the valleys and through to a destination like Bristol, but when the trains came back on the main line they could run into reliability problems. The vast majority of people using them would be waiting at a station like Cardiff Central because their trains had been delayed outside the system."

"The other thing was the completely different needs. In the days of the old DMUs, short-distance journeys with high-density stops were ideally served by Class 116s which had lots of doors. They were not suitable for cross-country runs, any more than the cross-country units were suitable for start-stop services. When the Class 150/2 Sprinters were introduced, there was a proposal (described in Chapter 5) that some of the allocation of 27 would be used for a number of services through from the valleys to the main line. They would have been used on Birmingham services – a Merthyr to Birmingham working was planned. But there were a lot of arguments for making the Valley Lines a separate railway."

Integration of services has happened on the Maesteg line since the formation of the South Wales and West Railway shadow franchise. Trains from Maesteg have run through as stopping trains to Abergavenny and, since June 1996, a daily Maesteg to Paignton working has seen Class 158 units on the branch. Extending long-distance services to start at valley stations was considered by John for the core Valley Lines routes. Class 158 services from Pontypridd and Trefforest to Portsmouth or Manchester are possibilities.

WalesRail

The area of the Provincial Sector which most inspired John was not a PTE region but Scotland, where Chris Green's ScotRail branding had met with the same immediate success as the Valley Lines identity in 1985.

"I thought ScotRail did much better than we did, particularly after Sprinters were introduced. There was a much more positive attitude to the Sprinter services around Edinburgh. I went there every two years to see Scotland play Wales at Murrayfield and I always took the chance to ride on the trains. I was impressed by the way the trains and stations were turned out and the positive marketing of the services."

"You've got to look a class act to attract people. It's getting more important now because the alternatives are so good. The alternatives for most people are cars. Most people's cars are tips inside but they tend to keep the outside looking clean. If they get on public transport and find it's down at heel they think, 'Why bother? They don't seem to want to attract me, so why should I use it?' Therefore public transport users tend to be people who have no choice," says John.

However, it was not the detail but the whole concept of ScotRail that impressed John, and he seized every opportunity to argue the case for a similar organisation to be created in Wales. He had a difficult task on his hands, partly because the passenger railways of Wales are in three sections connected only by lines in England. Scotland's geography favours a selfcontained transport network, because it has a narrow border with England and Glasgow and Edinburgh form two poles around which the country can rotate. Wales, by contrast, is smaller yet has a border that is twice the length. As a result there is far more inter-urban travel across the border than between the regions of Wales. Chester, Manchester and Liverpool are magnets to the North Walians, and Shrewsbury and Birmingham are popular destinations for folk in Mid Wales. Cardiff is a significant hub for South Wales, but Bristol is nearby and London and Birmingham also exert a strong pull. Just as the locals tend to travel on an east-to-west axis, so the incoming travellers – particularly the tourists who flock to the beaches, mountains and castles – tend to flow from north-west England to North Wales, from the West Midlands to Mid Wales and from London and southern England to West and South Wales.

Another factor opposing John's plans was the attitude of the English towards the prospect of their services being controlled in Wales! The entire ScotRail network was indisputably Scottish, but routes that would have been central to a WalesRail system – Cardiff to Crewe, Aberystwyth to Birmingham and Wrexham to Bidston – were partly or largely in England.

"In 1988 I started the Wales sub-subsector of Provincial," says John. "It wasn't a subsector in the true sense but it was intended to evolve into a subsector. It all got washed away by the Organising for Quality initiative in the early 1990s. We made the case that the inter-urban line from Cardiff to Crewe and Manchester should come under Wales, as would Birmingham to Aberystwyth. If the organisation had gone through to its logical extent I think I would have won my case there, because it would have made sense to link the parts. There was more difficulty with the idea of trains running into Birmingham being controlled from Wales."

The concept only gained approval because Provincial was undergoing profound soul-searching at the time. In 1987 headquarters seemed oblivious to the impending upheaval of Organising for Quality (a plan to make BR totally business-led rather than production-led) and was working on a new structure for the sector.

"Instead of having the subsectors split geographically, the structure they debated and decided to implement was to make inter-urban, urban and rural subsectors so that people could specialise in one type of service. Scotland and Wales would be separately managed, covering all three types of service. Provincial headquarters would hold them all together."

Although this structure was not adopted for any of the BR passenger businesses, it had a direct precedent in the railfreight sector, which had organised itself into different divisions to specialise in the various bulk commodities, in deepsea container haulage, in parcels traffic and in small consignments of freight. Other countries, such as the Netherlands, were dividing their passenger businesses according to traffic rather than geography.

In the event Organising for Quality swept like a whirlwind through the seedlings of this concept and no more was heard of it – with the exception of the Valley Lines being separated from the rest of Regional Railways South Wales and West in 1994.

Nevertheless, John was appointed manager for Wales but the job was a non-business role after 1991. From then on he was responsible for representing all railway sectors in liaison with councils, development agencies, the Welsh Office, the Confederation of British Industry and other organisations.

"The appointment was born of frustration by the managing director for Provincial at the time, John Edmonds. If truth were told, he was fed up with answering questions from all parts of Wales about the different approach of the various subsectors. He asked me to take on the role of pulling it all together. Initially, because it was too complicated to create a new subsector, I would be responsible to Provincial Western, but for operations in North and Mid Wales I would be responsible to Provincial Midland. I had never worked for such a complicated matrix of responsibilities. I tried to take a longer-term view, and thought we should take one step at a time and try to get it properly constituted in the course of time."

"Organising for Quality stopped it. During the discussions for OfQ I put in my claim that Wales should be a region. I was in a minority of two who argued that. I believe Paul Prescott was the other. He was marketing manager at Provincial and is now managing director of Railtrack Scotland. I think he saw the sense of it. Although Wales was a disparate country there were things like tourism which were quite significant to a lot of Welsh railways. Through all the trouble we had in pulling this together we were successful in showing that it could be managed better from Cardiff than it could be from Swindon, Birmingham and Manchester."

"It never happened and I think that was a shame. It's all history now, but we'd at last have got an all-Wales dimension for regional services."

DMU Resource Problems – Pacers At Last!

In essence, the story of success on the Valley Lines is an essay on devolution. In the early days, when Provincial sector headquarters was like a blind baby hedgehog, John had the freedom to institute radical changes in Cardiff at the drop of a hat. Conversely, it is no simple coincidence that the graph of passenger miles begins to fall just at the point where headquarters starts throwing its weight around.

Notwithstanding the fracas of the 1987 timetable change, the first severe setback to the Valley Lines' growth occured in 1989 and is attributable to decisions taken at a senior level which, in turn, can be traced back to government policy on investment in new trains.

"In the early part of 1989 the whole of the Class 155 fleet of Leyland-built Express units was grounded overnight because doors were sliding open while the trains were moving," says John. "There was a crisis, which was mostly alleviated by delivering brand-new Class 156 units from works to Provincial Western, instead of going to ScotRail. That in itself caused problems in Scotland. What couldn't be covered by Class 156s could be covered by more efficient use of old DMUs. In West Wales we had 16 units for 12 diagrams and for a period we had 13 diagrams for 16 units. In the Cardiff valleys we managed to improve the availability of the Class 150s and we reduced some formations from four-car to two-car where we could get away with it. we ceded three Class 150s for main-line work initially."

"Some months latter, there was a nagging problem arising from the difficulties caused by the Class 155 withdrawal. The Bristol to Weymouth line was having appalling problems with reliability. It was being run by Class 119 DMUs on long diagrams, and the trains were breaking down. We had a lot of debates in Swindon and various solutions were postulated for the Weymouth line, such as putting in temporary maintenance facilities at Westbury. They were all rejected as too expensive and not seen to be solving the problem, so the eyes were cast on the Valley Lines fleet. They wanted to take three further Sprinter diagrams out of the valleys to cover the whole of the Weymouth service with Class 150s."

"'Problem solved,' they said. I said, 'Yes, that's one problem solved – but at the expense of creating another one in an area where we've got a mass market.'"

"They said the old DMUs would have shorter turns in the valleys and could return to the depot more easily, but I argued that if they were breaking down on the Weymouth line they're certainly going to have trouble on the heavy grades in the valleys and with the wear and tear of stopping and starting at all the stations."

"By a majority vote, I lost. I must admit, I took it with very bad grace. Shortly afterwards I was asked by someone from the press whether I'd fought my corner on this. I said, 'Of course I did but I lost and I think it will be bad for business.' I spilled the beans that they were improving one service but making another one worse, which didn't seem right to me. I was reported verbatim and I got hauled over the coals for it. In retrospect I was wrong to be so outspoken, but I felt very annoyed.

"In the event, everything I predicted happened. The whole service went to pieces. Three more Sprinters went out from the valleys and four or five MetroCammell DMUs wheezed their way around. They couldn't keep time, therefore on the single-line sections the timetable just went into mayhem. At the end of summer 1989 I just didn't dare look at the statistics - they were just too horrifying and I knew it was going wrong but there was nothing I could do about it. Canton was working as hard as it could to keep them going. We might have been able to reorganise maintenance procedures, but by the time that had been done the crisis would have been over. We just had to soldier on. We lost a lot of business then – people were just fed up."

This situation was, of course, temporary but the process of improving a local railway in the 1980s was such a steep uphill struggle that a pebble dislodged could quickly cause an avalanche. The City Line at the time was a microcosm of the snowballing process that was soon to affect the Valley Lines, and possibly other Regional Railways services.

"It was difficult to tackle the problem of unreliability on the City Line but we needed to advertise if we were going to hold out against the stiff competition from Cardiff Bus. At the end of the 1980s and in the early 1990s our budget for advertising was chopped. We in Cardiff were no longer masters of it. It was imposed on us and the feeling was that it was not worth advertising local services to any extent. Putting up the case to advertise heavily in a five-mile radius of Cardiff to get back the business we'd lost to Cardiff Bus was laughable. That was not the business we were in, and the services were allowed to fall," says John.

"The other problem was that the county council had no advertising budget for the City Line. It was the councils' responsibility to advertise the services they had started under the Speller Act. We did manage a bit of joint advertising with South Glamorgan, but of course they didn't have an advertising budget because their money had been spent on getting the line up and running."

"This is one of the weaknesses that people should be addressing. These schemes should be appraised in terms of the money they will need from the councils for their whole lives, not just the money needed to start them off. That's easier said than done, of course, and I'm not sure whether councils could vote in advance that certain sums of money would be spent on advertising the services in future years."

"The City Line is one of those disaster stories where, once things started going wrong, one thing compounded another. The unreliability caused falling income, so there was no justification for spending on advertising. If we had got the advertising money the City Line might have succeeded."

The crisis precipitated by the withdrawal of Class 155s in 1989 flushed out the last of the weaknesses in the design of the 1987 timetable. Turnaround times at the termini were too short, even for Sprinters. If a train was late arriving it would be late departing and could quickly disrupt the entire Valley Lines timetable, particularly through forcing other trains to wait to enter single-line sections or to enter the double-track section through Cardiff in the correct sequence. When the time came to implement the hourly service on the Aberdare line, the opportunity was taken to rewrite the timetable from first principles. The best features of the 1987 timetable were kept but longer recovery times were built into the diagrams. The City Line was converted to an independent service, rather than being served by Merthyr trains. Theoretically, the system's reliability was improved overnight but, in practice, little changed because so many other wolves were at the Valley Lines' door.

"Because the business is resilient in the valleys, most of it came back after 1989 but problems were starting to occur with the Class 150s. The troubles of age started creeping in and weren't being tackled perhaps as well as they might have been," says John.

"And then the Pacers came in." Removing Sprinters from the Valley Lines to deal with the Class 155 crisis inevitably exposed again the difficulties John had encountered when trying to justify an allocation of Sprinters to the Valley Lines. Using Class 150/2s on long runs like Bristol to Weymouth indicated that the Sprinters could find better ways of meeting Provincial's all-consuming target of maximum earnings per vehicle. The option of removing Sprinters from the valleys grew more attractive as the sector's financial difficulties deepened. In fact, the Class 150/2 design was the ideal train for the Valley Lines. It had the power to cope with the fierce gradients and the acceleration to maintain tight clockface timetables despite frequent stops. Its axle-loadings were light enough to allow the track to survive with the minimum of maintenance. It had the wide doors and standing spaces needed for busy commuter work, as well as a high enough quality of ride to make a Merthyr to Cardiff journey comfortable. Such niceties, however, went out of the window in the last, desperate years of Regional Railways and the valleys could not escape Pacers.

"I didn't resist," says John. "I felt that a small fleet of Pacers was very sensible because we couldn't go on running our old DMUs for ever. We couldn't justify Sprinters for the City and Coryton lines and some of the peak workings. I felt that about eight or nine Pacers would have been sensible. I'd talked to some of the engineers and they said some of the serious problems with Pacers occurred because they were doing work which they weren't designed for. They were designed for light, short-distance work, but in many cases they were being run hard. Quite often I used to see them in North Wales, all the way from Manchester to Bangor. They weren't up to it, but I thought if we had Pacers that never strayed more than five or six miles from Canton, on City Line and Coryton diagrams, that would be only 150 miles a day compared with nearly 300 miles for diagrams to the heads of the valleys."

"That might have been the solution but, in the event, when they came – and it's still the case today – there was great indiscipline in the use of Pacers. They are used on what should be Sprinter diagrams."

The main problem was not a mechanical one but the lower capacity of Pacers, which have 122 seats per unit compared with a Sprinter's 149 seats. Although some routes, including the Aberdare line, could be overcrowded on Saturdays few attempts were made to restrict Pacers to quieter routes like the Cardiff local lines and the Caerphilly shuttle turns. "This is lack of attention to detail. They can do better but people often don't," says John.

The 1989 experiment to create all-powered three-car sets failed because of indiscipline in provision of units for service at Canton depot. This train was working to its correct diagram when seen approaching Cardiff Queen Street on a Bargoed to Barry Island working. Set C902 comprised a Class 108 power car sandwiched between Class 116 power cars to give extra capacity without compromising train performance. *Stephen Miles*

The problem is familiar to him from the period shortly before Pacers arrived in the valleys when some peak workings called for three-car sets. Provincial headquarters wanted John to return to traffic the Class 116 trailers which were removed in 1987 but he was determined that the three-car DMUs must be able to match the acceleration of Sprinters so that reliability could be maintained. Several sets were enlarged by the addition of another driving car to give three powered vehicles per train. The presence of a driving cab with no corridor connection in the train was not a problem because there would be assistant ticket examiners as well as conductors on the crowded peak workings.

"They were booked mainly for Rhymney Valley morning and evening peak services. In practice they kept turning up on the City Line and the Aberdare line, where the platforms are only long enough for two-car DMUs so we couldn't use a third car anyway. I remember a conductor telling me one day it was a stupid idea forming those trains because they had to lock the third car out of use. I said it was a perfectly good solution which was being abused. I asked Canton to sort it out, but they said the flow of trains out of the depot in the morning was such that they couldn't marshal the trains. So the three-car sets would leave the depot at the wrong time in the sequence and they'd work the wrong services. You'd have a two-car train on the seven-something service from Bargoed and it would be severely overcrowded. Those three-car sets in the valleys didn't last long. I gave up. We were wasting our effort."

The Pacers weren't all bad. The drivers preferred them because they had more spacious cabs than the Sprinters, where the driving space was confined by the passageway to the corridor connections. The passengers also preferred the ambience of the Pacers, although this is more of an indictment of the sombre and claustrophobic interior design of the Sprinters than a plaudit for the spartan bus-type seats of the Pacers. The Pacers are still pretty free of graffiti, possibly because conductors and passengers can see right through the train. Mechanically, too, they were superior to the Class 142s which had played havoc in the Greater Manchester area, although they were far from reliable when they arrived in Cardiff from Heaton.

"Gradually they were modified – given better transmissions, engines and door operating mechanisms – but by this time a lot of damage had already been done. They were worse than the old DMUs in some cases. The upside was that when a Pacer failed it could be rescued by a Sprinter. If an old DMU failed you had a hell of a job because the couplings were incompatible. Some things improved but others got worse because the Pacers failed more often. That was partly due to the learning curve with the staff and partly to serious design problems. They caused some pretty horrifying unreliability - fortunately after I had stopped being responsible for the Valley Lines."

Whatever the problems Pacers were causing, management could at least rely on the Sprinters which remained on valleys duties. But in the early 1990s the entire fleet of Class 150 Sprinters

on BR needed major overhauls. One way to release them to the workshops, where several were needed at a time, was to take one unit at a time from each of the various centres operating the Sprinters. Instead, a decision was taken to replace with Canton units the Sprinters that were going for overhaul from any depot except Canton. Their valleys diagrams would be taken over by Pacers.

"Word was spreading round that this was only while this major overhaul work was being done and the Sprinter fleet would be restored to its normal strength afterwards. I suspected that this was wrong and that it was their final means of getting the Sprinters out of the valleys to put them on other business - and I was right. I was not in a position to do anything about it so I could only look on and, when it happened, say, 'I told you so.' There are now three fewer Sprinters in the valleys than there should be, in my view."

In fact it seemed that the Valley Lines were about to become exclusively Pacer-operated shortly before John moved on from his post as business manager for Wales. "The whole of the Heaton fleet was coming to the Western Region, it had been decided, and they felt the best thing was to put them all together on the Valley Lines. I knew this was just one of the options but I thought, 'If we're not careful, this is what will happen.' By lobbying various places I could see that the decision had been made in Euston House, headquarters of the British Railways Board. I was up there one day for a meeting and I passed the office of the Provincial resources manager, Martin Shrubsole, on my way back. I thought I'd tackle him on this issue if he was there. He was in, and he was very obdurate. He said, 'We've got to do something with these Pacers. We've inherited these things and they've got to work somewhere. You can't justify Sprinters on the Valley Lines because your earnings per vehicle aren't high enough.'

"Of course, I saw red. I shouted, 'What happens to our agreements with the local authorities? Do we just tear them up?' What started as a reasonable discussion ended up as a slanging match. We were literally shouting at each other down the corridor in the end. I went away feeling angry, because I could see it was a fait accompli. I was going to have to justify all this and tell the local authorities that we'd let them down after they'd trusted us. On the way back to Cardiff I was preparing my defence, and my speeches to the press!"

"A couple of days later I got a letter from Martin which was very apologetic. He said, 'I think we both lost our temper. I should have told you that this is only one of the options and that we're not going to ride roughshod over you.'"

The Pacers are the perfect illustration of what happens when a railway has to replace ageing rolling stock on a shoestring. The Pacers may have been cheap to build, but the savings have been lost several times over already.

"The Pacers were more expensive to maintain than the Sprinters, although they cost the same since being re-engined. In terms of units for passengers carried, a Pacer is still more expensive to maintain because, for the same maintenance price as a Sprinter, you get 27 seats fewer."

The Pacers may also be exacting a heavier toll from the somewhat brittle permanent way in the valleys. Their axleloadings are 12 tonnes, compared with a little over nine tonnes on Sprinters. The more jerky movement of four-wheel vehicles also places greater stress on track joints, the most critical part of trackwork in maintenance terms. A further cost attributable to the Pacers, although incalculable, is the long-term revenue lost because people abandoned the railway during periods of unreliability.

Such a period in the valleys coincided with Regional Railways taking a much firmer control of its profit centres. The Valley Lines identity was unceremoniously dumped, despite the opposition of the local management. Marketing practices had to follow what the head office experts decided was best for each area and advertising budgets were controlled centrally.

The greatest damage was caused when Regional Railways headquarters took a cursory look at the fares being charged in the valleys and decided they should conform to the levels elsewhere in Britain.

"We were told we had to burn off extra demand at peak periods because we didn't have the extra rolling stock to accommodate it," says John. "We introduced the practice of charging peak fares on Saturdays before Christmas. It was seen as a rip-off. As for the real peaks, there was a tremendous amount of pressure after Sprinters came in to push prices up. I went along with this for a period because we had new rolling stock and, with the exception of the period in 1989 when the service quality plummeted, we really didn't lose anything significant through real increases in prices. We made a big impression on the bottom line. The revenue improvement was significant and loss of passengers minimal."

"But in these cases the law of diminishing returns sets in, and you can take things one stage too far. Around 1990 we took it too far. We went over the threshold of what people perceived to be value for money. We started to get a big drop in passengers, although the revenue was still increasing. In terms of the business we were avoiding putting more rolling stock in. We were reducing overcrowding but it was only a short-term thing. I felt I was looking long-term, but I'm not sure that everybody was. I knew the customer reaction could develop from a dribble to a cascade. When fares increases were associated with bad service and unreliability, then that was what started the unravelling process."

"We had a large organisation with a large headquarters that was taking responsibility for many things back to headquarters level. They said the Valley Lines fares levels were generally lower than in other places but they failed to notice that the propensity to spend was lower and that the basic income in South Wales, not just in the valleys, was below the threshold for most of England. Once you start fighting people who are looking from a position of not knowing the real facts, then you're fighting with a hand tied behind your back. They were taking more decisions away from the people who knew, and saying, 'We don't want to know the big picture.' When we started losing our grasp we could see the abyss coming. People weren't listening. They knew better, and national policy was their guiding star."

The abyss, of course, coincided with the recession which Britain suffered in the early 1990s, just as the halcyon period of the Valley Lines had coincided with the boom years of the 1980s. The effects of the property boom and the recession on the Valley Lines, however, were mostly indirect, and were felt through central government's cash settlements with local authorities and through further pressure to reduce BR's subsidy. To fall into recession, an economy has to have a height from which to topple but the valleys didn't climb to a significant economic plateau in the 1980s. While property developers were having the time of their lives in London and elsewhere, the valleys were going through the pain of having their coal industry amputated with minimal anaesthetic. Perhaps the nearest thing to recession that the valleys experienced was the long miners' strike – and yet that period of deprivation coincided with spectacular growth on the Valley Lines.

The Wider Perspective

The fortunes of the Valley Lines were nowhere near as closely linked to the fate of the British economy as Network SouthEast's commuter services. Instead, the rise and fall of the Valley Lines were mostly down to factors of British Rail's (and the Department of Transport's) own making.

As an organisation that existed to provide communication – and ran trains between various parts of Britain, had a huge internal phone system, internal mail, a computer network and various staff magazines – Regional Railways was surprisingly poor at internal communication. Messages could travel with ease from headquarters to regional offices, but communication between profit centres, even within one subsector, was sparse. John Davies, and other managers no doubt, partially overcame this handicap by observing rail businesses elsewhere in Britain and abroad and thereby received the kind of inputs that a more effective company might convey through best-practice bulletins, networks or seminars.

The same was true looking from the Valley Lines out. It is hard to imagine that a management approach which achieved a 40% increase in passenger numbers in two months would be of no relevance and use to managers running similarly depressed businesses in 1984. (Indeed, a carbon copy of the Valley Lines fares reduction occurred in winter 1995–96 when Central Trains reduced the fares on the Cambrian Coast line because the fares had been pegged to national levels but were too high for the local people. The result was a 60% increase in usage – enough to result in a higher income despite the lower fares.) Yet nobody seemed eager to find out what had happened behind the scenes in South Wales in 1983.

Lessons from the valleys may have been applicable even to other passenger sectors. John noticed that Network SouthEast was missing out on custom to various regional shopping towns because it was so strongly oriented around commuting to and from London.

"Lots of trains were running around practically empty, in places like Kingston. I remember thinking that some parts of Network SouthEast needed route managers, to look at the total potential."

However inappropriate the methods used in the valleys might have seemed for the bigger canvas of south-east England, nobody could deny that Valley Lines management had been successful in promoting off-peak travel. It was possibly the only local system in Britain where Saturdays were the busiest days. Taking a few leaves out of John's book might just have helped NSE to generate some income from the vast resources lying idle between the peaks and at weekends.

"I would say we looked at the totality of things that were going on around Britain and came up with some interesting ideas," says John. "Other parts of BR were reluctant to learn from us. They thought the success we had was due to unusual circumstances. I would have expected some people to be banging my door down and asking how we did it. OK, it might sound a bit conceited, but I had a lot to offer people if they'd only ask."

"There wasn't much synergy between people. They were compartmentalised. I felt that when we had meetings in Swindon there should have been more discussion between us where we could exchange ideas. There was such a crisis over the need to cut costs that it consumed all the waking hours of Provincial headquarters. I know that the people attending management meetings with subsector managers tended to concentrate on examining their navels. That went down to the subsector group meetings. When you raised questions for discussion there was no time to talk about those subjects. I think that was a terrible, terrible shame."

"Later at Regional Railways executive meetings, occasionally we'd get a presentation on marketing or something but when it came to discussing the nitty gritty you couldn't do it. I used to put an item on the agenda which was simply 'Making money'. I don't think most people knew how to address the subject, let alone have a useful discussion."

Area business group meetings in Cardiff threw up excellent ideas from all quarters – the engineering solutions described earlier in this chapter being excellent examples. But collaboration between different functions happened only spasmodically in BR. "We were able to discuss at local level issues that were not discussed at sector and subsector level, which is where they should have been aired. The discussion seemed to stop. People interested in the local area would contribute ideas but the exchange of ideas didn't exist at the higher levels. They'd say, 'South Wales has got nothing in common with anywhere else.' But some things it did have in common – best practice."

In 1989 John, through his pan-Wales management post, got the chance to prove that best practice from South Wales could apply elsewhere. "On the North Wales coast line the situation was so bad that it was a matter of despair as to whether we could ever put it right. We studied the problems hard but we could only do one thing at a time. It pained me to see passengers being treated as they were. Reliability was poor, and it was the only Sprinter service with declining patronage in the whole country. I came under attack from all quarters – not just from the operators but from the business managers higher up. I could get away with saying I'd inherited the mess for while. By the time that excuse was wearing thin we'd started the turnaround."

"North Wales was uncompetitive and overstaffed. It couldn't compete with the new A55 dual carriageway. I said, `If we don't do something quickly we'll be dead meat.' I took over in January 1988 and I remember going up before that, in July 1987, and spending a weekend with Eric Roberts, then the area manager at Chester, going down the coast and being utterly depressed at the shambles. We came back from Llandudno on a relief train, a two-car DMU that was on its last gasp. We were the only passengers on this train which was put on to relieve a Sprinter, which was jammed to the doors. Nobody had been told about the relief train. It was put on at short notice – the crew and unit happened to be there. I said, 'This proves one thing, if they can just pick out the crew and train on a Saturday afternoon.' "

"One of the first things I did was go through the traincrew establishment with a fine toothcomb, find out how many we needed and many we had. That was the easy part. The hard part was getting them to change. If I thought we had problems on the Western Region they were nothing to the problems on the London Midland!"

Just as in the valleys in 1983, there was simply not the time to go through the motions of commissioning market research, waiting for data to be collected and presented, analysing results and deciding on the correct course of action. So John did the same as before, and studied the market in person to see what the people themselves needed and wanted.

"Steve Sharpe was my manager for North Wales. He and I intensively studied the market by observation - not just what the railway was doing but the road competition as well. We talked to local authorities and got a view, and then used our judgement to come up with a solution."

"Within 15 to 18 months of taking over we introduced a radically new service which increased train miles by 40% on the North Wales coast. Instead of having a stopping service every hour from Chester to Bangor and Manchester to Chester, with shuttle services to Llandudno and a shuttle service to Holyhead, we converted it into a fast limited stop service every hour from Crewe to Bangor and a stopping service from Manchester to Llandudno. We cut out all the shuttles, which were costing a fortune to run but carrying hardly any passengers."

"Fortunately, in all the chaos of getting everything set up in the headquarters of the new Regional Railways, nobody noticed what we were doing until we'd done it. And then the s**t hit the fan, as the expression goes. We were told to justify making such a radical change and increasing train miles by 40% without carrying out market research. The service was successful and a similar service runs today."

John Davies's method of reviving rail services by administering first aid was not, of course, a universal solution. But the fact remains that the North Wales coast line had declined while someone, in another part of the same BR sector, had been there before and could have pointed the way to the solution. It is impossible to estimate how many other run-down services could have been resuscitated simply by local management applying John's methods or – as John himself had done – applying the best practices that could be observed in various places.

The lack of exchange of ideas contributed to one practice that gnawed like a termite at the Valley Lines and other parts of Regional Railways.

"There was a problem that if you did really well and cut your costs and improved your bottom line significantly better than your contemporaries elsewhere, you could well find that disadvantaged you. Frequently they'd say, 'There's to be a 10% cut across the board.'

"John Pearse, as Provincial manager Western, had to fight his corner because the whole of Provincial Western was far better at managing its resources and costs than many of the other subsectors. That was brushed over, however, and we had to cut another 10%. Whereas other companies were cutting into the fat, Provincial Western was increasingly cutting into the bone. Sometimes it could be counter-productive because you could worsen the service and you'd start losing passengers. Fortunately we managed to keep afloat, but it was a cause of concern and resentment among people who'd worked hard that they would then be told to make more cuts. It happened in BR and probably most other big organisations that had similar policies."

"There were big disparities between subsectors of Provincial and some of those only came to light after Regional Railways was formed. There was a general view held at a high level that Provincial Western was a bad performer but when the systems for monitoring things were improved I think a lot of people were surprised by how good Regional Railways South Wales and West was in terms of the efficiency of its service. By that time it was too late for some things, because people elsewhere who hadn't done as well at cutting costs had received much more resources."

"I think it will manifest itself in the franchises. Everybody's got to look hard at cutting costs. If you've got a franchise that's had a fairly easy time in the past then you've got more chance of making money in the future. I don't know whether that might make South Wales and West Railway a bad buy, while North West could be a good buy in some respects."

John believes ScotRail was the most impressive of all the subsectors. Although it was a little over-staffed, it had established a quality product and employed some good ideas. It also had great success on income.

"Other subsectors had impressive parts, but other parts appalled me. There were real problems towards the end of the 1980s, when they had to cut back investment substantially because costs had been going up in some areas. In parts of North East and North West there were Sprinter services that were costing more to run than the services they replaced. We had nothing like that on Western. The result was that Provincial's bottom line went pear-shaped. That was when production of Class 158 units was switched to Network SouthEast to form the Class 159 fleet for its South Western division. There was a chop on the number of Class 158s Provincial could afford, even though traffic was growing at a hell of a rate on the inter-urban routes. The resourcetightening became chronic, and it still is. That decision was right at the time because Provincial would have gone under if it hadn't been taken. Government was in no mood to bail anybody out, and you had to achieve your budget."

"The reduced number of Class 158s would have affected the Valley Lines through cascading. Class 156 units had to make up the shortfall, and the gap left by the Class 156s had to be filled with Class 150/2s. At the end of the day, the Valley Lines lost some of its Sprinters as a result."

THE PENARTH AND BARRY LINES

Top Left: A healthy complement of passengers leaves a Class 150/2 unit at Eastbrook in February 1992. This was the only new station to be provided on the Barry line, and was opened in November 1986.
Rhodri Clark

Centre left: Penarth station remains intact in September 1967 as a driver prepares for another run to Coryton. By then, however, passenger services no longer continued beyond Penarth on the coastal loop line to Barry. This view illustrates the lined green livery carried by Cardiff's DMU fleet before BR's corporate blue was applied. *Western Mail and Echo Ltd*

Below left: In December 1986 the old station building at Penarth is still in place, on the right, as a DMU waits to return to Cardiff. The station might have lost its buffer stop had plans in the mid-1980s to restore half a mile of track into Lower Penarth not been thwarted by householders living beside the trackbed, which is now an urban linear park south of Penarth station. *Stephen Miles*

Below right: This picture taken at Penarth station exactly four years later shows a new train, new shelter, new platform surface and a new building on the site of the old station building. The Countyride branding denoted public transport supported by South Glamorgan County Council. Here the branding reflects the council's investment in station improvements at Penarth.
Rhodri Clark

Barry Island station used to be the destination, on summer Saturdays, of numerous excursion trains but by July 1987 one platform sufficed. In 1996 the area occupied by the excursion platform and carriage sidings on the left is being converted into a steam railway with the aid of a National Lottery grant.

A pair of Class 37 locos rest in a siding as a Sprinter rounds the curve into Barry station from Barry Island.

The driver of a DMU bearing the full Trên y Cwm branding looks back for the conductor's signal at Barry in August 1988. The unit has been shortened to two-car formation so that it can keep time on Sprinter diagrams. The line to Barry Island diverges to the left at the ends of the platforms. The lines straight on are the Vale of Glamorgan route, which lost its passenger service in 1964. Restoration of the service, partly to serve the burgeoning Cardiff International Airport at Rhoose, has been considered several times but has yet to happen.

In January 1992 a Sprinter rolls into Barry station past the solid-looking signal box at the eastern end of the island platform.
Stephen Miles (4)

CHAPTER 8

PUBLIC TRANSPORT UNDER SIEGE
Competitors On The Roads

Long before any serious thought had been given to the concept of open-access competition between rail operators, Britain's railways had begun to face serious competition from road transport. The Valley Lines were not spared this rivalry and when John Davies took up the reins in 1982 several new roads were at various stages in the planning and construction processes. The challenge of the A470 dual-carriageway road between Merthyr and Abercynon was successfully anticipated but there were plenty of other substantial new roads in the pipeline to exercise the minds of the rail operators. In some cases the new roads did little to dent the railway's business, but in others the new roads were to tug the market from under BR's feet with significant consequences.

Road competition to passenger railways takes two forms - bus services and private cars. The latter form is always more difficult to tackle, partly because the competing service is hard to define.

"If you take on the bus companies you can monitor the outcome of your actions," says John. "You don't know the size or the nature of the competition from the private car. You're dealing with individuals who make their own decisions and can travel when they like and where they like. If you want to find out what journeys people are making by car you have to set up expensive surveys where you stop motorists and question them. The only measure I ever used for cars was to say to anybody who thought there was no more potential for the Valley Lines to expand that they should drive up the A470 from Cardiff and see how many cars were still on that road."

A consequence of this split was that rail managers often went for the soft option of attacking bus competition, even though the other form of competition was bigger and likely to have a longer term effect on business.

"If you went for the bus competition you tended to have the thrill of the chase with someone you could recognise. From time to time the bus and train operators would get together and talk. We were on pretty friendly terms with most of our competitors and we'd have a reasonably intelligent conversation once we'd got the slanging matches out of the way!"

In the early 1980s considerable efforts were being made to co-ordinate public transport. A joint ticketing agreement allowed passengers arriving in Cardiff by train to continue by Cardiff Bus to certain destinations around the city centre. Mid Glamorgan County Council convened meetings between the public transport operators with the aim of fostering co-operation and the rail development strategy described in Chapter 6 was conceived as a public transport strategy, although the attitude of the National Bus Company subsidiary in the area, National Welsh, soon put paid to hopes that the strategy would encompass all public transport.

"Basically, public transport was under siege and there was a lot to be gained from co-operating – as well as from competing with each other to push ourselves forward," says John. "Three or four times a year Mid Glamorgan brokered a meeting with the public transport operators. It was very convivial. South Glamorgan did that sort of thing in a different way, but it was equally matey. Mid Glamorgan had grand ideas of trying to bring public transport together. In the early 1980s, of course, this was coming at the same time as the Government was trying to tear it apart."

The forums were well supported by the municipal companies but even before deregulation National Welsh was adopting a combative stance. This attitude could be traced back to the early days of the public transport strategy for the valleys, when National Welsh declined to get involved with the other operators as it feared the councils would let out its commercial secrets. Despite assurances from the councils that the sole aim was to ensure co-operation, and that any confidential information would not be passed on, National Welsh would not join in. The other operators, mostly municipally owned outfits serving the district and borough council areas, were less significant than National Welsh.

"They lost out in the long term because no investment was directed towards bus-rail integration or bus development on corridors that weren't rail served. There might have been investment in improving the infrastructure for passengers – bus stations, bus stops and possibly bus lanes – but in the event there was never a concerted effort to look at helping the bus industry in a more strategic way. There could have been joint ticketing arrangements, for journeys from the Rhondda Fach to Cardiff for example, but National Welsh were totally opposed to this as a concept. They said, 'Why should we give up our passengers at Porth and have the railways take them to Cardiff?' They didn't think of what the passengers wanted, or they were simply interested in rejigging their express services to compete with the trains. The railway got nearly all the local authority funding that

Refurbishment of Caerphilly station in 1990 involved replacing the forbidding wall between bus and rail stations with a fence. Its potential as an interchange was not developed, however, partly because of lack of co-operation from National Welsh, whose minibuses can be seen in this view. The green garden sheds on both platforms were provided as shelters while the main part of the station was closed off for work to proceed. *Stephen Miles*

was available under the development strategy, and the buses got very little. They lost heavily, and it was through the obduracy of National Welsh that they did."

Nevertheless, BR enjoyed good relationships with many of the municipal companies.

"Rhymney Valley District Council's bus operation was an excellent company to deal with. They were committed to co-ordination. A lot of people interlined with the train at Pengam and Hengoed. They weren't very profitable but they were always smartly turned out and seemed to be a well-run company."

The bus and rail stations at Caerphilly offered enormous scope for integration, because of their excellent location and the fact that the go-ahead Rhymney Valley District Council was the predominant bus operator there. Mid Glamorgan County Council was beginning to think of ways to improve the physical interchange site, but any hopes of such progress were about to be shattered by bus deregulation.

Elsewhere in the Rhymney Valley an independent operator was proving to be a thorn in BR's side. Evans of New Tredegar had capitalised on the rail strikes in the late 1970s and early 1980s by running express coaches for commuting to and from Cardiff. People were so fed up with the disruption to the trains that they stayed with the coach services. At the services' peak, five or six coaches ran from Rhymney, Pontlottyn, Bargoed, Pengam, Hengoed and other towns to Cardiff and returned after office hours. Some went to the city centre and others direct to the Ty Glas office complex in northern Cardiff. When John sat down to analyse this competition he realised the railway had a difficult task in the case of the Ty Glas services, as the offices lay some distance from Llanishen station.

As was described in previous chapters, the Rhymney Valley was given special treatment in the 1983 fares reduction, and afterwards, because its custom was so poor.

"We started picking off the express coaches, one by one," says John. "We made further judicious fares reductions. Ian Evans, then managing director of Evans of New Tredegar, would say to me, 'Every time we're just starting to stabilise our position again, you lot come and drop the fares or improve the service and we have a further decline.' Eventually they dropped out of the market altogether. It was the railway's fault that those services started in the first place, and I was determined that the railway would recapture that market."

Merthyr Tydfil Transport held great scope for co-ordination with the trains because Merthyr station was not ideally sited for such a large sprawling town. Although the bus station was a short walk away, co-ordination could have given the outlying housing estates a better service. In the event integration came from a different direction when the small independent operator Silverline, assisted by Mid Glamorgan County Council, established a connecting bus which started in the cramped station forecourt and ran via the Brecon Beacons to Brecon. It still runs today.

"Merthyr's buses had appalling productivity. They were running up huge losses in what was natural bus territory. They had low car ownership, concentrated settlements and a centrally sited bus station. They lost £750,000 in their final year, partly because they weren't the slightest bit commercially aware," says John.

Merthyr Tydfil Transport was controlled by a rather cumbersome democracy cum bureaucracy, as was highlighted by the tale (recounted in Chapter 3) of its inability to respond quickly to the sudden aggressive marketing of BR's Merthyr line. No co-ordination was ever achieved, although John did once attempt to short-circuit the system as a way of cutting the Merthyr line's operating costs.

"In 1983, when we were looking at the costs, we felt - at the negative stage before we decided that the answer was to expand - that we could save money on evening services. We wanted to do an experiment, with Merthyr Tydfil Transport providing services in lieu of trains between Merthyr and Cardiff after 19.00," says John.

"I discussed it informally with one of the officers at Merthyr. He said the councillors wouldn't buy it. I said I'd write to him with some costs so he could at least have a look at it. He said, 'If you write to me, the letter will be opened by the councillors.' I didn't

believe him and wrote the letter. Of course, it blew the cover. We never did have rail-replacement buses with rail tickets valid. The council didn't want it. The conspirators would have said it was the beginning of the end, but in fact it was the end of the beginning. We were looking at all sorts of options at that stage."

Bus services in the Rhondda were operated by National Welsh rather than a municipal firm, so Cardiff Bus was the only other municipal bus company of great interest to the Valley Lines management.

"We had a relationship with Cardiff Bus but it wasn't strong. We mutually withdrew from the joint ticketing system. It was so little used and so expensive to administrate because of the railway's archaic accounting practices that we decided it wasn't serving any useful purpose. That was the last real co-operation we had with Cardiff Bus"

Bus Deregulation

In October 1986 the Transport Act of 1985 came into force, freeing bus services from regulation in an attempt to inject free-market efficiencies into bus operation. In South Wales, and many other areas, it effectively set back public transport integration by 10 years - and accelerated the drift to private transport in similar measure. The worst aspect was not that bus firms were allowed to compete but that co-operation of any sort was outlawed as an anti-competitive practice. The whole initiative was based on the false premise that there was scope for competition within public transport, a premise which ignored the tough competition already existing between private and public transport. Some companies in South Wales attempted to follow that premise and went bankrupt within a few years.

Some municipals lost the fight because of inefficiency. The first to go in South Wales was Taff-Ely Borough Council's transport undertaking, which had stubbornly kept its bus conductors almost until its dying day. National Welsh's attitude before deregulation didn't bode well for the chaotic period after 1986, and John had to take seriously the company's threat to compete with the trains in the valleys even before October 1986.

"In some areas we had pitched battles," says John. "One of those was Pontypridd to Cardiff. When National Welsh introduced their X4 service from Merthyr to Cardiff they were providing four express services an hour between Pontypridd and Cardiff. That seemed ridiculous. We've got four trains an hour there now, but in the mid-1980s four buses an hour seemed quite a challenge. The X8 from Maerdy to Cardiff ran every hour, the X5 and X6/7 between them provided half-hourly services from Aberdare, and the X4 filled the gap. National Welsh staked out the ground for a war. They slashed their fares and improved their service. We reduced our day return from Pontypridd to Cardiff from £1.30 to 99p. We included Trefforest for good measure. It wasn't served by buses but was a large part of the Pontypridd urban area. National Welsh then put their fares down to 90p, and for a while we level-pegged at 90p each. Interestingly we both earned more money at 90p than we did at £1.30. The battle was in the newspapers - deregulation was causing intense interest. We didn't really need to advertise because the press did it for us. Eventually the managing director of National Welsh and I met and decided this was going nowhere. We formed a slight cartel and agreed to be sensible and both raise our prices back again."

Another of National Welsh's initiatives was to extend its X9 service from Ystrad Rhondda to Cardiff to begin at Treherbert instead. Although the service ran via Talbot Green rather than Pontypridd, the change was designed to siphon some of the railway's custom from the upper Rhondda. BR responded with an advertising campaign, stressing that the trains were better value than the bus even though the rail fare was a little higher. Within a year not only was the extension from Treherbert withdrawn but the whole X9 service was cut back to peak-period journeys only.

"During that period we monitored the bus competition closely," recalls John. "We would get out and about on the buses sometimes. When we had management trainees we would give them a project to look at the bus competition. They hated it because I made them get up first thing in the morning to travel on the early commuter buses. But I did it myself, as did Alan Beardsworth. One day I drove to Treorchy and caught the first X9 service of the day to Cardiff. I asked the divisional manager's chauffeur to take me back to Treorchy so I could take another X9 to Cardiff at 9 or 10 o'clock. By the time we got back to Treorchy I said, 'I've had enough of travelling on buses. Just one journey is enough.' So we followed the bus to see how many got on and off. When we got to Talbot Green the bus waited five minutes for time and we stopped the car nearby. The next thing we knew was the bus driver standing by the car window and threatening to knock my block off! 'I've been watching you all the way down the valley', he said. 'You're spying on me. Who are you?' I told him we were British Rail and prepared for the worst. He said, 'Oh, that's all right then. I thought you were National Welsh management trying to catch me out.' That goes to show what the staff thought of their management, doesn't it?"

National Welsh threatened to upset the rail service to Aberdare when it was launched and introduced a peak express service from the main towns in the Cynon Valley to Cardiff. It was shortlived, because the local people were so determined not to lose their train service for a second time.

"We knew we weren't competing with the buses for journeys within the Cynon Valley. After deregulation three operators slogged it out – Cynon Valley Borough Council, National Welsh and Shamrock, a local independent. There were buses every two or three minutes down the whole length of the valley so we weren't even trying. We were anxious to compete on the main route to Pontypridd and Cardiff, and it's significant that before National Welsh went under they withdrew the large part of their express services. They'd been running them in the Cynon Valley for many years – slow journeys down the valley but fast from Pontypridd to Cardiff. Shamrock ran minibuses, and later bigger buses, but they still haven't threatened the railway. The then proprietor, Clayton Jones, told me himself that his market tended to be between Mountain Ash and Abercynon, because that was not well served by the railway, and he did not get much business from Aberdare and places between there and Mountain Ash. So the bus and train were tending to complement each other."

National Welsh tried its best to stop Mid Glamorgan County Council funding the reopening of the Aberdare line.

"There was constant harping that the money would be better spent on improving coach services. For the subsidy that went to the rail services they could provide everybody with deluxe buses fitted with carpets. They knew they were onto a loser but they were opportunists and they kept on and on," says John. "The public wasn't with them. The public reaction was, 'Why aren't you making these improvements now?' There was a lot of cynicism from the public that when new rail services were introduced the bus services got better. They said they wouldn't use the buses because they should have been improved before. There was a lot of sour grapes. The county council told National Welsh, 'If you'd come in with us in the first place we could have helped you with some investment and we'd have had a more rational transport policy.' "

"The performance was repeated four years later, when the Maesteg line opened. Local bus operator Brewers, now part of the FirstBus group, made the ritual complaints about unfair investment and, a few weeks before the trains started running, replaced its wheezing Leyland Nationals and other ageing vehicles in the valley with smart new buses. The frequency of the express buses up and down the valley was doubled to half-hourly and the new services marketed strongly. They had some strong competition with the trains but the public voted with their feet. As with the Aberdare line, the public wanted the trains back and were determined to use them. There was an interesting collective will amongst the population. They were grateful for the train service."

Collective will could also work against the railways, as John discovered when Cardiff Bus began operating direct services to Cardiff from the outskirts of Caerphilly. Those services were aided by the fast dual-carriageway that had been created to link the A470 near Taffs Well with western Caerphilly (illustrating how private bus operators benefitted from public investment just as BR did on the Aberdare and Maesteg lines). We just didn't see the competi-

tion coming. They were picking up quite a lot of business. People were used to coming into Caerphilly bus station and changing to the train. It was convenient but it cost more. The direct buses hit us harder from Aber than Caerphilly station itself. When we had changed the infrastucture so we could turn trains round in Caerphilly instead of Aber, we reduced the service level at Aber. People at Aber didn't take that well. They had been used to having the only decent service in the Rhymney Valley north of Caerphilly. When the direct bus services started they seemed happy to transfer."

Along the entire length of the Rhymney Valley, however, BR was handed custom on a plate as a result of the kind of suicide pact which the 1985 Transport Act seemed designed to encourage. For decades the long bus route between Newport and Rhymney Bridge had been operated jointly by municipals and the National Bus Company. By the mid-1980s this involved Rhymney Valley District Council and National Welsh both running every hour at evenly spaced 30-minute intervals. Just before deregulation Mid Glamorgan County Council urged both operators to sort the service out so that one operator took it over and ceded another route of similar value to the other operator. Neither company would have it and they decided to slog it out. Instead of two buses an hour from Newport to Rhymney Bridge there were four, but there was still a half-hourly service because they were running neck and neck. The inevitable happened there. Inter Valley Link (as the Rhymney Valley District Council operation had been renamed) went bust, followed after a few years by National Welsh."

"We just watched this and picked up the business. There's quite a lot of local business within the Rhymney Valley, particularly to Rhymney and Bargoed, and I'm sure we benefited from the nonsense on the buses."

In most parts of the valleys, however, competition between bus and rail was something of a damp squib. John discovered this shortly after deregulation when a BBC current-affairs programme in London asked him to host a journalist who was compiling a report on bus deregulation. John decided to take his visitor on the train to Merthyr, where they would stop for lunch, and return on National Welsh's rival X4 service.

"The first thing I found was that this guy had never been to Wales before and he was fascinated," says John. "He normally dealt with foreign stories and exciting trips to trouble spots around the world. On the way up to Merthyr he interviewed a number of people who, almost to a person, said they enjoyed the train and wouldn't go on the bus – no matter what the price was – because the train was what they liked. When we got to Merthyr we popped across the road for lunch. We caught the X4 back. It didn't have many passengers on it and it was a little bit cheaper than the train. He asked the driver for permission to interview the passengers and, almost to a person, they said they enjoyed the bus and wouldn't consider the train, no matter what the price was, no matter what the service was. There was no story there, which I thought was a shame really."

One corridor where National Welsh did gain the upper hand over BR – and quickly too – was Cardiff to Penarth. National Welsh and Cardiff Bus laid on fast and furious minibus services which penetrated the city-centre shopping area to the Hayes – even deeper than the railway stations – and circled the houses at the other end as far as Lower Penarth. This formidable competition coincided with the troubled introduction of Sprinters.

"I put in a 20-minute frequency to Penarth because such a short line needed a frequent service to develop. Initially it was very successful but reliability suffered because the turnarounds at Penarth were very tight and late-running trains were often terminated short at Cardiff. If a train was late running to Penarth, it would be late coming back and late going up the valleys, where it would cause all sorts of trouble with the single-line sections. One can understand why these cancellations happened, but they weren't sensitively handled. People would arrive at Penarth and, even though it was staffed, often nobody would know the train wasn't going to run. Members of the Glamorgan Rail Users' Federation and others were saying we should go back to a half-hourly service and make it reliable, but I didn't see that reducing the frequency would make any difference. We'd decided a 20-minute frequency was what the market must have and we had to make sure it ran. But it didn't. It carried on being unreliable for a long time, just when Cardiff Bus and National Welsh introduced a joint minibus service every six minutes. They slaughtered us. Their service was reliable, even if it wasn't as comfortable as the train."

One of the remarkable transformations in this period of inter-necine rivalry was that of the relationship between Cardiff Bus and BR. In 1983 Cardiff Bus was one of relatively few bus operators in Britain which had a through-ticketing arrangement with BR, but within a few years they became rivals in a contest which Cardiff Bus won hands down.

"During the 1980s Cardiff Bus became more aggressive to-wards us. They saw us threatening them quite seriously in some areas. Deregulation was the turning point there," says John. "Cardiff Bus bitterly opposed the City Line. They fought tooth and nail to stop it happening by making representations to the county council. They said they served the area well, which was true. In terms of frequency and journey times they were good, and still are. Their commercial side, with the exact-fare system, was basically customer unfriendly, and their standards of information are diabolical. They didn't succeed in stopping the City Line scheme, but they got the last laugh because they successfully targeted the City Line stations."

None of the other local operators dared take on a giant like Cardiff Bus for fear of bringing a ton of bricks raining down on their heads in the form of retaliatory competition. Only in the 1990s did Cardiff Bus face its first significant competition, from the Cardiff Bluebird operation. Cardiff Bluebird's owners are well outside South Wales and have flooded relatively old buses onto a few of Cardiff Bus's best routes. In response, Cardiff Bus has put extra buses on those routes and the result is the gross over-provision of capacity and additional traffic congestion which appeared like a rash in Merthyr, Caerphilly, Bridgend and many other towns for short periods after deregulation. In the late 1980s, however, no other bus firms threatened Cardiff Bus, which was free to go for the Valley Lines' jugular in Cardiff.

"They targeted places like Llanishen and Lisvane and put their best buses, ones with coach-type seats, on routes that competed with rail. Our business in the inner suburbs of Cardiff took quite a knock. One of the sad things was that we concentrated almost all our efforts on ruining National Welsh and their express services without noticing that Cardiff Bus were doing the same to us. By the time we woke up to the situation it was too late. It was more important for us to maintain our longer-distance business than to fight to the last drop for local business in Cardiff, but I kick myself for not noticing what was happening until it was too late. Our efforts to regain the business we'd lost were thwarted by the fact that places like Llanishen, and the City Line in particular, were suffering train cancellations. The City Line had appalling prob-lems, with trains cancelled without explanation. Cardiff Bus took us to the cleaners there, and still do, but the fact that they still have these passenger-unfriendly systems suggests that the railways could still bounce back and take the business. The perennial problem of reliability was difficult to tackle but I think we could have done more to fight for a bigger advertising budget. If we had got the advertising budget the City Line might have succeeded."

Passengers on the Coryton line remained deaf to Cardiff Bus's serenading. They demonstrated a strong affinity to rail, which was surprising considering their service had consisted of peak period trains only until the mid-1980s. The Barry line also rode out the storm of bus deregulation. National Welsh and the local independ-ent, Thomas Brothers, were going through the kind of unimpres-sive squabbling in which National Welsh was also engaged on the Rhymney Bridge to Newport route. The trains, meanwhile, were dependable and considerably faster than the buses to Cardiff.

By the mid-1990s the once-seething bus battlegrounds of Mid Glamorgan are quiet, the calm rippled by the occasional belch of satisfaction as Stagecoach, FirstBus or another giant operator ingests another local outfit. Islwyn Borough Transport is the only municipal company to have survived in the valleys. Anyone who knows where to look, however, can easily find relics of that era of thoughtless attrition. The bus station in Bridgend was owned by the National Bus Company and has been 'developed' into offices since the demise of National Welsh. Now the buses stop at ramshackle shelters dotted around the town centre and passen-gers queue for services on narrow pavements in busy streets.

Caerphilly is the most poignant remnant – the site that came so close yet is now as far as ever from being the perfect transport interchange. The local buses come and go without attempting to connect with train arrivals, and passengers wait for trains and buses in the cold because the railway waiting room is boarded up and the railway booking-office building is closed off with steel shutters for 16 hours of every 24. Information on delays to rail or bus services is minimal. All these things might not be so had National Welsh behaved a little less petulantly when the local authorities had the will and the cash to improve co-ordination of public transport, and had deregulation not outlawed the most basic integration in the interests of the passengers.

"The situation in Caerphilly was one which a rational transport policy would have addressed," says John. "It's a superb inter-change site where bus-rail competition could be turned into bus-rail co-operation, with benefits to all sides. It's still there, and something could still be done with a little bit of imagination. God forbid, the imagination still isn't coming from Government and the Office of Fair Trading who seem to stamp on anything that's seen to create a public transport monopoly, so private transport thrives on the poor facilities competing with it. That story is not unique to Caerphilly – it's the same all over Britain."

New Roads

The low proportion of families which owned cars in the valleys was a boon to the Valley Lines in the short term, but the reverse side of the coin was that the same area had an enormous potential for growth in car ownership. Quite apart from the many attractions of the private car, the mushrooming of new roads and improve-ment of existing ones provided a strong incentive for families to invest in cars.

"No matter how successful the Valley Lines were, the market share kept on falling because motor traffic was going up all the time. The number of passenger miles travelled was increasing faster by car than by train," says John.

In 1983 imminent road schemes in the valleys posed less of a threat to the rail business than the westward extension of the M4 motorway into Carmarthenshire. However, John and his fellow managers uncovered plans which had been drawn up by the county councils - with the blessing of BR - to close the railways at the upper ends of the valleys to create a ready-made route for new roads.

"The roads in the valleys were poor. While that was good for the railways it was bad for the people who had cars and who were frustrated because they couldn't move fast enough. It's still the case in parts of the Rhondda and the upper Rhymney Valley," says John. "They had carried out an exercise on the effects of shutting the railways and it was quite seriously contemplated that the trains would terminate at Porth in the Rhondda and the trackbed would make an excellent arterial road up to Treherbert. That was a ridiculous suggestion because the Rhondda line was so well used, even in the dark days of the early 1980s. I don't think the constituents in the Rhondda Valley would have been happy with their councillors if they'd taken the railway away."

The exercise showed that the lost income from stations between Treherbert and Porth and the effect of that loss on the Porth to Cardiff section made the scheme less viable than retaining the line to Treherbert. Abercynon to Merthyr and Ystrad Mynach to Bargoed produced the same results. Bargoed to Rhymney, how-ever, showed a net benefit from replacing the railway with buses.

"The railway was taking a very negative view of the future and the councillors had jumped on this as an opportunity to expand their roads programme more easily and more cheaply than if they had built new roads in topographically difficult areas."

Urgent action was needed in the Rhymney Valley. The threat of closure north of Bargoed had to be fought off by inducing better patronage of the trains. There was also a live proposal to reduce the infrastructure between Ystrad Mynach and Bargoed to a single line.

"Thank God I got hold of that quickly enough," says John. "It was all ready to go through the system. Again it comes back to Frank Markham, who agreed with us when we said this was horrific and we couldn't contemplate any expansion if it went ahead. We knew how much reliability could be affected by singling after the Rhondda line was singled in 1981. I regret that was carried out. In the circumstances it would have been better to have kept the double track up the valley to Treorchy."

The provision of the crossing loop at Ystrad Rhondda permitted a half-hourly frequency but did little to improve reliability. If a train was late coming from Treherbert it would delay the up train in the loop, which in turn could be late on its down run.

Once the possibility of building roads on the trackbeds had been abandoned, BR still had to deal with the competitive advantage other new roads would give its rivals.

"New roads were coming on stream at a furious rate. A number of councillors took me on and said they weren't coming fast enough. That was a cryptic statement at the time," says John.

Fortunately road schemes have an even longer gestation period than rail capital schemes, so BR had time to brace itself for the shocks. In the Rhymney Valley planning was underway for bypass roads in Caerphilly and a new dual-carriageway from Caerphilly to Ystrad Mynach. The Bargoed bypass was also being considered, although its dependency on land reclamation caused delays and allowed the Aberdare rail reopening to be brought forward.

In the Rhondda a new road had involved building a new platform at Trehafod, where the railway's former three-track formation provided useful spare space once the formation was reduced to twin tracks. The mid-Rhondda road between Dinas and Llwynypia was imminent, along with better roads from Tonypandy to Llantrisant to reduce journey times to Cardiff and the M4 motorway. Each of these projects posed some threat to the railway.

Road construction was racing ahead in South Glamorgan. Cardiff's lavish Peripheral Distributor Road was extending eastward from the M4 in strides. A slight loss of rail custom on the Penarth and Barry routes was an omen, as the PDR was planned to be extended across Cardiff Bay to provide easy access to southeast Cardiff and the city centre. However, the Cardiff Bay regeneration project could ill afford to have a major arterial road running though its heart, so the road had to be accommodated in a tunnel beneath Butetown. This increased the price and the design and construction work involved, and postponed the day of reckoning for BR. When Neil Kinnock, European Commissioner for Transport, opened the road in 1995 it had become the most expensive road ever funded by a local authority in the UK and the projected maintenance burden had caused a few heart palpitations in South Glamorgan's new county hall nearby.

"One of the reasons for us going to a 20-minute frequency on the Barry and Penarth lines was to pre-empt the PDR. I had the view that we would go to a 15-minute frequency but we never got the reliability right. The new timetable was put into place to pre-empt the competition but the qualitative follow-ups never got off the ground, partly because of the change of rolling stock and introduction of Pacers. That caused problems which management were so anxious to solve that other considerations were forgotten," says John. "What's been inexcusable in the last few years, when the road was imminent, is that the Valley Lines management have done nothing to get people to stay with the rail mode. There's been a huge drop in business, as far as I can see."

What the management apparently failed to do was focus on the Barry and Penarth lines as John and his colleagues had focused on the Merthyr line when the A470 extension north of Abercynon was about to open. The marketing aspects of this exercise are described in Chapter 3, but the threat of the road influenced BR's thinking in many other ways. Merthyr is a large town at the head of a relatively sparsely populated valley, so the train service to Pontypridd and Cardiff is inter-urban in character. Trains in the other valleys tend to pick up more passengers at communities along the way. This difference meant that end-to-end journey times were crucial in combating the potential effect of a new dual-carriageway trunk road but various factors seemed to be ganging up against BR.

"The Merthyr line was beset by problems above Abercynon. When the Deep Navigation colliery at Treharris closed, the underground passages were unstable and it took a few years for that to settle. There were long and crippling speed restrictions that added to the schedules on the Merthyr line, which was most unfortunate at the time," says John.

Another obstacle to faster running was Black Lion loop, which had been retained principally to serve the sidings at Merthyr Vale colliery. It was also used to cross two pairs of passenger trains a day, one each in the morning and evening peaks. This permitted a half-hourly frequency at the busiest times of the day.

"Black Lion loop was a stop between stations. It was adding a minute or two to the schedules. That might not sound critical but every minute counts when you're trying to get the end-to-end timings down. We and Mid Glamorgan County Council looked at the options for Black Lion loop: take it out completely and resign ourselves to an hourly service; convert it to No Signalman Token (Remote-controlled) to save costs; or move the loop to Merthyr Vale station with normal signalling or NST(R). We ruled out NST(R) at Black Lion because we would have to provide a platform for the driver to get out and it would add two minutes to the journey time each way. If we put NST(R) in at Merthyr Vale station we would have a two-minute stop but a net increase of 90 seconds, which was still unacceptable. The cost of putting in conventional colour-light signalling at Merthyr Vale was prohibitive because cabling would have to be provided from Abercynon signal box. We decided - and in retrospect I think wrongly - not to proceed with any of these projects but to remove Black Lion loop and signal box. The council and I decided that Merthyr was a different case from the other valleys. It seemed unlikely that it could justify a half-hourly service because Merthyr was a self-contained town and there wasn't as much commuting out of Merthyr as there was out of other areas.

"I think the crossing loop will be revived in due course, especially as the bus competitor is now running every half an hour. The Merthyr rail service is stymied now. There was a scheme to upgrade the speeds on the line but there were budget cutbacks. The speed is generally about 40 m.p.h. between Merthyr and Abercynon. With stops as well, the journey time is not very competitive."

The new roads in the Rhondda were less of a threat because they didn't cut road journey times as drastically as the A470 and the railway had improved its service since the provision of the Ystrad Rhondda loop. The new road between Caerphilly and Ystrad Mynach, however, cut as much as 10 minutes off some road journeys. It was opened after John had left BR, and its inauguration approximately coincided with the recasting of the Rhymney line timetables to eliminate the long layovers at Bargoed. Although this saved on resources, it lessened the attractiveness of the rail service by creating uneven frequencies which are difficult to commit to memory.

"When new roads open you're bound to lose some people to the car but you have to improve your loadings by getting people to travel more often. You have to try to improve your penetration of the market by offering a better service," says John.

New roads could affect the railway in other ways besides offering faster journey times. Newport station had long since been cut off from the town by a new dual-carriageway road, and in the early 1990s there was a prospect that the same might happen at Pontypridd, where an expensive inner relief road was being built to ease chronic traffic congestion. This road involved the remarkable construction of a bridge under the railway to the north of the station without stopping train services. The tracks were underpinned by a metal web before a concrete box, forming the walls and roof of the bridge, was pushed underneath using hydraulic jacks. The road scheme also provided funds for the new side platform at Pontypridd, since the road precludes restoration of the down passenger line by occupying a sliver of land where that line once ran.

Pontypridd station is close to the centre of this lively shopping town, which has indoor and outdoor markets, but its elevation forces passengers to climb steps to reach the platforms. The unimposing entrance was previously cramped and the approach placed pedestrians and road traffic in uncomfortable proximity

Now the inner relief road interposes several lanes of swift traffic between intending rail passengers and the station.

In the early 1990s the Welsh Development Agency and others proposed redevelopment of Pontypridd station with an eye on commercial gains. Redundant railway land could be freed for office buildings and the listed structures underneath the station's huge canopy could be transformed into a small shopping mall. A footbridge was considered so that people parking at the large Sardis Road car park, to the north-west of the station, would reach the town centre via the station platform. In the event the scheme was abandoned, partly because forecasts suggested the steps up to the station would discourage too many people from taking that route. The station's adaptability was another factor.

"The Taff Vale Railway built Pontypridd station to last 200 years and they made damn sure it would be difficult to make any modifications," says John. "They reinforced the stone and brick-work with iron railings. It was almost impossible to make structural alterations because of the expense. The TVR wanted to leave a legacy for all time, and they've got a lot to answer for!"

The listed structures on the station were something of a liability for BR. The only way John could find the money to repaint the giant canopy was by using money - some £60,000 - that was spare towards the end of one financial year. The magnitude of this liability was one reason for BR to shy away from building a second station in Pontypridd, further to the north. Although this site would have suited bus-rail interchange, it would have been a little further from the town centre than the present station and could have been served by Aberdare and Merthyr trains only.

The Pontypridd inner relief road and the planned Bargoed bypass involve railway land and consequently funding for new station platforms. Similarly, the proposed Mountain Ash bypass raised the prospect of improving the Aberdare line because the road would occupy the site of the present station. When the project was first discussed John floated the idea of providing a crossing loop at Mountain Ash to allow a half-hourly service to Aberdare.

"I wanted to improve the track lower down where there were sidings which had been used fairly recently to load waste coal. Every attempt to get somebody to straighten the kink in the track there failed. It would have cost about £50,000. The purpose was not so much to speed up services as an end in itself but to get trains to Abercwmboi fast enough to run a half-hourly service. When I proposed a loop at Mountain Ash it was so that freight and a half-hourly passenger service could be accommodated."

One of the problems was that half-hourly services on the Aberdare and Treherbert lines plus hourly trains on the Merthyr line could not be knitted into an evenly spaced pattern south of Pontypridd. In trying to produce an acceptable timetable John even considered running the Merthyr trains outside the clockface pattern and non-stop from Pontypridd to Cardiff, so they could compete better with the A470.

"I think they're still planning to have a loop at Mountain Ash. The diversion of the line would be funded by the road scheme but a loop might not be. It would involve replacing a single-platform station with a double-platform station."

Park and Ride

Heavy investment in new roads with little corresponding upgrading of railway lines was bound to increase the competitive edge of the private car, but John Davies and the county councils were also keen to exploit the opportunities cars presented for the rail business. Instead of going for out-and-out competition they wanted to make it easy for motorists to access the train service, giving them the best of both worlds. Mid Glamorgan, in particular, embarked on an extensive programme of providing new, improved and enlarged car parks at stations. Many have been poorly used, chiefly because of poor security. One of the best used station car parks is at Radyr, where a hill makes pedestrian access from a large settlement somewhat laborious. The station car park at Taffs Well is conveniently sited for the A470 road and has been extended to meet demand.

Some car parks, including Caerphilly, were fitted with closed-circuit television cameras but still most park-and-ride facilities lacked whatever it was that would attract significant numbers of motorists to transfer to rail. Consequently Mid Glamorgan decided to take a fresh look at its park-and-ride policies.

"They came up with the idea, which has yet to be translated into reality, that there should be two mega park-and-ride sites which would be strategically located for trunk roads and would have the whole panoply of security systems. The new stations would have a lot of facilities, like bookstalls and cafes, covered accommodation and heated waiting rooms," says John. "Two locations were selected in principle. One was Power Station Hill, south of Trefforest, where a new link road to the A470 was being planned at the time and has now been built. It's a difficult site to build a station but there's lots of land for car parking. The other was about half a mile south of Caerphilly station, near the north entrance to the tunnel. The proposed Caerphilly bypass was to come round there and an old tar works provided lots of land. I imagine the new stations would have been called Pontypridd Parkway and Caerphilly Parkway. Whether the planners still have their eyes on those stations I don't know, but it seemed like a good idea."

"There is a danger that park-and-ride could abstract rail traffic if people drove part of the way instead of using their local stations, but that presupposes people would use their local stations. We were looking at what people wanted. They wanted to use their cars, park somewhere and get easy access to Cardiff. If easy access and cheap parking was available in Cardiff it would have defeated the object of the exercise but peak congestion is bad in Cardiff and parking is expensive, although it's plentiful now. We needed to look at luring the motorist out of his car at a place where it was convenient to do so and with a very frequent train service. In fact, frequencies of at least every 10 minutes, and possibly seven-and-a-half minutes or five minutes at the margins, were talked about. From south of Caerphilly that might have been possible. Let's forget about the investment costs of new rolling stock to make that possible – this was the thinking that was emerging."

Whereas cheap fares, better frequencies and new stations had fuelled the early years of the Valley Lines' revival, it was evident in the 1990s that quality of service had become a prime consideration. In 1995 a Class 47 locomotive hauling four air conditioned Mk 2 coaches, all belonging to Waterman Railways, was introduced on commuter services on the Rhymney line. Despite occasional problems with locomotive reliability, passengers seem pleased with their 'posh' train. They seem to value leg-room after being used to the cramped three-plus-two seating of the Sprinters and to value the smooth, quiet ride after the bouncing and jolting of the Pacers.

"What I would have liked to see the county councils do was to provide money to improve the quality of the service," John says. "A lot of the research we did found that people weren't worried so much about the time the journey took, they were more concerned that the train arrived on time. People found the journeys were good value for money and were happy with the staff and other aspects of the service, although they didn't like unstaffed stations – nobody does. I felt it was important that customers should have easier access to the trains. When things went wrong people needed to be informed on the platforms and they needed somewhere comfortable to wait. When we talked about the future direction of the rail development strategy in 1991 I made some strong points about qualitative improvements. I said, 'So we've got capital improvements planned. If we decide to do them they'll take a few years to be approved, so what about spending some money in the intervening years to build up quality?' That would have had a great bearing on the councillors' constituents."

"I'm sorry to say that it wasn't the county councils who failed to warm to this idea, it was other people in BR who said we shouldn't waste money on this sort of thing. I was very unhappy about that. Regional Railways did pilot a satellite-based train information system in 1993 and used the Valley Lines as a trial area, but the scheme was expensive and the benefits have not been universally evident to the customer even three years on. I was disappointed with the railway's view because I thought we'd achieved so much and now we needed to keep abreast and get ahead of the customers' qualitative view. That view was moving fast. Cars were getting better, roads were better, and people were looking closely at the quality of the rail service."

THE MAESTEG LINE

Maesteg station on its first Saturday in use, 3rd October 1992. The Sprinter unit was substituted for a Pacer to provide a little extra capacity because crowds were flocking to the railway for the novelty of a ride. The Gateway superstore visible in the background gained planning permission on condition that its car park could be used to access a possible future station. *Stephen Miles*

British Rail's trainload freight sector raised repeated objections to the Maesteg reopening, on the grounds that part of the mothballed line would be used for coal trains again. This train is being loaded with coal recovered from a tip at Pontycymer, in the Garw Valley, before proceeding to Margam via Tondu in October 1992. *Stephen Miles*

A few days before the launch of the Maesteg service, an old DMU passes Tondu signal box on a route-training working for staff. The line to Blaengarw leads off to the right and that to Margam diverges at the bottom of the picture. The line running round the signals was formed into a passing loop so that trains from a tip recovery site at Maesteg could pass passenger services on the branch. *Stephen Miles*

On the second Saturday of the Maesteg service extra trains were run to Tondu while the scheduled hourly services were further up the branch. Here a Pacer is seen waiting in the loop ready to return empty stock to Cardiff after working a relief service to Tondu. The loop was not equipped for passenger use, precluding the running of half-hourly services to Maesteg. *Stephen Miles*

The station at Pencoed, on the main line between Bridgend and Cardiff, was built with staggered platforms either side of a level crossing so that the barriers – a source of frustration to local people - could be raised while trains were making their station calls. This view, in March 1992, shows the down platform complete and awaiting fencing and a shelter. The platforms on the main line stations are long enough for four-car trains, so that some services could be provided by Class 158s en route to Swansea. *Rhodri Clark*

Pencoed and Pontyclun stations were built before those on the Maesteg line so a limited service could be provided by Cardiff to Swansea trains. This Class 158 unit, on a Swansea to Portsmouth Harbour working on 11th May 1992, was the first train to call at the up platform at Pencoed. The red and blue platform shelters used on the Maesteg line were designed in-house at Cardiff and proved to be attractive as well as durable and odour-free. The design has been perpetuated at all subsequent new stations in South Wales. *Stephen Miles*

CHAPTER 9

IT AIN'T NECESSARILY SO

How The Tide Could Be Turned Again

By 1996 the Valley Lines have come full circle in more than one way. The first is that usage of the system has declined, after surging ahead so quickly in the 1980s, to levels not much greater than 1983. Also the Valley Lines, under a separate infrastructure body, may revert to the compartmentalised engineering versus operations mentality of BR in the 1970s, having passed through an intermediate stage where both disciplines came under the control of the same business management.

Naturally, there are significant differences in both cases – the wheels may have turned full circle but they are now farther down the track. Whereas parts of the Valley Lines were under threat of closure in 1983, such action is inconceivable now. The local authorities, in particular, appreciate the value of their rail services and are investing in the Taff-side lines. Confidence in the rail system was practically absent when the Valley Lines were declining in 1983 and it is a credit to the achievements of the 1980s that the local authorities and others remain committed to a system that, between March 1994 and March 1995, saw its passenger miles shrink from 61 to 52 million, its passenger journeys slump from 6.9 to 5.8 million and its passenger revenue decline from £6.5M to £5.7M.

As to the split between operations and engineering, the big difference between the present and the past is that engineers will for the first time come under genuine commercial pressure. Although the separation of infrastructure and rolling stock from the operators inevitably creates bureaucracy and inflexibility, the new situation could usher in efficiency gains on the engineering side to match the ones made on the operational side in the 1980s.

Rail privatisation should be a success in the valleys only if all the players on the railway's side work together as a team and exercise their attacking skills rather than using the railway's old tactic of continuous defence.

The Need for Local Management

One of the ironies of the United Kingdom in 1996 is that a highly centrist Government, committed to controlling matters from London via its system of quangos, has created the most devolved layout of railway operations since before 1923. Scotland, for example, now has complete control over running its internal passenger trains with nobody looking over the managers' shoulders from a tower block in London and telling them what their country needs. Most of the Welsh railways are controlled from English bases but the Valley Lines, at least, have for the past two years been run from Cardiff by people who ought to be close enough to their specialist market to understand it.

However, as this book has already shown, the Valley Lines have declined further in their period of control under the Cardiff Railway Company shadow franchise, partly through failure to anticipate and cushion the shock of two large new roads in the Valley Lines' heartlands. This seems to prove that local management is not a panacea.

"Let's say 'it aint necessarily so', as the song goes," says John Davies. "It's happened here because the railway doesn't seem to have been as well managed as it ought to have been. They've had no marketing manager till recently. How an organisation can continue without marketing playing a major part I don't know."

It must be said that the Cardiff Railway Company devised a number of useful promotions, the most innovative of which was a scheme for unemployed people to travel for half-fare if they were using the trains to look for work. The operating company held joint marketing promotions with shops and restaurants, produced colourful leaflets aimed at visitors and relaxed its rules on carriage of bikes by train. It also immediately reinstated the Valley Lines identity.

"The jobseekers' fares I thoroughly applaud, and they've done quite a bit on development of the tourist market. But the big bread and butter business has been neglected. The sustained advertising campaigns that we ran in the 1980s majored on the main features of interest to customers - value for money and frequent services. We had lots of publicity telling people what was there for the mass market, but now the mass market has been clobbered while a few niche markets have been developed. The Chiltern Lines shadow franchise has had a huge rise in passengers since it was managed locally, albeit with total route modernisation and new trains. Thames Trains, managed locally but sharing tracks with other operators, has done extremely well since the signal-workers' dispute in 1994. Again they have a modern fleet, but that's all. They didn't have total route modernisation. The trouble is that the other bespoke networks, Merseyrail Electrics and the Isle of Wight, have performed miserably. Maybe it's down to the railway hierarchy not knowing how to run a small operation. It thinks big and can't organise itself to run local services effectively."

The existence of the Valley Lines franchise as a separate undertaking from South Wales and West Railway is partly attributable to John's input into the formulation of the privatisation process. Having experienced the ebb and flow of local freedom in the 1980s he was convinced that a local urban system like the Valley Lines needed its own management.

"The idea was forming in my mind in the late 1980s, when privatisation was first being discussed, that the Valley Lines were a candidate for a separate system. My ideas were based on the situation in various European countries, notably Switzerland. Nevertheless, I'd seen these services and felt it would be sensible to have a locally managed system in South Wales where management concentrated on urban services and meeting the needs of local people."

"The train operating units and train operating companies are still grossly over-managed, in my opinion," says John. "To make it easy to deal with the unions in 1994 they simply carried on roughly the organisation, and organisational style, that was there before. It's a pity they didn't start thinking how to change the style of a local company. I'm not sure that the way the organisation was created was the right thing on a much larger scale, in many cases."

After the Conservatives had won the 1992 general election, BR managers were invited to throw into the melting pot their views on the way rail privatisation should be prepared.

"I took the opportunity to write to the Department of Transport to say it would be sensible to have a local network based on the Cardiff Valley Lines. It should also be a specialist in urban services in South Wales and possibly in Avon, because Avon was so close. The DoT called me up to Marsham Street and we had an interesting two hours' discussion. They were keen on the idea because the Valley Lines were self-contained. I think they felt it was a chance to try out – the Chiltern lines and Merseyrail Electrics were others – the concept of urban networks which were managed separately."

In fact, the self-contained nature of the Valley Lines, right down to their own exclusive island platform at Cardiff Central, appealed rather too strongly to the DoT. Consequently, half of John's proposal was adopted but the other half – to place all the urban services in South Wales under a specialist urban operator – was ignored.

VALLEY LINES
Passenger statistics 1982–1995

	Annual Pass. journeys M	Annual Pass. income £M	Daily Pass. journeys (6 day week average)
1982	4.7	2.6	15 000
1983	4.8	2.8	15 300
1984/85	6.8	3.3	21 700
1985/86	7.0	3.5	22 400
1986/87	7.8	3.9	24 900
1987/88	9.3	4.6	29 700
1988/89	9.8	6.2	31 300
1989/90	8.7	6.3	28 000
1990/91	9.5	6.6	30 400
1991/92	8.6	7.0	27 500
1992/93	8.1	6.8	25 900
1993/94	6.9	6.5	22 000
1994/95	5.8	5.7	18 500

The Maesteg line suffered immediately. Mid Glamorgan County Council had insisted that at least some of the Maesteg line trains should run to and from Cardiff Queen Street, so that passengers would have quick access to the shops and offices close to Queen Street station. The Maesteg line, however, was entrusted to the South Wales and West franchise and Cardiff Railway Company was to be the sole passenger operator on the short section from Cardiff Central to Cardiff Queen Street. Consequently, through running from Maesteg to Queen Street was withdrawn. Worse, passengers suddenly had to pay higher fares for the privilege of changing trains and platforms at Cardiff Central and continuing to Queen Street because the single fare bracket covering all stations in central Cardiff, including Cathays and Bute Road, was abolished in favour of a surcharge for the short ride onwards from Central to Queen Street.

Other local services, such as those from Cardiff to Chepstow and Abergavenny, could have been developed by an urban operator for South Wales, John argued. The Swanline local service between Swansea and Bridgend, which was then about to open, could also have been incorporated. All this, however, would have required agreements between operators sharing the same tracks. On the South Wales main line there would have been three operators, specialists in InterCity, inter-urban and local services respectively. The rail privatisation programme was going to be complicated and costly as it was, and had to be pushed through in a short timescale against considerable opposition. For simplicity's sake, the DoT opted to restrict the Cardiff local franchise to lines not shared with other passenger operators.

"When they came to the Maesteg line, it would be too complicated to have this as part of a franchise that was otherwise self-contained. I realised while I was at Marsham Street that I was onto a loser pushing this thing and I withdrew. Basically, there's a danger you'll lose the damn lot unless you trim your sails to meet the conditions. That's what I did."

The DoT's attitude was strikingly similar to that of Richard Beeching in the 1960s. Both were attempting wholesale reorganisations to very tight timescales, and both opted for simplicity wherever possible.

The main line between Swansea and Cardiff is an excellent illustration of what went wrong under Beeching. For simplicity's sake, he categorised all long-distance trains as profit makers and all stopping services – local trains on main lines – as loss makers. In as far as he went, he was probably right. The stopping service between Swansea and Cardiff was outrageously inefficient with a DMU service at odd times of day not much changed from the previous expensively-operated steam service. What Beeching failed to do was to differentiate between stopping services in urban areas, which had the potential for growth, and those on

long stretches of rural main line, which had little or no potential. The Swansea to Cardiff stopping service was in the former category. Its potential has been proved in the 1990s when councils alarmed at the forecasts for traffic growth have spent millions of pounds rebuilding six of the stations axed after Beeching on that route (plus a new station at Baglan) and reinstating stopping services between Swansea and Cardiff.

The compartmentalised thinking of the two companies now operating between Swansea and Cardiff also bears an unfortunate resemblance to Beeching's attitude. Neither Great Western Trains nor South Wales and West Railway, which runs two-hourly class 158s plus hourly Maesteg and nearly-hourly Swanline services, seem to acknowledge the synergy between their services on that corridor.

"I think there's tremendous potential for business travel between Swansea and Cardiff," says John. "Business travellers require good-quality services but they also require a frequent service so that when they've finished their business they can come back without delay. The train operators now provide that, but there's no joint marketing about the benefits of the more frequent service. That's shown to great effect on the Swanline. One of its biggest advantages is in providing more frequent services between the main stations, Swansea, Neath, Port Talbot and Bridgend, but has not been advertised. That's where most of the traffic is and where most of the growth would come from."

"A third operator, running between Bridgend and Cardiff with the Maesteg service, could make that situation even worse if they were also compartmentalised in their thinking. Great Western Trains was privatised in February 1996 and I hope that now that South Wales and West Railway is privatised, both operators will get their heads together and do the best for people between Bridgend and Cardiff."

Ironically the Maesteg line, which is remote from South Wales and West headquarters in Swindon, appears to have fared better in the shadow-franchise period than the Valley Lines, which of course were controlled from Cardiff.

"Maesteg to Cardiff has done well recently, largely because the local manager based in Cardiff saw the service going downhill in 1995 so he decided to do something about it. I don't know how much support he had from higher authority – they don't seem to have paid much attention to letting it be known what they achieved. They've shown that a local service which is remotely controlled can achieve things if the local managers and staff get their act together."

John's vision of a specialist local rail operator in South Wales, incorporating services in the Cardiff valleys and on the main line, was frustrated by the Department of Transport but the vision has not melted away completely. John believes much could be achieved by basing an urban rail manager in Cardiff to develop the unique advantages of local rail services and liason with their communities.

"There would be sense in looking at the market to bring inter-urban services into the Valley Lines area – perhaps Pontypridd or Barry. I think all sorts of things could happen once the network has been privatised. People could start thinking about their core businesses, their core competencies. With open minds, a lot can be done."

The Regional Railways Era

In the last 15 years Britain's railways have passed through three contrasting management patterns. The first was the method of corporate BR, where the engineers went about their own work often with little reference to what the business managers wanted. The engineering disciplines had their own hierarchies, at local, regional and board level, and the whole system carried bureaucratic baggage by the caseful.

The third management pattern was set up in advance of privatisation. Operating and marketing the Valley Lines have been entrusted to one organisation while the engineering functions are the domain of separate companies. Again, there is a danger that bureaucracy and lack of communication could have a stifling effect on development.

John is no doubt that the system in between those two was the best for the Valley Lines. That was the system in which the business managers had control over all disciplines so the local railway should, in theory, have gone into orbit around its customers' needs. Although the period leading to that system allowed John to exploit local freedom and a new atmosphere of cooperation with the engineers, the system itself when it was fully established in 1991 never matched expectations.

"In many respects, because service performance had been pretty bad and there had been lowering of responsibilities, the introduction of Regional Railways in 1991 started pulling things together and producing improvements because everybody, no matter what their function, was focusing on the same thing. It didn't work as well as it ought to have done but I think that was largely down to personalities. I'm not sure though that creating another monolithic organisation was necessarily the best thing.

The mid-1980s were undoubtedly the best period for the Valley Lines. That situation was unstructured, I know, but if local management had been strengthened it would have produced even bigger opportunities. For the first two years I was lucky enough to be well supported by a divisional manager who was prepared to stand between me and other people when we took risks. We took risks with the business, not with safety or anything like that. If that had been allowed to flourish in lots of other places, the urban railway in Britain would be far better off than it is now."

"When Regional Railways was created, they produced once again a national template which was slavishly reproduced in different sizes in various regions of BR. There are certain advantages in that, certainly in an organisation like railways where you need strong lines of command because safety is so vital. You can't have blurred distinctions. But the reproductions of that template all had the stamp of a central, bureaucratically thought-out organisation."

"All through the piece the Provincial sector and Regional Railways had to deal with the feeling on the railways generally that their services were unimportant, that they were heavy lossmakers which weren't worth bothering with. It took a while for the managers to come round to realising that those services were to be managed in the same way as any others. In the early days of Provincial some managers took up the challenge very quickly – it was a good challenge to take up. We had a hell of a battle against people who ran the other sectors who said we should be kept down. They said railways were not meant for local services, they were meant for moving masses of people and freight over long distances. But the fact of life is that a lot of people need to move around the urban areas. The railways don't make a lot of money out of it but they're damned important, particularly in terms of reducing congestion."

"If there'd been much more real support from a high level for the idea of the business sectors deciding what the customer wanted, Regional Railways might have been a greater success. What tended to happen was that some people didn't like it. They said this wasn't the way to run a railway and they obstructed. It didn't happen a lot in the Cardiff valleys, where we had a good relationship with those people, but I saw it happening, very destructively, on the London Midland Region when I was responsible for Mid and North Wales. It was difficult to get business decisions through because too many people would stick their oars in and say, 'This has always been our area of responsibility in the past and we've got to keep it.' At the local level South Wales was good, although there were serious tensions at Western Region level sometimes."

South Wales, however, had other adverse factors to counterbalance any advantages it had in co-operation across the functions.

"It was a fundamental error to put the Regional Railways South Wales and West headquarters in Swindon," says John. They said it was because they needed to be close to the InterCity Great Western headquarters to make sure that Great Western wasn't running all over them and pointed to the synergy with their regional cross-country services. I think it was more to do with the

senior management being unwilling to move from Swindon. I thought Cardiff was the natural centre because all the express services were centred on Cardiff. Swindon had only one Regional Railways service, to Gloucester, whereas Cardiff was the centre of most South Wales and West routes.

"Some people said it didn't really matter where the headquarters was. I think it did. There was too much concentration of power in one place and it was too far from most of the business. You could say that if they'd been based in Cardiff they wouldn't have had much contact with their customers in Bristol and Plymouth, but they had a nodal point for so many services and the major maintenance facility in Cardiff. Besides that, it would have been a nice gesture to base one part of BR in Wales. People used to say, 'What's so special about Wales?' We had it a number of times and it used to raise my hackles."

Another problem for the Valley Lines was that South Wales and West served small cities separated by vast tracts of farmland, whereas the other Regional Railways subsectors derived much of their income from huge cities with their own local networks and travel between huge cities which were relatively close together. Scotrail had Glasgow and Edinburgh, North West had Manchester and Liverpool, North East had Leeds, Sheffield, York and Newcastle, but South Wales and West had Bristol, Plymouth and Cardiff.

"I felt the Valley Lines needed to have its corner fought against tremendous pressures from elsewhere. I still think that anybody who buckles under on that is lost."

Privatisation will help the train operators to tackle some of the problems which hampered Regional Railways, and that help will stem from the fact that the people managing the train operations will be released from the perennial headaches of complying with directives from higher authorities and of keeping the trains running.

P. Cardiff would have been a more suitable base than Swindon for Provincial Western and Regional Railways South Wales and West because so many of its services centred on the Welsh capital. Instead Brunel House, seen here towering over a Bute Road to Barry Island train reversing in Queen Street station, housed only a satellite management team. *Stephen Miles*

"The greatest opportunity missed by Regional Railways was putting their retail activites right. They created what they called a retail organisation but what I saw developing was retail safety managers, rather than retail managers. The retail organisation came in at a time when safety paranoia was at its greatest. I saw a huge concentration on getting stations and other premises so safe that it was practically impossible for anyone to be involved in an accident, so they thought, but I didn't see any revolution in the way we served the customers, the way we provided tickets and information."

"Certainly the idea of real-time information was subsumed into other organisational problems. The way you buy your ticket has still not changed. It hasn't changed much in my lifetime, apart from the use of glass-fronted ticket offices and computerised ticket machines."

"If you go to almost any other transport organisation, airlines in particular, and any other retail organisation you'll find that everything has changed. Open stations was the equivalent of open shops, but the railway never embraced that concept and wanted to go back and close things up, making them less friendly to the customer instead of finding a way to manage the difficulties which open stations raised. Shops went open-plan because that's what the customer wanted. They weren't as secure as the previous system. Pilferage increased and they had to find a means of sorting that out. They did find a means, because they had to keep it the way the customers wanted.

"On the railway the focus on the customer didn't develop much. I think privatisation will focus on that. The Valley Lines under private management will have new pressures. Whoever gets the franchise will be silly to think the subsidy will continue on its present level. The pressure is going to come on further reducing subsidy. The pressure on costs continues, but the pressure on increasing income must be applied. I may be proved wrong, but if the new franchise operator pursues a scorched-earth policy of running only what they've got to run and screwing down other things like wages, I don't believe they'll achieve the result in terms of reducing the subsidy. It will be the same as the syndrome of the early 1980s –cut costs and don't worry about income and you'll be all right. But you have to constantly develop your markets. People die and they stop working, so present markets are always in decline. New people are born, they leave school, they start work, children need to travel, and unless you keep up the marketing effort they're not going to know about you."

At the same time, of course, the competition is developing. Rarely does a television commercial break not include at least one advertisement for cars. Cars are attractive and full of creature comforts. Car ownership is rising in the valleys and usage of cars is projected to increase well into the next century. More new roads are being planned or built and, for all the talk in Whitehall and Westminster of balancing public and private transport, public transport in South Wales is still viewed as a social service while roads are seen as a basic ingredient of economic prosperity.

Clearly the railways cannot rely on their existing assets alone to develop new markets and increase their modal share. The qualitative improvements mentioned in Chapter 8 will still need to be carried out and the biggest unanswered question about rail privatisation is whether the new railway will be able to deliver the necessary improvements to the hardware.

The Need for Investment in Local Railways

The vision of many politicians, officials and lobbyists for the Valley Lines in the next century is as a light-rail system or a system mixing light and conventional rail. The practical problems of this are highlighted in Chapter 6. In 1996 the idea of converting some lines to light rail is litle more advanced than it was five years ago. Clearly, the local movers and shakers are hankering after something in public transport. That something is novelty.

"Conventional rail has a credibility problem. Because it's had so many years of bad service and even worse publicity, the public can't perceive that heavy rail can be good," says John.

"A few years ago, the first consultants' report on public transport for Cardiff Bay recommended a guided-bus system with overhead electric wires. It was on a test track in Belgium at the time but it was unproven in service, and it's still unproven a few years later. But they recommended it because the public would think it's a nice, new sexy thing and it must be better than what they had before. (Incidentally, the only city in the world to adopt this system, Caen in France, has now dropped the idea). Now they're talking about light rail on the Valley Lines. If they're going to contemplate spending £200M on light rail, why don't they spend a fifth of that on putting in some lovely stations with good interchange and park and ride, refurbishing the trains or even buying some new low-floor diesel trains from Germany? They could get far better value for money, but people run away with the idea that they've got to have a novelty."

Trains and stations are not the only things which will need to be given a new face to attract new passengers. To compete with the convenience of the car, frequency will be a key issue. New roads are in the pipeline in Merthyr and Mountain Ash, so half-hourly rail services will be desirable in both valleys to keep the trains competitive. Such schemes, however, require investment, and investment is likely to be the crunch point of the privatisation programme.

One problem is likely to be the extra complexity of the new system. As described in Chapter 7, the solution of moving the crossover from Aber to Caerphilly was arrived at through the close relationship between operators and engineers in the 1980s and was justified as a solution on the grounds of cutting operating costs or, as it turned out, increasing income.

"If that situation arose now, I'd hope that Railtrack would talk to the operators of the services and see what would be the best thing to do. The same process could be gone through as in the 1980s but it would be a lot more bureaucratic because they'd be obliged to tell the rail regulator and would have to consult with the Valley Lines management and the freight operator and everybody else. The train operators would suggest a solution to Railtrack and negotiations would begin. The saving of the extra unit might be reflected in a higher track access charge in the future, and that higher access charge would justify Railtrack spending the money to move the crossover. I think the same result would be reached but it would be a very contorted process."

Unfortunately, contorted processes cost money, money that is spent on managers, consultations, and lawyers to draw up contracts. So there remains a danger that, if the solution were spotted, the financial gain to the train operator between saving a unit but paying higher track access charges could be so small as to be outweighed by the cost of organising the engineering change.

Another factor which will determine the amount of investment in the Valley Lines is the relationship between local authorites and the rail businesses, particularly Railtrack. Over the 15 years described in this book the railways have lost any obligation and funding they might once have had to develop new services for the general good of local communities. Instead, development capital has come increasingly from local authorities. Now those authorities have a greater bearing on the Valley Lines than ever before, partly because the Welsh Office will still not give grants for public transport investment along the lines of the grants available from the Department of Transport for English rail and bus schemes.

One immediate threat to the relationship is that Railtrack is a centralised, profit-driven creation of a right-wing Government, while every one of the local authorities covering the Valley Lines area is predominantly left-wing, necessarily parochial and ideologically opposed to the privatisation of Railtrack. Some local authorities are already unhappy with the stations they funded being handed over to Railtrack without a penny being paid in compensation and by the franchising director's proposal in the passenger service requirement to subsidise only a two-hourly Swanline service, after the council had invested millions of pounds on the understanding that an hourly service would run throughout the day. Within a month of being privatised, Railtrack paid its shareholders a £69M dividend and some local authorities could be reluctant to pay for rail investments if they believe the funding should come out of Railtrack's profits.

That relationship could well be strained unless Railtrack changes its attitude to development partnerships.

"One of the problems with Railtrack at the moment is that they're not prepared to speculate to accumulate. They will only do something provided somebody else pays for it," says John. "When you want a job done in your house you ask a tradesman to come and give you an estimate. He doesn't demand £100 to come and give you the estimate. Railtrack say, 'Sorry, but we don't know whether you're really going to do this if we give you an estimate.' The answer is that some things will be affordable, others won't, so Railtrack has to take a chance. Railtrack won't take that chance and this is causing a lot of resentment around the country. I don't suppose it's any different in the valleys. Whether Railtrack will be more commercial now that it's privatised I don't know, but I hope so."

Railtrack's attitude contrasts with the attitudes to be found in two of the most successful development relationships with local authorities. One of those is the relationship between the superstore companies and the planning authorities. A feature of that relationship was a certain amount of give and take. Supermarket chains like Sainsbury's were prepared to construct sections of road well beyond the boundaries of their stores as part of their projects, despite the fact that local authorities were responsible for local roads. In Railtrack's case the cash flows in the opposite direction but the organisation could do well to take a leaf out of Sainsbury's book.

Prehaps the most fruitful relationship ever to exist between non-metropolitan councils and a railway company in Britain was that between BR and Mid and South Glamorgan county councils in the 1980s. John Davies helped to establish that relationship by making BR work with the county councils rather than at their request. A rail development strategy was drawn up and millions of pounds were spent by the councils on its implementation. Many of the projects involved a contribution from BR, particularly through centralised functions like station safety and design, but Railtrack has already shown itself to be unwilling to make that contribution.

One of the foundation stones of the rail development strategy in South Wales was trust. The county councils trusted John Davies to wring the best possible value for money out of their rail investments. Chapter 6 described the temptations to go over budget on the engineering of the Aberdare line because the county council was paying, but the council trusted John to keep an eagle eye on the engineers and keep costs to the minimum. More spectacularly, the BR which the county councils had previously known would have turned the Ystrad Rhondda loop project into a massive investment involving signalling controlled from Porth signalbox but the BR of 1986 quickly spotted a way of cutting the costs by installing the No Signalman Token system. It remains to be seen whether the new unitary councils in South Wales will view Railtrack and the franchise holder with the same trust as their predecessors viewed BR under John Davies.

"If a situation like the Ystrad Rhondda loop arose now, I suppose there is a danger that Railtrack could come and do things that might not be in the best interests of the business. That would be like going back to BR before the 1980s, when the civil engineer would put in continuous welded rail whether we needed it or not," says John.

Despite all the potential risks, John believes the current situation can work to the advantage of the Valley Lines.

"Regional Railways was created in 1991 in the hope of reviving the spirit of local business managers dictating what happened on the railway. It was hijacked by people who wanted to have the power back to the centre and railwaymen reverted to what they knew best, which was how to run and engineer railways. There's nothing wrong with that except that the business side wasn't allowed to flourish as it should have. That's why I, in a minority of people, think the idea of creating a separate infrastructure authority is right, despite the bad points of Railtrack. I think it's inevitable that we would have the strategic infrastructure managed by a separate business. Now the business of the train operating companies is not about running trains, it's about carrying people. If they can embrace this business of creating service for people, rather than playing trains, then they'll succeed."

"With reasonable people the current situation is probably workable. It's important that things are done in the proper way, for safety reasons and with regard to spending public money, but the problem is you've got people in the rail industry who are still not commercial in their thinking. Railtrack is protective in too many ways and whether, as a big national monopoly, it can change is a problem. We've got the right solution but not necessarily the right thinking behind it. Our situation has been contrasted with Sweden, which has had an infrastructure authority for some years. It's said that Sweden has a better system because the infrastructure is publicly owned. It's not necessarily better. They've been criticised for doing things without reference to the train operators, Swedish Railways and the municipal railways, and there's a lot of tension there. What's fortuitous is that the Swedish government has decided that the infrastructure authority will have a lot of money to improve the railway as a whole. They're spending vast sums of money with strategic government direction because they're treating railways and roads on a level playing field, which is difficult in this country."

"If a future Government is going to change anything, one of the things I would look hard at is putting the subsidy into the infrastructure and basically getting the train operators to run profitably except where, like fringe bus services in rural areas, they go for top-up payments for social services. I think, for the great many services, the train operating companies can be profitable provided they pay for use of the infrastructure in a comparable way to road users."

One of the points proved by the rise and fall of the Valley Lines is that local railways and central control do not mix. Throughout the last 15 years the Valley Lines have been swimming, or attempting to swim, against the tide of centralisation that characterises the British way of life. The corollary is that the European countries which are noted for their excellent local rail services, countries like Switzerland and Germany, have highly devolved political structures where the regional and local authorities can control their local transport. In France the power is concentrated on Paris, and in France the high-speed rail network is highly developed but local trains are poor or non-existent in many areas. Yet even France has some impressive urban systems – most of them funded by municipal authorities.

The reason for this is that people live their day-to-day lives in towns, valleys, districts, boroughs and neighbourhoods. Central control might be fine for the long-distance InterCity services which connect the regions with the centre, but it is impossible for the people at the centre to grasp the details of daily life in each urban area. Road traffic is forecast to double between 1990 and 2025. 60% of all journeys in Britain are less than two miles in length and 73% of all car journeys are less than five miles in length. It is obvious, therefore, that local railways are the key to providing a well-oiled transport system in cities like Cardiff, where the stations are centrally sited.

The devolved structure of the rail franchises should enable systems like the Valley Lines to exploit their potential to the full. However, even the new company running the trains in South Wales will be subject to numerous pressures from outside, notably from the London-based franchising director (who controls the subsidy), the London-based rail regulator, centrally controlled Railtrack, and the centrally controlled rolling stock leasing companies. Changing that situation could be a matter for politicians in the future, but the immediate task of the private franchise holders will be to use their knowledge of local travel patterns, traits and opportunities to gain as much custom as possible within their various constraints.

The lesson from the Valley Lines in the 1980s is that successful local rail operators must increase their income as well as cut their costs, and the best way to increase income is to apply the maxim which British Rail often forgot: passenger railways are not about trains or tracks or signals, they're all about people.

GLOSSARY

Aptis	Computerised ticket-issuing machine used at principal stations
Bay platform	Dead-end side platform, usually for connecting branch services
Block post	A point between two block sections. Term usually used to denote an additional signal or token instrument on a single line to enable higher capacity.
Block section	Section of track between two home signals
Clockface timetable	Pattern of trains calling at the same minutes past each hour
Conductors	New term for guard introduced on BR in the 1980s
Crossing loop	Extra parallel track on single line permitting trains travelling in opposite directions to pass each other
Crossover	Track connecting parallel lines
Diagram	Programme of work for train or traincrew
Division	A local geographical unit within a BR Region
DMU	Diesel Multiple Unit – a Self-propelled diesel train driven from either end
Down line	Normally the track for trains heading away from London, but in the South Wales valleys the track for trains heading towards the coast
Down time	Unproductive period between train or traincrew duties
Exact-fare system	Method of collecting fares without giving change
Facing point	Point diverging in normal direction of travel
Layover	Time spent by train at terminus between services
Light rail	Modern tramway
Locked in	Train on single-line section isolated to permit other services to run with the single-line taken
No Signalman Token (Remote)	Single-line token dispensed by driver-operated machine in lieu of signalman
Open stations	Stations with no ticket barriers
Pacer	Modern DMU consisting of two four-wheeled vehicles, Classes 141, 142, 143 and 144
Park and ride	Station with adjacent car park provided for rail users
PayTrain	Local train on which all tickets are issued by the on-board conductor
Portis machine	Portable computerised ticket-issuing machine
Region	A large geographical division of BR replaced by business sectors in 1991
Route knowledge	Required familiarity of traincrews with routes on which they operate
Sectional council	Body representing staff at strategic regional level
Sector	Business division of BR
Sprinter	Name given to modern DMUs of Classes 150, 153, 155 and 156
Turnaround time	See layover
Up line	Opposite of down line (see above)
Zonal fares	Grouping of fares by geographical bands of stations

ACKNOWLEDGEMENTS

The authors would like to thank Stephen Miles, Ian Walmsley, John Hodge and Peter Clark for help with illustrations and Neil Sprinks for checking the draft manuscript.

Front Cover: The opportunity and the threat for the Valley Lines are encapsulated in this 1991 view of a Sprinter train at Trehafod in the Rhondda Valley. The dense housing was a source of custom, but the new road beside the railway provided an attractive alternative to the trains.
Rhodri Clark

Back Cover Top: The early years of the Valley Lines' resurgence relied on staff getting the best out of the Class 116 trains, which had served the valleys since 1958. Here one such train rounds the curve into Abercynon station on a service from Cardiff to Merthyr in 1985.
John Davies

Back Cover Bottom: Since the break-up of British Rail for privatisation, a locomotive-hauled train privately owned by Waterman Railways has been hired to provide daily commuter services on the Rhymney line. On a summer evening in 1996 the four-coach train is soon heading northwards over Bargoed viaduct.
Rhodri Clark